SUCCEEDING AS A MANAGEMENT CONSULTANT

―――

Learn the skills used by the leading management consulting firms, such as McKinsey, BCG et al.

―――

2nd EDITION

By Kris Safarova

STRATEGYTRAINING.COM & FIRMSCONSULTING.COM

We believe in the power of logic, reason, and a compelling narrative to teach our clients to solve mankind's toughest problems.

SUCCEEDING AS A MANAGEMENT CONSULTANT

Learn the skills used by the leading management consulting firms, such as McKinsey, BCG et al.

© 2010 Firmsconsulting LLC

A Kris Safarova | StrategyTraining.com & FIRMSconsulting.com Original

February 2020

Published & Printed in the United States of America by Firmsconsulting LLC, a member of The Strategy Media Group LLC, Los Angeles.

www.firmsconsulting.com

Firmsconsulting and The Strategy Media Group are registered trademarks of The Strategy Media Group.

Firmsconsulting business books are available at special discounts for bulk purchases for sales promotions or corporate use. Special editions, including personalized covers, excerpts of existing books, or books with corporate logos can be created in large quantities for special needs. For more information please contact **info@firmsconsulting.com**.

All Rights Reserved. This book or parts thereof may not be reproduced in any form, stored in any retrieval system, or transmitted in any form by any means–electronic, mechanical, photocopy, recording, or otherwise–without permission of the publisher, except as provided by United States of America copyright law. For permission requests, write to the publisher, at the address below

FIRMSCONSULTING L.L.C.	THESTRATEGYMEDIAGROUP L.L.C.
187 E. Warm Springs Rd.	8605 Santa Monica Blvd
Suite B158	West Hollywood, CA 90069-4109
Las Vegas, NV 89119	USA
info@firmsconsulting.com	

Disclaimer: This work contains general information only and is not intended to be construed as rendering accounting, business, financial investment, legal, tax, or other professional advice and/or services. This work is not a substitute for such professional advice and services, nor should it be used as a basis for any decision or action that may affect your business and/or career. The author and publisher disclaim any liability, loss, or risk that is incurred as a consequence of the use and applications of any of the contents of this work.

Terms of Use: This is a copyrighted work, and Firmsconsulting LLC companies ("Firmsconsulting") and its licensors reserve all rights in and to the work. Use of this work is subject to these terms. Except as permitted and the right to store and retrieve one copy of the work, you may not reproduce, modify, create derivative works based upon, transmit, distribute, disseminate, sell, publish, or sublicense the work or any part thereof without Firmsconsulting's prior consent. You may use the work for your own noncommercial and personal use. Any other use of the work is strictly prohibited. Your right to use the work may be terminated if you fail to comply with these terms.

Firmsconsulting and its licensors make no warranties as to the accuracy, adequacy, or completeness of the work or results to be obtained from using the work, including any information that can be accessed through the work through hyperlink or otherwise, and expressly disclaim any warranty, expressed or implied, including but not limited to implied warranties of merchantability or fitness for a particular purpose. Under no circumstances shall Firmsconsulting and/or its licensors be liable for any indirect, incidental, special, punitive, consequential, or similar damages that result from the use of or inability to use the work, even if any of them have been advised of the possibility of such damages.

ISBN 978-1-7340327-2-7

THIS BOOK IS DEDICATED TO MY FAMILY.
MAY THERE BE MORE PEOPLE LIKE THEM
IN THE WORLD.

IT IS ALSO DEDICATED TO OUR CLIENTS
AROUND THE WORLD WHO WORK HARD
TO SOLVE MANKIND'S TOUGHEST PROBLEMS.

WOULD YOU LIKE TO VIEW
EXCLUSIVE PREVIEW EPISODES
FROM THE PROGRAMS
ON THE PREVIOUS PAGE?

———

Visit

Firmsconsulting.com/promo

to submit your email.

You will be emailed the content at no charge

———

All content by
ex-McKinsey, BCG et al. partners.

CONTENTS

EXHIBITS		9
EDITOR'S NOTE		11
INTRODUCING THE ENGAGEMENT		15
ETHICS AS A COMPETITIVE ADVANTAGE		21
BUSINESS JUDGEMENT		43
PROLOGUE		49
WEEK 0	Week Before the Engagement	55
WEEK 1 - DAY 1 & 2	First Week at the Client	71
WEEK 1 - DAY 2	Top-Down Analyses	81
WEEK 1 - DAY 2	Engagement Charter	105
WEEK 1 - DAY 2	Work Plan	115
WEEK 1 - DAY 3	Thinking about the Value Tree	121
WEEK 1 - DAY 3	Operations Strategy & Productivity	131
WEEK 1 - DAY 3	Developing the Value Tree	149
WEEK 1 - DAY 3	Developing the Model Architecture	163
WEEK 1 - DAY 4	Drafts of Week One Planning Documents	175
WEEK 1 - DAY 4 & 5	Wrapping Up Week One	191
WEEK 2 - DAY 1	Mine Site Visit	201
WEEK 2 - DAY 2	Context After the Site Visit	211
WEEK 2 - DAY 2	Debating Metrics with the CFO	219
WEEK 2 - DAY 4	All the Planning Is Done	229

WEEK 2 - DAY 4 & 5	Designing and Conducting Focus Interviews	245
WEEK 2 - DAY 5	Feedback from the Focus Interviews	255
WEEK 3 - DAY 1	Preparing the Draft Storyboard	267
WEEK 3 - DAY 2	Building the Model	285
WEEK 3 - DAY 5	Output from the Financial Analyses	299
WEEK 4 - DAY 1	Presenting Feedback from Focus Interviews	315
WEEK 4 - DAY 1	Pre-presenting	331
WEEK 4 - DAY 2	Identifying Quick Wins	339
WEEK 4 - DAY 5	Steering Committee Meeting	347
WEEK 5 - DAY 1	Mid-Engagement Reviews	357
WEEK 5 - DAY 4	Services Workshop	365
WEEK 6 - DAY 1	What Is Big-Picture Thinking?	377
WEEK 6 - DAY 3	Managing a Crisis	391
WEEK 6 - DAY 5	Operations Improvement & Services Feedback	399
WEEK 7 - DAY 2	Aggregating the Business Case	417
WEEK 7 - DAY 3	Business Case Sign-Off	425
WEEK 7 - DAY 4	Final Storyboard	431
WEEK 8 - DAY 4	Consulting Values	439
WEEK 8 - DAY 5	Did the Engagement Team Succeed?	445
EPILOGUE		453
ABOUT THE PUBLISHER		457

EXHIBITS

EXHIBIT 1	Elkhart, Indiana Unemployment Rate	44
EXHIBIT 2	Decision Tree Analyses	64
EXHIBIT 3	Checking Issues	65
EXHIBIT 4	Overall Analysis Approach	85
EXHIBIT 5	Charter Template	109
EXHIBIT 6	Draft Work Plan	120
EXHIBIT 7	Productivity Definition - Output Lever	138
EXHIBIT 8	Productivity Definition - Input Lever	138
EXHIBIT 9	Operations Strategy Options	141
EXHIBIT 10	Commodity Company Strategy	143
EXHIBIT 11	Saudi Oil Example	144
EXHIBIT 12	From an Operations Strategy to an Operations Plan	145
EXHIBIT 13	Building Value Trees	158
EXHIBIT 14	Draft Financial Model Architecture	172
EXHIBIT 15	Draft Charter	180
EXHIBIT 16	Draft Financial Model Description	181
EXHIBIT 17	2nd Draft Financial Model Architecture	182
EXHIBIT 18	Draft Work Plan	183
EXHIBIT 19	ROCE Value Tree	184
EXHIBIT 20	ROCE Detail	186
EXHIBIT 21	Final Work Plan	233
EXHIBIT 22	Final Charter	234
EXHIBIT 23	Final Model Architecture	235
EXHIBIT 24	Final Model Description	236
EXHIBIT 25	Final ROCE Value Tree	237
EXHIBIT 26	Final ROCE Detail	238
EXHIBIT 27	Draft Value Chain	240

EXHIBIT 28	Opportunity Chart Template	264
EXHIBIT 29	Benefits Calculation Template	265
EXHIBIT 30	Overall Presentation	272
EXHIBIT 31	Headlines	273
EXHIBIT 32	Where Are We in the Story?	273
EXHIBIT 33	Writing Headlines	274
EXHIBIT 34	Deficit Communication Approach	277
EXHIBIT 35	Aspiration Communication Approach	279
EXHIBIT 36	Business Case Objectives	290
EXHIBIT 37	Types of Analyses	291
EXHIBIT 38	Bottom-Up versus Top-Down Analyses	293
EXHIBIT 39	Business Case Storyboard	295
EXHIBIT 40	Model Structure	296
EXHIBIT 41	Worksheet Structure	297
EXHIBIT 42	Update Chart	302
EXHIBIT 43	Mino 1 Value	321
EXHIBIT 44	Overall Feedback from Focus Interviews	322
EXHIBIT 45	Mino 1 Competitiveness	323
EXHIBIT 46	Mino 1 Priorities	324
EXHIBIT 47	Morale at the Site	325
EXHIBIT 48	Rating Senior Management	326
EXHIBIT 49	Employee Feedback	327
EXHIBIT 50	Employee Advice	328
EXHIBIT 51	Services Matrix	372
EXHIBIT 52	Completed Services Matrix	373
EXHIBIT 53	Explaining the Services Matrix	374
EXHIBIT 54	Managing the Service Functions	375
EXHIBIT 55	Core Services at Mino 1	403
EXHIBIT 56	Measuring Value in Services	404
EXHIBIT 57	Customer Ratings of Services	405
EXHIBIT 58	Investment Required in Services	406

EDITOR'S NOTE

THE SECOND EDITION of this book, eight years in the making, resulted in several changes. We listened to extensive reader feedback and added new chapters on ethics, top-down analyses, operations strategy, productivity and business judgement, and clarified existing concepts. This edition summarizes and builds on the advanced concepts available to our loyalty members, Firmsconsulting Insiders, who have access to over 6,000 digital training episodes all taught by ex-McKinsey, BCG et al. partners.

That said, the original goals of the first edition are still relevant.

We were once partners and engagement managers in leading management consulting firms. We commenced our careers as business analysts and worked our way through the ranks. We vividly remember our first engagements and training programmes. We were given a lot of support, encouragement, and training. We had high-quality training materials at our disposal. Such materials included >200 slide manuals on calculating economic profit, >150 slide templates on developing business cases, weeklong mini-MBA sessions in the USA, 300 slide guides to change management, specialised weeklong training programmes in Europe, internal training books, and more. Actually, there was much more.

Therein was part of the problem. Despite all the support we had, our first assignments were not easy, and the support was not always appropriate. There was too much information, and it was difficult to know where to focus. Analytical tools were taught as isolated analyses, as if we could simply learn and magically use them on an engagement to solve a client's most pressing issues. Training was stripped of the emotional challenges posed by clients. Moreover, the emphasis on the analytics resulted in critical facilitation and management skills having to be learned in real time and sometimes even in front of clients. With such a significant difference between the information given to us and actual life on an engagement, it was often confusing to know what was required to become an outstanding management consultant. Of course, we eventually worked through these teething problems. Yet, it would have been far more rewarding if the training catered to this gap.

In hindsight, it would have been much more useful if we had been given a detailed field guide that walked us step-by-step through a complete engagement. We did not visualize a guide that gave us all the answers. That would be impossible. Instead, we envisioned a guide that would introduce us to the fundamental consulting concepts and teach us how to use them in a real situation:

- It would teach us how management consultants learn their purpose on an engagement while navigating client challenges, diagnosing the problem, and developing a set of recommendations that work.

- It would show us how different analyses are used within the context of a complete study, how the engagement team should manage client relationships, the decision-making process, the mistakes they make, and ultimately how all the different pieces of data should be used.

- We envisaged following one engagement team through one problem and over their entire study. We wanted to understand the context.

EDITOR'S NOTE

At the time, such a field guide did not exist.

When we left management consulting, we heard the same feedback from both consultants and aspiring consultants. Younger consultants wanted to learn the tools and techniques of the major firms, such as McKinsey, Bain, and BCG. Unfortunately, available books only taught them the basic mechanics of analytical approaches. That is not enough. Less experienced consultants and aspiring consultants wanted to know what it was like to be on a consulting assignment. They did not have an adequate answer. Executives wanted to learn to think like consulting partners without working at the firms.

This book focuses on these gaps and brings our vision to life. We have distilled the tools and techniques from the leading firms to produce the essential guide for a management consultant. Any person who works through this book will be able to understand much better what is required to be successful in leading management consulting firms.

For every tool and technique used in this book, you will find advanced online training at Firmsconsulting.com, a website dedicated to providing compelling and realistic strategy, operations, implementation, and leadership training programs. All Firmsconsulting.com training programs are developed by former consulting partners from leading consulting firms.

We sincerely hope that you will find this book to be useful, inspiring, and educational. We hope that it will help you to genuinely understand what it is like to be on a management consulting engagement and what is required to be a professional.

As you will learn, the essence of management consulting is our value system. An outstanding leader anywhere always has the correct value system.

Kris Safarova
Los Angeles, California
January 2020

INTRODUCING THE ENGAGEMENT

WE WILL WALK YOU THROUGH an engagement over an eight-week period. The story explains in great detail the challenges faced by the engagement team, how they developed hypotheses, built the analyses, and provided the final recommendations. We have placed the explanation of management consulting techniques within a lively and engaging storyline, which allows you to truly understand the challenges faced on consulting engagements, connect with the characters, and understand both how and why they debated elements of the study.

Firmsconsulting.com & StrategyTraining.com are dedicated to helping you master those consulting skills needed to effectively serve clients. This book continues this theme. It is written so that the reader may *follow*, *understand*, and *replicate* a strategic engagement using the same techniques used by the leading firms, such as McKinsey, Bain, and BCG.

To make the story realistic and useful, we have worked with one client engagement throughout the book. Using different examples and different clients to explain concepts would have made it difficult for readers to see the data linkages and development of the final recommendations. The client and engagement are fictitious. The data presented are also fictitious, but they are based on actual consulting engagements and the real experiences of the partners and engagement managers when they were management consultants.

THE CLIENT

The client is the Brazilian gold mining company Goldy Mineracao (called Goldy). The company grew to become an emerging markets champion lauded in the business media and Brazil, but it has struggled to perform over the last four years. Its share price has been punished by investors, and key mining operations have underperformed their peers. Salient details about Goldy create the impression of a once-proud company that has lost its way and is unable to manage its core mining operations:

- The head office is in Rio de Janeiro, Brazil, and Goldy has always been managed by Brazilian nationals.
- Fifty-five percent of Goldy's operations are deep-level gold mines in the interior of Brazil.
- Goldy owns and operates three of the five largest gold mining reserves.
- Goldy also has mines in Russia, South Africa, and Australia.
- The company is listed on the New York and Sao Paulo stock exchanges.
- Although 35 years old, Goldy has grown through a series of acquisitions over the last 10 years to become one of the three largest pure gold mining companies in the world.
- It has incurred considerable debt to fuel its M&A.
- The company has a reputation for being a "rebel" and not playing by industry rules. Management is known for publicly going against conventional wisdom.
- Over the last 12 months, Goldy has unsuccessfully tried to buy several large mines, which has stalled its growth.

- Efforts to improve performance of its operating assets appear to be moderately successful. Operating margins and tonnage (volume of ore extracted) have declined, while the share price trades at a discount to peers.
- Strong cultural differences exist between the corporate office, who are generally of Italian/German ancestry, and the workers, who are of poorer African ancestry from the developing areas of Brazil. This has led to unrest at some of the mining sites.
- Goldy is very independent and generally hostile to outsiders. Their one and only previous interaction with management consultants resulted in a lawsuit due to a failed systems implementation.
- Morale is believed to be an issue, and the investor community has been demanding to see a coherent strategy to turn around the company.
- The Brazilian government is the majority shareholder, but it is a passive investor and has not pressured Goldy to increase employment or undertake populist measures. Goldy effectively operates as an independent company.
- The Brazilian government has publicly championed Goldy and encouraged the company to use its secure national base to grow internationally.

GOLDY EXECUTIVES

The engagement team will interact primarily with the following executives at Goldy:

- **CEO** : Carlos Selgado
- **COO** : Heinze Brito
- **CFO** : Flavio Semer
- **EVP - Mino 1** : Gavrilo Pinto
- **Finance Manager** : Sergio Gabrielli

ENGAGEMENT TEAM

The engagement team consists of five business analysts and associates along with the engagement manager, engagement partner, and director:

- **Director & Senior Partner** : Hendrik Lotke
- **Engagement Partner** : Marcus Capple
- **Engagement Manager** : Luther Matthau
- **Associate (Business Case)** : Max Kraus
- **Associate (Operations)** : Klaus van Hertzog
- **Associate (Services)** : Nadia Melinka
- **Business Analyst (Business Case)** : Alana Cruz
- **Business Analyst (Operations)** : Rafael Pedro

The consultants have been retained to understand why production value is down and develop a set of recommendations to correct the decline. At the commencement of the engagement, the team had not been told which of Goldy's mining sites would be analysed first.

INTRODUCING THE ENGAGEMENT

Although different work streams[1] (operational improvement, services, and the business case) will be completed on the engagement, this book will primarily follow the engagement through the viewpoint of the business case team. We wrote the book from the business case team's viewpoint since they take a broad view of the entire engagement. This is their experience.

---

[1] A work stream or work team refers to a group of consultants within the engagement team focusing on a distinct cluster of analyses. Two work streams are present at the commencement of this engagement: the business case team and operations improvement team.

ETHICS AS A COMPETITIVE ADVANTAGE

―――

articles from firmsconsulting.com

MAX PONDERED HARD AND LONG how to teach Alana about ethics and values. The firm uses the terms often and religiously, but he had never found anything that explained the concepts well enough. He had personally struggled to understand the concepts during his first few years and he felt this had held him back. So, he searched around and found the following explanation of the concept, which he converted into an email and sent to Alana.

From: Max Kraus

To: Alana Cruz

Date: Tuesday 22 March at 16:22pm

Subject: The beating heart of consulting

Hi Alana!

Hope you are settling in well and excited about the new engagement! I know I am. You would have heard the firm speak about values and ethics so much, but I thought the following articles (inserted below) do an outstanding job of explaining the concept in a practical way that you can use.

Read it and let's discuss it over lunch when you have time.

Max

*** Articles attached

Management consultants have access to data that moves markets. We advise companies and industry leaders who make multibillion-dollar decisions on investments, new plants, hiring, firing and more. What we do matters. Yet, who watches us? We are not a regulated industry. Senior partners cannot and should not have to check every decision younger consultants make. And who checks the senior partners? Young consultants are given significant autonomy, as are partners. In the absence of detailed rules, no regulations, etc., how do consultants make the most appropriate decision? Does it even matter if you are not breaking the law or will never get caught, let alone lose your job?

Let's take it to the extreme case. If you never got caught, why bother? Simply because the benefit of being ethical is a more important reason to be ethical than the fear of any penalty of getting caught.

Ethics is not about criminal behavior. This is not a discussion about why being ethical is the right thing to do. What we will show you is that being ethical gives you a formidable competitive advantage to accelerate your career. That should be enough reason to be ethical. We also help you understand ethics and how to think about the concepts. There are no absolute rights nor absolute wrongs.

YOUR CAREER

Being ethical gives you a sustainable competitive advantage. Values and ethics are not feel good concepts that should be taught at the end of an MBA program, as it is currently often done. Values is a material competitive advantage that is difficult to replicate and has a tangible financial impact. In Michael Porters' thinking, ethics is the ultimate competitive advantage since it requires one to adjust every aspect of their life, thinking, philosophy and activities to achieve this advantage. Doing that is very difficult which means many would not do it. This means it is hard to copy your competitive advantage. This means you are unique. It is worth understanding and building your life around this. It is one of the most formidable tools you can have to build your career and life.

When you begin your adult life, your ethical position is determined mostly by what you tell people. Since you do not have much of a track record and since working with you is usually of a low financial risk (your salary is lower when you start out versus probably much higher later in life) people merely assess you based on what you say. As you mature and/or the financial risk to being associated with you increases, your ethical position is increasingly determined by your actions and track record.

When we are young, we tend to use the few signals we have to show our worth and standing. These typically include having Harvard and McKinsey on your resume and a GMAT score north of 760. That is why people are obsessed with accumulating them. You don't yet have a track record of being outstanding in a specific line of work so people use these metrics to determine if you have a good standing in the world.

Your worth and standing in life is determined by accolades. As your career progresses, you begin to be judged more by your actions and less by these accolades. If you lack character and integrity you always need more hard skills and career enhancing data points to compensate for your lack of ethics/weak reputation. Think about this, if you are a horrible person who screams at staff and throws a tantrum on a daily basis, you will probably still have a job if you create wealth or have the accolades which signify the ability to create wealth. It forces you into this skills arms race because you do not have a reputation which encourages people to work with you. You need some other incentive to encourage people to work with you.

If you are someone whom people trust implicitly, they will hire you just because having you there signals enormous credibility and because they know you will do the right thing. That is one of the reasons the most elite consulting and law firms are hired. It is not just because they can do something many other consulting firms cannot do. It is because when the chairman of the board is offered a report from these firms, there is an implied credibility. It is known that these firms have a reputation for walking out of the engagement if it is wrong for the client. The fact that they completed the engagement is a credibility stamp on the report.

In other words, these firms have developed a track record of taking short-term pain (walking out of engagements or not undertaking engagements and losing revenue from such engagements) to do what each firm thinks is right. It takes years to build true credibility.

Other firms whom do not have such credibility look for other ways to be hired. They look for technical skills to impress the client. They may claim to have a new methodology, lower prices, etc. So, you see how this plays out. Without credibility and a strong ethical standing they have to bear a steep cost to entice clients to work with them.

Also note that two consulting firms growing very fast may be enjoying high growth for very different reasons. One could be growing fast because it is benefiting from its credibility in the market, which was built years ago. Another could be growing fast since it is discounting fees and paying too much for talent. In other words, not all growth is equal. The drivers of that growth matter enormously.

WARREN BUFFET

Of course, ethics is a major sustainable competitive advantage outside of consulting as well, for those of you not in consulting. Let's use a well-known example, but analyzed through the lens of integrity, credibility and ethics. In 1956 Warren Buffett returned to Omaha, after a stint at Graham-Newman in New York City, where he worked for his teacher and idol Ben Graham. Warren had about $174,000 and he was going to "retire."

In pursuit of his goal of becoming a millionaire he started a partnership like Graham-Newman's sister hedge fund, Newman & Graham. This would allow him to raise money to manage and invest it from his house, putting money into the same stocks as he bought for himself. The plan was to invite friends and family into the partnership. The key for Warren was to deal only with people whom he was sure trusted him.

Eventually he opened multiple partnerships and partners no longer had to be his family and friends. His name was passed along like a secret with advice to "invest with Warren Buffett if you want to get rich." But one thing stayed the same – the people who invested trusted Warren. The reputation that Warren developed by being consistently transparent and honest with his partners became his sustainable competitive advantage. This is in addition, of course, to his highly intelligent approach to investing and phenomenally hard work.

By 1960 Warren no longer asked people to invest, they had to bring it up. This is the same strategy as Marvin Bower used for McKinsey. If the other party asks you for your service, they don't have a "prove you are worthy" attitude. You are doing them a favor and not the other way around. Of course, this only works when people trust you, as they did in Warren Buffett's case and in Marvin Bower's case.

Imagine how tough it is to work for a client who does not trust you, constantly checks your work and always wants you to prove your worth? In the worst cases distrustful clients ask for changes that may not be helpful, refuse your advice and then blame you when their approach failed. That is a pretty horrible experience. Yet, if you do not take the time to build your selfless credibility that is where you will be in life.

What does this mean for your career in practical terms? It means that at a certain point technical skills and career enhancing degrees/

designations have declining returns. They tend to have the most returns when you are young and then quickly decline like the resale value of a car. Someone with adequate skills from an unknown school who is seen as highly trustworthy will almost always, over the long-term, be appointed over the vastly skilled person who studied at an elite school but is seen as untrustworthy. Too many young consultants focus on technical skills and career enhancing designations. Yet, credibility is more important in the long-term to get to the next level. Technical skills, and at that just good enough technical skills, are the foundation.

Think about it. Let's say you are the world's greatest financial modeler. What does that mean?

Does it mean your models are technically perfect, but no one hires you since you have a poor reputation?

Does it mean your models are technically perfect, you are hired, but not listened to much since clients question your motives?

Does it mean your models are good enough and you can influence the most senior decision makers?

Which of the three options above creates the most value to clients?

In another scenario, does it mean that when you will be 59 years old you are still going to build financial models?

I hope not. Because by the time you are 59 years old you hopefully should have been CEO and now chairman of the board. We erroneously think if we have technical skills and impressive career enhancing designations everyone will want to hire us. That is not always true. At a certain age you have to break out into managing people and leadership. And when it comes to managing people, and leadership, the trust element becomes crucial.

Do people trust you to follow you? Do people trust you to put you in a leadership position?

This is where a reputation for being ethical, which is earned by being consistently ethical over a prolonged period of time, leads to a formidable and sustainable competitive advantage. It cannot be won overnight via grandiose action, it cannot be bought, and it cannot be faked. And the true, and only, test of ethics is whether you can cite numerous examples of when you left money on the table because it was not the right thing to do. Unless you have left money on the table without hesitation, you probably have never lived by your values or your values are inappropriate.

You either earned it or not, so you better get started while you have the runway to get this done. And it will not be easy to do. Like Michael Porter said, a competitive advantage is not one single thing you do, but how you organize your life to produce this advantage. That means you need to change everything. Far too many people will not understand the importance of values and ethics. And of those who understand, the majority will give up in trying to organize their lives to make this a sustainable process.

ARE YOU ETHICAL?

We recently put out a note about a trend around the world where candidates record their telephone-based case interviews with McKinsey, BCG and Bain. They are doing it knowing full well it is wrong to do so. Moreover, they are sharing it with us and their network, and asking for comments.

We believe that they should not do this, since it is illegal to record someone without his or her permission. A few people wrote back to me and said they did not know it was illegal or it is not illegal in their country, that's why they did it.

This highlighted a great misunderstanding some candidates have about what is ethics, how to approach ethical decisions and how to determine if you measure up to be considered a person with high ethical standards.

Our concern is, as it stands now, some of you will struggle unless you spend sufficient time understanding what ethics is, how to think about ethics, how to make ethical decisions and what changes you need to make to build an unquestioned reputation for high ethical standards.

However, we believe ethics can be taught and mistakes can be fixed with the appropriate guidance.

First, it is important to understand that ethics usually applies to three types of actions. Actions not covered by law, actions for which the law is not enforced or actions for which the law is clearly wrong.

Therefore, when someone tells me, "Kris, I made this recording because it is legal in my country", what we hear is that the individual is very unethical. This is because even though the person would not like to be recorded without permission and knows it is wrong, they have gone ahead and done it because it is legal to do so. They are using a legal shield to do what is wrong.

Ethics generally covers actions which are not covered by law. However, for this act where the law does exist but is not appropriate and we rely on our ethical judgment, the person has demonstrated poor ethical judgement.

This does not make the person evil or bad. Wonderful people sometimes do unethical things. And it is very important not to shame someone for making mistakes nor punish them in perpetuity. Just talk to them and teach them. That is often all that is needed.

Many people believe that ethics is an absolute concept, that you know what is ethical with absolute certainty, you know what is not ethical with the same certainty, it is clear as night and day. That is not true.

In the West we have a tendency to think with absolute certainty that our beliefs are ethical and correct. However, the best way to think about ethics is that it is evolving, what is ethical is often a hypothesis and sometimes there is no right answer. When judging people for ethical breaches, we have to understand the context. Depending on the person you are analyzing you have to apply more severe or less severe definition of ethics. And because you will rarely know the context when reading about a situation, it is best to hold off on harsh judgment. Imagine someone who grew up in a challenging part of central Africa, surrounded by warlords. The social construct they are part of is probably not as ethical, assuming a Western definition, as that of someone who grew up in Vancouver, the home of Greenpeace. For someone growing up in the strife-torn context in central Africa, we would expect him or her to not be as ethically conscious aka self-aware as someone who was raised in Vancouver.

If both people breach the same ethical value, we should look at the situation and also consider what were their unique circumstances, what was normal for them and did they do what was abnormal for them. That is why our legal system allows judges discretion when casting judgement. It recognizes the importance of context. It realizes that the law is not absolute. The law must be interpreted in the context of the situation.

Anyone who tells you that they know with absolute certainty that they are absolutely right is absolutely wrong. You can only be reasonably certain of being right.

Many times, when we judge people for ethical breaches, we assume context homogeneity. We think that a person who was raised by a loving family in the United States and went to a great school should have the same punishment as someone who was an orphan in rural northern China and hardly had exposure to anything good his entire life. You cannot measure people this way because their actions are shaped by their social network and their environment. We must compensate for this context.

Now let's look at some examples of different ways to think about ethics, and why knowing something is right with absolute certainty cannot work, and why you need to develop the ability to assess these things for yourself. If they are so hard to judge, there will be no rules, only principles and there will never be a guidebook to make this easy.

Paradox 1

Let's assume you are walking down a street and you see a burning building. You see a baby in that building and you want to save that baby. The only way to save that baby is to jump on the car parked on the street and put some kind of garbage can on a car to reach the window where baby is, but to do this you will need to damage the car. Would you damage the car to save the baby? Most people would.

Would it change your mind if I told you that the car belonged to someone who needed a very important treatment for a life-threatening illness and they needed the car because they were going to sell the car next morning to pay for the treatment?

Clearly, that is a tough decision to make. Do you save the baby now knowing full well that you could kill this person because they won't get the money for treatment? A lot of people will choose to save the baby. Not because they know with any certainty that they can find an alternative means to pay for the treatment without the car, they may not even be committed to look for additional funds, but because if they don't save the baby they appear to be evil or unethical in the present moment.

Many times, when people do things that are ethical, they are not doing it because it is ethical, they are doing it because they are trying to avoid being labeled as being evil or unethical. The flip-side of this is that a lot of actions that we see as being unethical, we see without context. And of course, a lot of seemingly kind decisions are not intended to be kind. They are done to manage one's image in the present even if the future consequences are dire.

People struggle to compare and contrast the short and long-term consequences of a decision. They tend to only look at the short-term consequences.

Therefore, just because something looks unethical does not mean it is. You can only make that judgement call when you know the trade-off.

We need to think about trade-offs. There is always a trade-off. A lot of discussions about ethics do not consider trade-offs. That is the problem with an absolute view of ethics.

This is typically a Western view. We assume we know with absolute certainty what is right and wrong. We like lecturing other nations. We assume that if we decided that x was the "right thing" to do in 2018, then every other nation who did not come to that same conclusion at the same time as us is evil. To lecture others is to assume your rate of development in testing and accepting ethical concepts is the norm. Other nations may take longer to get there but who is to say the speed of arrival is the main issue. Is it not the quality of the implementation when it does arrive that matters? If we fight for the right for children to learn at their own pace, shouldn't a nation have the same right?

This is one example of a way to rethink ethics.

Paradox 2

Let's look at another example. Let's assume that you run a company and you have a supplier, TD Furniture, who lost all other clients and is now totally dependent on you. You want to lower your purchasing price from TD Furniture. You are buying chairs for $200 and you want to lower the price to $150. TD Furniture proved to you that if they lower the price to $150 they go out of business, but on the other hand if they do not lower the price you need to lay off employees to pay for the chairs. Let's assume you really need these chairs for your business.

What would you do in this situation? Would you say, "I will do the right thing and lay off people. I will not put someone out of business"?

What is *a* right thing and what is *the* right thing?

What if you knew that the reason TD Furniture will go out of business if prices drop to $150 is because they hire mostly family members, overpay them and deduct numerous personal expenses from the company? What if you found out TD Furniture charges so much for these chairs since their labor costs are very high because they moved the business to Malibu to be close to the beach? Should you subsidize their personal desires when you could import the chairs from China at 25% of the price? Should you subsidize this unproductive business and keep them in business when they are clearly not competitive? If you keep subsidizing them will they ever be forced to change their cost structure and is it good for them if you enable this unproductive behavior?

What would you do knowing this new information?

There is no right answer. But there is a guide. Do things ethically, provided it does not put you in a situation where you will cause harm to yourself or anyone else. When I say harm, I mean what the average person will consider being sufficiently harmful to justify sacrificing your values, such as putting yourself or your family in physical danger, etc.

Paradox 3

Now let's look at an example of an extreme situation of being too ethical, whereby being too ethical could, and we pick that word carefully, be damaging to you and others. Let's look at the massive, and justifiable, debate taking place in the United States about raising minimum wage. Let's further assume we wanted to do the ethical thing – generously raise the minimum wage.

Economics indicates that could be harmful for a couple of reasons, including the following:

First, by increasing money supply, inflation will spike. The price of goods will eventually go up because there is more money in the system. Even though people are getting paid more, things will end up costing them more to buy, therefore, cancelling the impact of the salary increase. Therefore, in the medium term, the salary increase will not really matter. The system will adjust itself.

Second, what does it do to the system on which capitalism is built? You should reward people not for how hard they work, not for skills they bring to the job but for the supply/demand ratio of the skill they bring to the job. That is, the more in demand a skill is and less there is supply of that skill, the greater the salary paid.

If you raised the minimum wage across the United States, you will undertake what is called a populist economic measure. You will do something to make people happy because the social construct to which you belong dictates that it is an ethical thing to do. Yet, you could be causing extreme damage to the system because you are giving away money without any commensurate return. Therefore, you can take extreme ethical stances that actually cause more harm than good.

What if the low salaries are being caused by an excess of low-skilled labor driving down prices? Or there is just no demand for some types of work.

Personally, we would like to see the minimum wage raised. However, we know this would not solve the problem since the minimum wage is driven by many factors which need to be fixed.

What happens if we raise the minimum wage by 30% but income inequality rises? Is this good or bad? What if the poverty rate declines but inequality spikes? Is this good or bad? Should we look at lowering income inequality or lowering the poverty rate. They are very different concepts requiring different fixes. It is possible to have high income inequality with fewer people in poverty.

Do you do that which sounds and feels good or what will fix the long-term problem even if it causes pain in the short-term?

Paradox 4

Let's assume you are a mother of two sons. Let's further assume you are from the middle of a poor emerging economy. There are a lot of kids in your community and your family is very poor. You've got one child who is incredibly promising academically. He is truly brilliant. He aces all the exams. He will probably end up at McKinsey and then as a CEO of some Fortune 500 company. You are almost certain he is going to change the world and take the family out of poverty. You have another child who is probably not going to end up at any college anywhere in the world. He will likely struggle economically.

Both need a kidney, but only one can get it. Which one will you give it to, assuming you are the only available donor?

This is an extreme ethical situation whereby you know on the one hand the child who is probably not going to go to some good university is not going to have financial resources in the future to take care of himself, so you should probably give the kidney to him. The one who is going to make it in the world probably will have financial resources, but it is likely he will not make it unless he gets a kidney from you.

If you give the academically weaker child a kidney, the rest of the family will most likely suffer. If you give the academically stronger child a kidney, the entire family will most likely be better off, but the academically weaker child will suffer.

Do the needs of the many outweigh the needs of the few? Who makes that decision?

There is no right answer. You have to determine what is acceptable.

Paradox 5

Let's go back to the first paradox. It's the same example with some new information. Let's assume the man who saved the baby is lauded as a hero but tragically perishes in the rescue attempt. Yet, he is remembered for his heroism. The city builds a statue in his memory, roads are named in his honor and the main bridge is renamed in his honor. He is feted in the press and the city holds an annual event to honor his memory.

He is a hero. Right?

To whom is he a hero? That is a more important question.

Let's assume he has a family with a wife and 3 kids. Let's further assume both his wife and youngest children are ill. His wife is legally disabled while his youngest child requires expensive treatment. His wife worked very hard from the age of 18 to 26 to pay the bills while he went to medical school. Thereafter, she became ill and had to retire. As a young couple their net worth is low, and they are still paying off many bills. They have no disability insurance, etc. At their age it did not seem necessary.

Are you a hero when you take actions which certainly hurt and probably devastate the only people who helped you, people who need you and people who would probably suffer immeasurable hardship without you? One could argue he is not a hero. His actions seem very selfish when viewed from the lens of the family.

On the other hand, you could argue that the baby could not take care of itself, so he is a hero, since his wife could take care of herself. Is the child's life worth more than the unwritten promises made to his family? Is he being a hero or selfish? If he is a hero to whom is he a hero? Is that the party to whom he should be a hero? What is the ethical thing to do in this situation?

Next time you want to be a hero, think of your family. It is not your decision alone to make.

Paradox 6

How many of you enhance your resume with your efforts travelling to Haiti, Peru, South Africa, Kenya, etc., to build homes for the impoverished and destitute? Why have you not travelled to Detroit, as an example, to help the citizens of that or a similar local city? Given the lower travelling costs would you not have more dollars to spend on helping someone versus using up the funds for travelling? Did you travel internationally for the adventure, since it sounds good and made you feel good? Where do your obligations lie?

Detroit was once an economic powerhouse in the USA. Taxes paid by Detroit auto manufacturers, their employees, their suppliers and the service industries supporting all three generated billions of dollars in tax revenue. Those taxes were sent to the federal government and redistributed across the country, and to foreign aid recipients, to help pay for schools, infrastructure, improved regulation, safety, security, etc. We all benefited from it.

Would it not make more sense to repay the favor by doing charity work for your fellow citizens in Detroit? You were an indirect beneficiary of their largess while a foreign country may not have helped you at all? Even in circumstances where a region may not have contributed economically in the past, they are fellow citizens, and does it not make more sense to help them?

On the other hand, who will help the people in Haiti? Why not you? There is no law expecting you to distribute your income to only help fellow citizens? What is the right thing to do?

Why not avoid charity work in total and just make a lot of money and pay higher taxes so that the government can do the work that you end up volunteering for? Would that not make a bigger impact? Are cheap Android phones not doing more to spread education and literacy than any charity-driven teacher training program in the world? Would it not make more sense to work at Google 100% of the time to help the world versus taking 4 weeks off to build homes in South East Asia? Would that not have a greater impact on helping people?

There are no right answers. However, a good rule of thumb, as Joey Tribbiani said, is if it makes you feel good, then it is probably not charitable work.

Addressing 2 myths about ethics

Let us conclude our discussion with addressing 2 myths about ethics.

Myth #1: If you are ethical, you are by default a nice person and usually a pushover. Being ethical does not mean you are a pushover. People can be tough and demanding, and yet still be values driven in every possible way. Being ethical does not mean you have to be nice to people. Personality and your value system are completely different concepts.

Myth #2: Following the rule, "the softest pillow is a clear conscience" is a sure path to ensure high ethical standards. It only matters if your conscience is attuned to what is actually right. If it is calibrated to things that are incredibly cruel, you will have fundamental problems making judgement calls.

YOUR SOCIAL NETWORK DRIVES YOUR ETHICS

The social construct to which you belong determines what you consider to be a clear conscience. You are your friends. When you are deciding whether you are ethical, or not, look no further than your friends and all those questionable things they do that you find acceptable. By condoning their behavior, you are desensitizing yourself to those elements you know to be wrong. You should think twice about whether those are things you should be a part of.

The social network you choose to join, and it is absolutely a choice, shapes your values, or lack thereof. When clients ask us if they are ethical we usually tell them we cannot answer this with any certainty. We say this if we do not know their significant others well enough. Your significant other is the most influential member of your social network. At the end of the day, when it really comes down to the wire, your decisions will be heavily driven by what your significant other considers right. Never ever forget that.

We say this because 95% of people who breach ethical values almost always cite personal circumstances. Here are a few examples:

> "I would not normally do this, but my husband and I discussed this and…"

> "My partner recently lost his job and we decided…"

> "I would normally never do this, but due to personal reasons…"

> "Unfortunately, my family must come first, so…"

You can fill in the rest. The last one is very telling. Somehow, many assume that a personal reason is a license to be unethical. It never was and never will be. Let's hope you chose your significant other well.

When did it become acceptable to be unethical for the sake of your family?

ETHICS IS NOT ABOUT THE LAW

Now let's examine further the role of judgement in ethics. Some points will be repeated and explained in a different way to make the connection that follows.

As described above, when we talk about ethics we are most of the time talking about actions where laws have not been written to cover your actions. If there was a law telling you how to behave in a situation, would it be an ethical debate given the law instructed you what to do? In most cases it will not be.

However, the world is not perfect.

There are times when the law is wrong. For example, when some ethnic groups were not allowed to attend universities in parts of the world. There are laws like that, unjust laws, right now in parts of the world. Therefore, in situations where the law is wrong, ethics should dictate your actions.

Think of countries that have exceptional constitutions. Their constitutions are so revered that other legal systems around the world quote from these country's constitutions and higher court opinions.

However, there are parts of that country that are lawless. Clearly the law is not enough if there is no enforcement. If there is no enforcement people will misbehave unless they are ethically bound to behave themselves. Therefore, there are two situations where we need to apply ethics to actions governed by law, when the laws are wrong and when the laws are not enforced.

To summarize, ethics is required when the law is not written, not enforced or wrong.

The application of ethical principles is inversely proportional to the correctness of the law, the reach of the law and the enforcement of the law. If there are no laws, or the law is weak, or the law is wrong, or the law cannot be enforced, you are reliant on your personal judgment to make decisions.

ETHICS IS ABOUT JUDGEMENT

The question is, how good is your judgment?

If ethics is about judgment, what drives our judgement?

We established that ethics is about judgment. Now let's consider 4 situations and we will show you what probably drives our judgment.

Imagine it is 1940 and you are a brilliant engineering student in Germany – blue eyes, blond hair, handsome but a bit naive. All you know is what is told to you, and you just happened to be a member of the armed forces. You are sitting at a hip Berlin bar. You are in a situation where everyone thinks it is just fine to persecute the Jewish and Slavic nations. Not only is this the kind of group you belong to, it is also aligned with the law in your country.

Let's take another situation. Let's assume it is 1910 in Canada. You are going out with your buddies, upstanding gentlemen who don't agree that women should have the right to vote. That is all you see in the press. That is what people talk about. That is accepted. How do you break away from that, when it is the only thing you know to be right? Some of you will say, "Well, we actually know that's wrong". However, the reality is, to a large degree, we are defined by our circumstances. It is easy to apply a higher ethical standard in hindsight. We can prove this.

In the first two examples I have presented scenarios that today, in hindsight, we know to be wrong. In the next two examples I will give you things that we don't necessarily know to be wrong today.

Think about eating animals. Human beings consume millions of tons, maybe tens of millions of tons, of animal carcasses every year. It is completely acceptable to do this. It is acceptable to make jokes about it. In a hundred years people may look back at us and be horrified. Statues of people we revere today will be taken down because they condoned the consumption of meat. We think it is acceptable because the network we belong to thinks it is acceptable. If you belonged to a social network whereby your friends thought it was horrible and distasteful to eat animals, you would probably not do it. If your reaction to this was, it is not so bad, so I am going to do it, then remember this is how unethical behavior becomes acceptable. We justify it based on what we see as being commonplace.

Let's look at another example. Something that we notice every single time we are in a group of people – sexist comments. It is remarkable how much we tolerate sexist comments on television and in social settings. In fact, social settings reinforce this behavior. Comments like "you are acting like a girl", "you throw like a girl" or "only girls do that" are basically accepted discriminatory banter. Just about every major comedy show in the United States has made some off-hand sexist comments. Some thrive on it and their ratings are directly proportional to this behavior.

One of the most popular shows in United States, "How I Met Your Mother", actually has a scene whereby the main antagonist, Barney Stinson, talks about how he may have sold a woman into slavery. That show went on to have one of the highest ratings in cable television for United States. It was a joke, obviously, but the fact is we find those things funny.

This happens right now. We think it is acceptable to belittle half of the human race. So why do we do that?

We do it because everyone else is doing it.

The social group you belong to shapes your ethics.

***After sending off the email, Max realized that so much of consulting and ethics was built on business judgement that he would also need to spend some time explaining this concept to Alana. Contrary to popular belief, one did not increase one's business judgement only by reading the Harvard Business Review, McKinsey Quarterly, and/or Wall Street Journal. Reading them mostly exposed one to facts and data which, in the end, needed to be interpreted with judgement. Yet, reading alone does not increase judgement. Max made some notes on how to explain judgement to Alana.

BUSINESS JUDGEMENT

W**HAT IS BUSINESS JUDGEMENT?** Is it your understanding of business? Can you have business judgement if you do not know much about business? Do you need an MBA to have business judgement? Can an uneducated person have business judgement? Let's explain business judgement using the example below. Here is an exhibit[2] from the WSJ. We want you to look at this and answer one question. Don't read the article since it's not relevant to the point being made. Is the unemployment rate dropping in Elkhart, Indiana?

[2] https://www.wsj.com/articles/the-future-of-americas-economy-looks-a-lot-like-elkhart-indiana-1522942393

EXHIBIT 1: Elkhart, Indiana Unemployment Rate

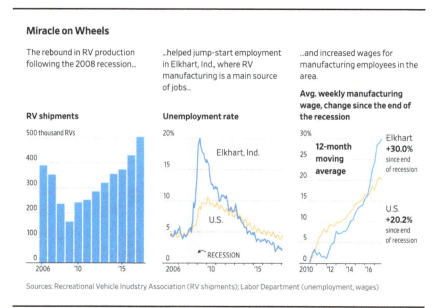

So, what are the things you see? Readers will likely notice one of two things, or both. There are other things you could see, but these two are the most common answers.

1. The majority would say yes, unemployment is clearly dropping. And they would be right.

2. A minority may realize that many potential employees left Elkhart over the last few years since the depression. Therefore, the drop in unemployment is driven both by more jobs and fewer workers to hire. In other more words, the percentage of people not being hired is smaller, but this is off a much smaller hiring pool than before. In this case, unemployment is dropping, but it is not something to celebrate. This group would also be right.

Yet, the latter explanation is more appropriate, or more right, since one can then craft policies to deal with a region lacking sufficient workers. Policies which attract new workers would be developed. These include better schools for the children of workers, new homes, etc.

With the initial answer, one could end up crafting completely different regional policies that did not factor in the primary reasons for the decrease in unemployment. In this situation, the region may raise taxes, since they think everyone that wants to work is working, further lowering the tax base if more workers choose to leave because of the high taxes.

As you can see, different people looking at the same data would almost certainly arrive at different conclusions. In fact, two people with seemingly similar profiles will arrive at a different interpretation. This is because their judgement differs. Judgement is the way one interprets information. And to interpret information we typically rely on our past experience, readings and teachings, what we see in the media, and travel experiences.

Let's think about what this means. A waitress, without a degree and no formal work experience, working at a café in San Francisco could correctly realize the drop in unemployment in the exhibit above is probably due to more jobs and people like herself leaving depressed areas. Her knowledge and past experience gives her better judgement here.

A brilliant consultant with an advanced degree working at an elite firm and only watching "Scandal" may not know this since the show, while very good, is not about average U.S. experiences. This consultant does not have the past experience, social network, media exposure, education nor travel exposure to realize this may be the reason the unemployment rate is down.

The point is that all experience matters when it comes to judgement. The mistake we make often is to ignore everything we have ever done in the past, and only think about things we read about in the WSJ, HBR, etc. To have good judgement, one must be willing to marshal everything they know and apply it.

If you want to build out your judgement, you need to think about the source of your knowledge:

1. **Past experiences** (packing trucks, waitressing, being mugged, etc.)
2. **Readings** (high school, university, media, books, comics, etc.)
3. **Education** (high school, university, ongoing development, etc.)
4. **Social network** (your significant other, friends, family, and their conversations)
5. **Media exposure** (cable, internet, streaming, etc.)
6. **Travel** (the trips you take daily and on vacations)

No one source is better, and a balance is not necessarily better. Television and media can be a great source of judgement, provided you distinguish between what is real and staged.

If you do have very narrow exposure to one set of views, you can either expand your exposure or compensate for your exposure when making judgements. For example, if you earn $300,000 / annum and are trying to estimate organic food consumption across the U.S., you cannot use your monthly organic food bill as a guide since your profile does not represent that of the average American citizen. That is one of the largest mistakes people make. In this case, just realize your data is not representative and adjust downward.

And do not be embarrassed about watching hours of Bollywood, K-POP, Turkish soaps, telenovelas, cooking shows, etc. You never know how that knowledge could be useful. We watch an incredible amount of television. And it helps with our reasoning. For example, you could very well one day be advising a large U.S. hospitality business and need to help them optimize their sourcing. Knowing types of food used by different nationalities could be useful to develop early hypotheses. If you take any case and break it down to its component issues, it stops being a profit, revenue, market entry, operations case, etc. It becomes a case about how to convince families in Chicago to buy insurance, which ingredients should be used to make medicine more "tasty" to children, how to stack more boxes in a semi that is travelling from Mexico to the USA. As you can see, very mundane sources of knowledge can help here. The point is you need to use what you already know.

So, try this. Look at some data in the media and draw conclusions just using textbook knowledge. Now try drawing conclusions using everything you know whether it embarrasses you or not. You should see a huge difference. Can you imagine how many bad decisions have been made in history because someone was too embarrassed to mention/use a data source from their personal life?

You get the point. Judgement is essential, and it comes from everywhere. Your job is not to assume you must ignore what you already know. You must learn to use it.

If you truly lack judgement, which is not possible, and it is more likely you just cannot apply what you know, then applying first principle skills we teach in *The Consulting Offer* will help but only up to a certain point. For example, in the drop-in-unemployment question, you could have brainstormed from first principles that the unemployment rate = (# unemployed / # total employees). Either the numerator is going down, the denominator is going up or stays the same, or the numerator went down but the denominator also shrank at a slightly lower rate. So, first principles analyses help you figure out what drove the issue, but you still need to apply judgement to determine what likely happened.

The big issue with solving problems only with first principles and leaving out judgement is that anyone can learn how to solve a problem from first principles. You are valuable because of the unique judgement you have. If you have no unique judgement, we could essentially hire anyone who knew how to solve a problem from first principles or simply automate the task. Analysis will only get you so far; how you interpret the findings is judgement and having the confidence to put forward a controversial interpretation based on your judgement is equally important. That brings us to the difference between responsibility and accountability.

The responsible person does what they are told, correctly. The accountable person thinks about why they are completing task x, determines if another task should be done to achieve the intended goal and makes those changes. They own the problem and not the solution. People who own the problem work harder, face tougher hurdles and are sometimes seen as arrogant, but they get the job done and ultimately are more successful.

PROLOGUE

From   Daniel Manicotti
To   Carlos Selgado

Date   Wed, April 5 at 5:23 AM
Subject Important: WSJ Story on Goldy

Carlos - we could have a problem.

I received a call from Edwin Welch at the Wall Street Journal. They are running a story tomorrow about Goldy and wanted our confirmation on some of the details. I gave him the standard response that we do not comment on internal matters, and our performance and plans are on track. This is what he wanted me to confirm:

1. Since taking over, you have uncovered major culture issues and production problems.
2. Your ideas and plans have met considerable resistance.
3. The board is not fully in agreement on some of the actions you want to take.
4. You are struggling to rein in the geographical regions.
5. Performance is continuing to drop, and planned quarterly results will be down again.
6. Either McKinsey or BCG is being retained to conduct a "One Goldy" study to reposition the business.

They are clearly not saying anything new. We expected some of this for your investor road show and talked about how to position this. It is what would be expected given your very recent arrival as CEO. So I don't think it's a big issue. The problem is that we don't want these negative sentiments to set the agenda for the meetings. So I think just the timing is bad.

I can talk at any time so please call as needed.

Best,

Daniel Manicotti
Executive Vice President - Public Relations
Goldy Mineracao

Assistant
Francesca Marchese

SUCCEEDING AS A MANAGEMENT CONSULTANT

*A*FTER A PARTICULARLY TIRING OVERNIGHT FLIGHT from Sao Paulo to London on which he had little sleep, Carlos Selgado was not pleased with the email from Daniel. After a rough few months, he was looking forward to this trip to break out of the negativity surrounding Goldy's future and put a positive spin on the business, its people, and assets. Such an email on the eve of his first major investor road show could hurt his plans. Since his appointment three months ago, the business media have given him a particularly tough time and virtually no room to settle in. It was not just the media who were having a go at him. He had been attacked by the labour unions, industry bodies, CEOs of rival companies, and investors. Walter Sydow, the imperious and brilliant CEO of International Mining Corp., publicly referred to Selgado's appointment as the "*. . . arrival of the friendly uncle, whom everyone loved, yet has the role of taking the sick dog (Goldy) out to the woods to be put down.*" Well, no one seemed to love him anymore. Selgado had not been expecting an easy task, but surely no one expected change in three months. He could only wonder what his friends at the WSJ had now cooked up.

Struggling through a packed terminal, Selgado looks for a newsstand and wonders about the throngs of travellers. Easter seems to have brought out an unusually large number of them. He picks up the WSJ and quickly skims the article while he is driven to his hotel. He breathes a palpable sigh of relief. Despite the negative slant of the article, the WSJ is not reporting anything new. They are using some

PROLOGUE

new quotes, but the story is still the same: new CEO, no change, and grave expectations of the quarterly results. Watching a London still struggling to shake off a particularly bad winter, Carlos briefly wonders about the path he has taken. It had not always been so bad. It was only six months ago that *Fortune* magazine called him "King Carlos" in a glowing story about his turnaround of the Brazilian state-owned electricity producer. At the time, he could do no wrong. Hoping to go into retirement and spend the promised, but perennially postponed, quality time with his wife of 35 years, Isabella, he had not been looking for anything new or strenuous. He was particularly keen on a few board positions or maybe even lecturing at the university–anything that allowed him to work on his yacht and go sailing with his wife.

With knowledge of his decision to leave the electricity producer already public, calls from headhunters and corporate boards did not take long to come. He dismissed most of them since they were just more of the same. They were not attractive enough to change course so late in his career. Then the calls from Goldy started coming. At first, he also dismissed them: what did he know about mining? But they became more and more persistent. After doing his own due diligence, Selgado was still going to say no. That's when the Goldy chairman started calling in the big guns. The Brazilian Minister of Resources eventually played the patriot card: "*Carlos, Goldy is a national institution in Brazil. It is your duty to turn it around. The very future, the very competitive fabric of Brazil is interwoven with Goldy's success. If Goldy unravels, Brazilian morale and competitiveness will unravel.*" Selgado eventually accepted the position.

The media sentiment changed within two weeks of his arrival at Goldy. In a remarkable twist from his days in the utility sector, *Business Week* kicked off the criticism with a cover story "*Is King Carlos about to be dethroned?*" Then everything just became worse. Everything that went on at Goldy was reported in excessive detail. No piece of information was too small to create speculation among the press. The criticism reached a crescendo with Sydow's comments, but who could blame them? Goldy was a behemoth by any standards—one of the world's largest mining companies, a major Brazilian employer, and one of a small group of emerging markets companies supposedly challenging established players. It was a story waiting to be written.

A month into his position, Selgado knew he would need help. His first management meeting was a disaster. The quarter had closed a mere month ago, and yet the organisation could not give him any indication of where the business was going. No single mining unit could report back on their cash or cost position. No one had a business plan, and certainly no direction had come from executive management.

The first meeting with the Strategic Planning Group (SPG) was another disappointment. At the very least, Selgado expected SPG to have a clear handle on the problems in the business. He was hoping they could tell him what was happening. Staffed with ex-bankers and young MBAs, the unit was designed for the sole purpose of generating acquisitions. Strategy in the company used to mean having an acquisition strategy and aggressively executing it. After all, that's how Goldy had grown. It seemed no one had a strategy for integrating the acquisition or extracting synergies once the deal was done. It was difficult to know if any SPG employees had ever even visited a gold mine. Goldy was like a huge supertanker merely carried by the momentum of its past success. Yet, even the largest supertankers can be stopped. It seemed Goldy was going in that direction.

It did not get any better outside the company. Two weeks into his tenure, Fleet Rock Investors wanted to meet him. The powerful and respected U.S. investment fund was the second-largest shareholder in Goldy and could quite rightly command the CEO's attention. In what started out as a cordial meeting, the eponymous Sir Albert Hall,

PROLOGUE

chairman of Fleet Rock, explained that it was too early for Selgado to present his plan for the business. Still, though, Sir Hall wanted to be crystal clear about Fleet Rock's views on Goldy and what needed to change. What followed was a 50-minute dissection of the perceived problems with Goldy's business. Sir Hall was kind enough to have a presentation prepared listing his thoughts and ideas to fix the business. While other investors were not so prepared with their recommendations, there was an overwhelming sense that Goldy was just not living up to its potential.

Realising the need to have an honest appraisal of the situation, Carlos contacted a consulting partner called Marcus Capple whom he met while preparing for his interviews with the board. He needed a top firm to come in and tell him exactly how bad it was internally and relative to the competition. He needed someone he could trust and whose findings would be respected—a consulting firm whose mere presence would signal that he was serious about change.

Getting out of his car, Carlos thought that at least the WSJ was a little clueless about the official mandate of the consulting firm, and that is as it should be. He would need to be careful in rolling out his turnaround strategy and employing consultants. The stakeholders at Goldy were powerful, entrenched, and resistant to new ideas.

WEEK 0

WEEK BEFORE THE ENGAGEMENT

READING THE WSJ ARTICLE ON GOLDY, Luther, the engagement manager, thought this was going to be a tough and high-profile engagement for the firm. In reality, it would be no different from the hundreds of other engagements handled by the firm each year. The team would just need to meet the standards expected. Luther was pleased that they managed to get a full week with the team for pre-engagement planning.

Week 0 is also known as the pre-engagement week. It is rare to have them. The team will work in the office and away from the client. The objective of this week is to ensure the team fully understands as much about the client and the problem as they possibly can and before they arrive on-site. At the end of the week, the team must actually develop their solution and thereafter use the engagement to test their hypotheses. Although this sounds counterintuitive, the process is explained below, along with examples from the Goldy engagement.

Engagement teams usually consist of experienced and inexperienced members. Consultants may be inexperienced because they do not understand a sector, client, or particular types of analyses. This initial week in the office provides inexperienced consultants a chance to understand the client and sector and not to appear "green" in front of the client. This is the general format of the week:

READING AND RESEARCH

Planning commences with the engagement team reviewing all relevant newspaper articles, research reports, equity research reports, annual reports, and regulatory filings about the client. They will also read competitor information and obtain advice from other consultants who have worked on similar engagements. The objective is to gain a broad understanding of the issues without going into too much detail.

ISSUES

As the team conducts its research, each member will write down any issues they *think* affect the client. The team is not worried about the accuracy of the lists of issues at this point. The aim is to generate a list of issues based on educated guesses and a careful reading of the material available. The team will try to go broad and identify as many issues across as many areas of the business as possible.

Over a series of one or two two-hour meetings, the team will use post-it notes to list every issue on a whiteboard. The Goldy team generates over 140 post-it notes. They can be in any order and any priority. The aim is to capture all possible issues affecting the client. It is similar to an educated brainstorming session. Luther facilitates the sessions to generate discussion and to capture the issues. The team will usually work together in one large room during this planning week, which allows them to create a war room, post information, and immerse themselves in the engagement.

WEEK 0 - WEEK BEFORE THE ENGAGEMENT

THEMES

Posting issues on a whiteboard helps everyone see a common set of items, potential patterns, and themes developing. In the second or third meeting, the team starts discussing the common themes from the list of issues. The session focuses on clustering the issues into common themes. For example, the following cluster of 13 issues scattered around the whiteboard can be listed under a theme called "rising costs" or "costs":

- Four salary increases to reduce labour walkouts.
- Fuel prices doubled in 16 months.
- Shortage of equipment and spare parts driving up costs.
- Mining taxes have increased.
- Water levy introduced seven months ago.
- Extended use of contractors.
- Tunnelling machines are in high demand and difficult to secure.
- Unrest in Thailand is forcing Goldy to buy electrical reticulation equipment from expensive Malaysian manufacturers.
- The Brazilian *real* is weakening against the U.S. dollar, driving up import costs.
- New mining act is creating uncertainty about future environmental costs.
- Steel and copper prices have increased 17 percent in two months.
- New shared-services centre rollout is delayed.
- Rising inflation is driving up domestic costs.

The team will go through every issue and add it to a theme. Once this is done, some themes may be combined, while others may be split apart. Generally, there are rarely more than eight themes for any one client and any one problem to be solved. Sometimes consultants take each theme and develop a hypothesis to test the theme. The challenge with this approach is developing an analysis framework on which to lay the hypotheses. Without the framework, it is difficult to apply the rules and techniques management consultants use to structure their analyses. To overcome this critical problem, another approach is presented below, which allows for the development of a hypotheses framework.

KEY QUESTIONS

The group uses this discussion on themes and key issues to spur debate and gain a better understanding of the engagement. This robust debate forces consultants to ask important, probing, and tough questions. It is as much planning for the study as an educational session for the consultants. It serves as a filter to weed out poorly formed ideas or weak thinking. After they are comfortable with the themes, *the team puts aside the themes and key issues for a moment.*

The group then takes the key question presented by the client and tests if this is indeed the key question they need to answer in the engagement. Sometimes clients raise the wrong question, which the client thinks must be answered. The engagement team tests if this is the right question.

Many consultants get too focused on answering the question posed by the client, but perfectly answering the wrong question will not help the client. The right answer to the wrong question will still not solve the root-cause problem. Therefore, the team takes time to ensure they are asking the correct questions in the engagement.

They ask themselves, *"If we solved this question posed by the client, would the problems at the client be resolved?"*

If the answer is yes, the key engagement question is confirmed and captured. In this case, the engagement team believes the key question posed by the client is indeed the correct question to answer and posts it on the whiteboard.

Key question: How can Goldy improve its production value?

Assuming they have the correct question, they need to think about how they would go about answering this question. Answering this one question is a difficult task. To make it easier and manageable, the team takes this question and splits it into smaller questions in a logical format. The next, level 2, set of questions would be:

Level 2 Question: Can Goldy increase its revenue?

Level 2 Question: Can Goldy reduce its costs?

Either way is a means of raising Goldy's production value.

As the team develops each layer of questions, they test each layer (e.g., layer 2, layer 3, layer 4) by asking themselves two further questions.

First, are these the complete list of questions in this layer that can impact the previous question? In other words, are raising Goldy's revenues and reducing Goldy's costs the only ways to increase production value? Is there any other way that should be added as a level 2 question? If the answer is no, this is called a collectively exhaustive list of questions or hypotheses.

Second, have the questions been sufficiently separated so that changing the variables that impact one question will have NO impact on another question? For example, the price of gold is a variable that impacts revenue, but the price of gold will rarely have an impact on costs. If each of the questions does not overlap through their variables, the team will say that the questions are mutually exclusive.

The principles of being mutually exclusive and collectively exhaustive (MECE) are fundamental concepts in management consulting. They are the foundations on which consulting analyses are built.

The first concept ensures that no stone is left unturned in analysing the key question of the engagement. For example, imagine there was another way to increase Goldy's production value, but the team overlooked this option. When the final recommendations are presented, it is possible that the overlooked option may have altered the recommendation. Having a collectively exhaustive set of options ensures that all avenues are explored.

When issues overlap and cannot be isolated, it is difficult to know why changes are occurring. It is also difficult to understand the issue. Isolating a question, issue, or analysis allows the engagement team to conduct a test whereby they can be sure that x, y, or z is responsible for the changes. If the hypotheses/questions fail the test of being mutually exclusive, the analyses and findings will be flawed because they are running analyses on hypotheses that have not been isolated for testing. The team takes the time needed to ensure the analyses fulfil these two requirements, but this is not easy to do. It can take an engagement team up to a week to ensure these two conditions are met for each part of the analyses. The team applies these checks and balances as they continue breaking down the key question.

A level 2 question can be broken down even further. Let us look at both revenue and costs:

Level 2 Question: *Can Goldy increase its revenue?*

    Level 3 Question: *Is there a way to increase the price of gold?*

    Level 3 Question: *Is there a way to increase the volume of gold sold?*

    Level 3 Question: *Is there any other way in which revenue can be increased? (Revenue from other sources, such as investment income,* is included here. Since this branch makes such a small contribution to overall revenue in mining companies, it is removed from the overall decision tree.)

Level 2 Question: *Can Goldy reduce its costs?*

Level 3 Question: *Is there a way to reduce operating (variable) costs?*

Level 3 Question: *Is there a way to reduce capital (fixed) costs?*

Again, the team will check to determine if they are mutually exclusive and collectively exhaustive. The team will continue building a level 4 and level 5 set of questions for each question. In the planning phase, some teams build out to a level 8 set of questions. Rarely will greater detail be needed at this stage. Later in the engagement, more detail will be added if required for the analyses. When questions are laid out from left to right, with the primary question on the left (*How can Goldy increase its production value?*) and the subsequent levels fanning out to the right, it tends to look like a tree with branches. This is the origination of the term value tree or decision tree.

EXHIBIT 2: Decision Tree Analyses

FIRMSCONSULTING.COM & STRATEGYTRAINING.COM

Decision trees can be effectively used to analyse the main problem statement

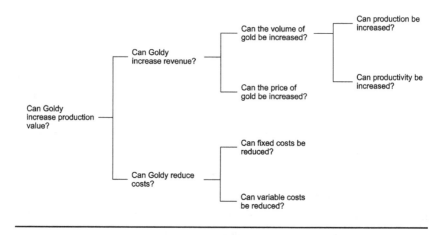

The team now goes back to the list of issues and themes it developed. Can they find a place on the tree where every issue and theme can be tested? If not, is the tree missing some questions? Are some of the issues irrelevant? Must the questions change? To accomplish this task, the team takes each issue and numbers it. A stack of post-it notes is used with each post-it note numbered to correspond to an issue. The post-it note is then placed on the decision tree where the team thinks the issue resides. Using this process, the team can visually see where most of the issues may lie. This can also serve as a check. First, is the analysis skewed to one or two parts of the question? Second, have they been unable to find issues in certain areas? If so, does this mean these areas have no issues? The team may need to go back and look at their issues again to understand why an area was ignored.

Once they are comfortable with their decision tree, they will proceed with the planning.

EXHIBIT 3: Checking Issues

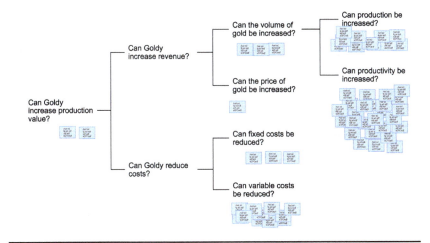

For the branches of the decision tree with the most issues, the team can conceivably assume that this is a priority area for the client. Since branches with issues will likely have different numbers of post-it notes, the branches will have different degrees of priorities. Therefore, the branches with post-it notes can be ranked in order of priority.

For the top three or five branches, hypotheses can be developed explaining why the problem is occurring or what can be done to fix the problem. This process for developing hypotheses ensures hypotheses are MECE and specific to a client problem.

Developing the decision tree is one of the most important steps of an engagement. Using the decision tree, the team can break down a hypothesis into manageable components for analyses. The team will revisit this in the next few days and test it further until it is finalised as a strawman.[3] Engagements are not static, and as information changes, the priorities of answering the questions may change, which may cause the tree to change slightly.

Given the amount of work required to rigorously analyse each branch in the tree, the tree will be split into different branches (set of questions), and different consultants will take over ownership to develop them further. It is critical to document and share all the work done on the decision tree and issues. It will be needed by the engagement team to review their thinking.

Using these detailed decision trees and hypotheses, the engagement team can determine the likely answer to the questions *before* they arrive at the client site,[4] i.e., the team looks at each question in the decision tree and based on their careful preparation, they estimate the likely answer by assuming the outcome of the analyses to test the hypotheses. Using the decision tree, the team also develops the storyboard for the engagement. The storyboard is the message delivered to the client based on the expected results. This is the counterintuitive part.

If this is done so early, then what's done during the engagement?

The engagement is therefore the process of proving or disproving hypotheses. The decision tree and hypotheses are written as questions. Over the course of the engagement, the team will develop

---

[3] A strawman is a draft version of a document.
[4] The client site refers to the client-owned premises within which the engagement team will be located over the duration of the study.

analyses to test each hypothesis and thereafter collect the data for the analyses. Depending on the results of the tests, the analyses are either proved or disproved, and the storyboard is altered.

The process can be summarised as follows:

1. Determine the key engagement question
2. Develop the decision tree to the 4th or 5th level horizontally
3. Check for MECE
4. Prioritize the branches
5. Develop hypotheses for the prioritized branches (explained later)
6. Develop analyses to test each hypothesis (explained later)
7. Develop the storyboard (explained later)
8. Collect data for the analyses (explained later)
9. Complete the analyses (explained later)
10. Refine the storyboard (explained later)

The process above is iterative. As analyses are completed and new information becomes available, the team may need to go back and create new analyses and repeat the process. It is not a linear process. This is the central technique used by management consultants. It allows the team to see the overall message and focus their work *before* the engagement begins.

BUSINESS CASE TEAM

The business case team has an overarching role on a consulting engagement. While the other teams focus on specific parts of a client's business, the business case team works across the entire scope of the engagement. The business case team will not be responsible for doing all the analyses. Rather, they will need to assess the opportunities for improvement *developed* by the rest of the team. Their job will be to determine the combined benefit to the client of implementing all recommendations. The business case team needs to ensure the opportunities recommended will actually deliver the benefits stated. Therefore, the business case must be independent and verify the opportunities presented. They ask such questions as the following:

- Are the opportunities mutually exclusive? In other words, are we double counting benefits?

- Does this opportunity make sense? Will it actually work as described?

- What is the impact of doing this?

- Is this opportunity worth pursuing? What are the returns and cash flow patterns?

The business case team will need to develop an Excel model of some kind to test various scenarios and options. A smart business analyst knows one does not need to be an Excel wizard to produce business cases. One needs to be highly analytical, understand how to analyse the problem, and translate that analysis into a simple Excel model. The best business cases are well thought out so that the models are simple and intuitive. Poorly designed business cases have highly complex models that are large, unfocused, cumbersome to update, and difficult to use. Excel models are tools that are the means to an end—not an end in themselves.

Although the key questions from the engagement still need to be confirmed with the client, the engagement team feels they have developed a very close strawman of the final key question and can begin their planning work. The business case team will also develop planning material (common to all streams) and some additional items that are unique to their work:

1. **Stream Charter:** a charter is a clear explanation of what the business case team will deliver. It is no more than a page in length and is shared with the rest of the team members to ensure there are no misunderstandings and gaps between the members' work. In some ways, it is the contract between the team and engagement manager.

2. **Model Architecture:** the architecture is a simple modular representation showing how the model will work, what it will do, and what it will produce. It is just one slide in length.

3. **Model Description:** a half-page description of the model. It forces the business case team to clearly explain what they are doing in simple language and to exclude unnecessary capabilities. Requiring the team to create a short description forces them to only describe the most important functions of the model.

4. **Decision Tree Tests and Data Requirements:** the decision trees are a set of questions. To answer each question, an analysis must be constructed. To run the analysis, data must be collected.

5. **Storyboard:** the storyboard consists of the headlines of the presentation that summarise the *expected* results from the business case stream. Using the planning materials listed here and completed decision tree, the business case team can develop a view of the likely analyses and results. The team will *only* write out the headlines so that everyone can understand what message they *expect* to deliver based on their *expectations* of the data analyses. Although the storyboard may change as the analyses are conducted, the initial thinking of the team will be sufficient to guide their colleagues.

The business case stream plays a central role in setting direction and providing guidance to the team. These five pieces of work take about a week to complete.

WEEK 1

day 1 & 2

FIRST WEEK AT THE CLIENT

THE ENGAGEMENT TEAM will initially be based in Goldy's gleaming new head office in Rio de Janeiro. They will be expected to liaise extensively with Goldy's operations planning centre in Belo Horizonte, Minas Gerais State, but for most of the engagement they will be based deep in the Amazon forest at the Mino 1 mining complex. Mino 1 will be the first mining hub studied. At this stage of the engagement, the team planning of the previous week has generated all that it can. It is now up to the work stream leads to take ownership for their activities.

The first week is always critical. Each team will need to prepare their planning material and analysis frameworks. Doing this is important for several reasons:

1. Building the overall work plan so early in the engagement requires the business case team to *understand the overall problem*, outline how they will design the solution, list their data requirements, and understand all the questions that need to be answered. Where there is an overlap of activity, the teams will need to agree on roles and responsibilities. This is a steep learning curve for a team with no gold mining experience. Yet, they know the management consulting processes work and are designed to overcome any information gaps they may have about the sector.

2. While they need to design the overall work plan soon, they also need to have a process that is *flexible enough to incorporate likely changes* in findings from the rest of the team. For example, what if the operations teams find a new benefit that was not identified earlier? The business case team's approach must allow for these uncertainties to be managed without disrupting the milestones and timelines.

3. The business case team must provide direction to the rest of the team but also requires inputs from everyone else to complete its work. The team must design its approach over the next eight weeks to account for this: *providing direction while also collecting information.*

4. The business case team *cannot work in isolation.* They need to present meaningful updates of sufficient depth, and at regular intervals, to provide direction to the rest of the team. These updates are critical input for the rest of the team and must be carefully planned. Remember that the business case team must conduct the initial top-down financial assessment of the operations. The result of this analysis, coupled with the focus interview feedback and benchmarks from Goldy peers, provides enormous insight to the engagement team. They direct the teams to possible areas of improvement or point out areas likely to generate little opportunity for improvement. Furthermore, the business case team uses these updates to test their thinking with the client and engagement team.

5. The business case team needs to find *allies in the client's finance department* who can share data, work with the team to test hypotheses, answer questions, and validate their approach. This can only be done if the business case team can clearly explain their approach and rationale and instil confidence among the finance department employees. They

need to build these relationships at several levels of the finance department—at the mid-level, where they will work with the finance team on a day-to-day basis, and at the CFO level, where they need to build rapport and trust to ensure he accepts the recommendations and defends the findings. Building these relationships is difficult to do if the team is unable to explain their objectives and approach.

FIRST CLIENT MEETING

Week one is always difficult for any business case team. It is especially difficult for this team, as the members have limited sector exposure. They need to start engaging the client at the same time they are developing their planning documents, and they need to build credibility among the client's employees as they are learning about the sector. Furthermore, the CFO, Flavio Semer, has recommended that the business case team join a finance session and present an overview of the study and the consultants' requirements. If they agree, Max and Alana, the business case team, will meet the CFO and finance executives (head of operations finance, 12 finance managers from each mine, head of investor relations, head of IT, and head of shared services) at 4 p.m.

Such an early unplanned workshop presentation is dangerous for several reasons. The CFO has a reputation of being very tough and harbouring a particular dislike for consultants. In the first meeting with any client, the consultants are trying to develop rapport and a working relationship. This is very difficult to do in a group meeting where the agenda and discussions are much more difficult to control. Furthermore, this early in the engagement the team will have little to present. They could end up looking unprepared. The reaction of the entire finance department is another unknown. The risk of damage to the consultants' reputation and hence, a setback to the engagement, is too great. Workshops must always be staged and managed events with defined outcomes. The consultants first need to prepare before they can participate in this workshop. Understanding the obvious risks and the CFO's dislike of consultants, Max, the associate leading the business case, understands that a workshop is the last thing they need on the first day of the engagement.

Therefore, Max decides it is best to initially meet Flavio alone. He politely suggests to Flavio's PA, Gabrielle, that they meet individually. He asks her to thank the CFO for the opportunity but suggests they meet alone to agree on any decisions before they are presented. He recommends pushing their meeting back to 5 p.m. or later in the week. Gabrielle confirms a meeting for 6 a.m. the following day.

For the first meeting with Flavio, Max has only one objective: *to start gaining the client's trust*. As the business case leader, he cannot be arrogant, he cannot take in a lot of documents with little context, he cannot have any extra people in the meeting, and he cannot create any risks by presenting information that may be erroneous. He first needs to understand the CFO and lay the groundwork for an effective relationship. Max prepares one agenda document:

Agenda

1. *Expectations of the engagement.*
2. *How would we define success for the business case work stream?*
3. *How should we share information and obtain approvals?*
4. *Decisions needed:*
    a. *Focus interviews with mid-level and senior employees.*
    b. *Allocating finance staff to assist the work stream.*

WEEK 1 - DAY 1 & 2: FIRST WEEK AT THE CLIENT

The agenda is prepared with great care. The objective is to draw out the CFO's concerns so that he feels he has been heard. If he feels his concerns are heard, he is more likely to work with the business case team. Although four agenda items are raised, depending on the client's mood, the last item will have to be covered very carefully or postponed to another meeting.

The agenda is written out clearly so that the CFO knows exactly what will be discussed in each agenda point. It is important to give a client time to prepare. Client relationships can be damaged if the client feels he was caught unprepared. As a professional courtesy, the agenda is sent to the PA within one hour of the *request* for the meeting.

The meeting at 6 a.m. begins ominously. There is a brief greeting and no offer of coffee or tea. Flavio is clearly not a people person or has had a very bad start to the morning. Max thanks the CFO for meeting him so early in the morning. He is very careful to weave into the conversation certain confirmations. This is a skill to ensure the client is reminded of any commitments made, which includes confirming the meeting is an hour in duration and asking if the CFO received the agenda sent the previous day. It is important to remind the CFO of these items early on without seeming to do so in a mechanical style. Max also mentions that the CFO probably knows all about the engagement, and the session was booked to elaborate on the approach used for the study. Implying that the CFO does not know anything about the engagement, whether true or not, is generally never a good idea. Just in case the executive has not been informed, it is always wiser to imply otherwise but still provide a brief update. Doing this prevents an embarrassing exposure about the executive's lack of knowledge. It's a skill consultants use to gain the support of executives who may have been sidelined by their superiors. Embarrassed executives can become uncooperative or defensive. Neither outcome will help the engagement team.

Flavio immediately goes into a point-by-point response to the agenda items.

Expectations of the engagement:

1. "Meaningful benefits that can be implemented."
2. "No wasting his time or that of his staff."
3. "No theoretical solutions."
4. He wants to know why the production value has dropped.
5. His staff and the operating teams must accept and validate the solutions.

How should we define success for the business case work stream?

1. "Clear explanation of the value creation gap and opportunities."
2. "Some early wins to show success."
3. "Improvement within nine months."
4. Acceptance by his team and the operating team.

How should we share information and obtain approvals?

At this point, he asks for Max's opinion. Max recommends a 30-minute meeting each Friday to present an update. On Thursday morning, he will forward a one-page summary of the progress made in the previous week. The CFO likes the idea.

Focus Interviews

The CFO wants to know why this is necessary. Max explains that some new problems and potential solutions may be known among the mine employees and executive-level employees. These focus interviews will allow employees to raise any concerns they have. Max also mentions that all information is confidential and that the interviews will last no more than 60 minutes each. He also points out that without this step the engagement could take longer since the consultants will need to analyse the business without any guidance from employees. Flavio agrees on the conditions that disruption to employees is minimised, confidentiality is guaranteed, and he can see a sanitized summary of the feedback.

Finance staff to assist the work stream

The CFO does not like this idea. Flavio mentions that all finance employees report directly to him, and some report directly into the operations. He feels that they are short-staffed and cannot spare anyone. He also feels that his employees should not be doing the work of the consultants.

Max indicates that he is correct on all these points.

Max further points out that he will need only about two to three hours a week from a senior finance person. This time would be used to test key ideas and help the consultants access information. The senior person will not need to do any actual work but will serve as a sounding board given the limited availability of the CFO.

A more junior finance person would likely be needed two days a week for the first four weeks to find data. Max mentions that the analyses done on the engagement will remain unused unless someone works with the consulting team to take over the material once they leave.

The CFO begrudgingly makes two personnel recommendations and suggests Max go see them.

Before Max leaves, Flavio provides one final word of caution. He mentions that a team of consultants were invited to try to fix a similar, yet more systems-focused problem about two years ago, but they failed miserably. He hopes "you guys" will be different and mentions that the only reason they were brought in is because the new CEO arrived after the last debacle and did not see the trouble consultants could cause. In the CFO's words, they are "walking on the footprints of failure." He asks if the team has ever visited a gold mine. He suggests the team do so soon to understand the environment. Max thanks Flavio for his time and goes off to see Gabrielle about the rest of the bookings.

The meeting seems to have gone well. Max has spent 90 percent of the time simply listening to the CFO and ensuring that his concerns are understood. Despite the hesitancy of the client, key decisions were made, and the engagement is moving forward. Max understands he must now respond to these comments in a professional way to continue building trust and respect. Hearing the CFO's expectations and ignoring them can create more hostility later in the engagement. If the CFO feels his concerns were ignored, he is much less likely to provide his feedback in the future.

Later in the day, Max will try to meet the recommended finance employees, book the focus interviews, and complete the work plan. Only when this is done will he consider having a finance department workshop. He knows it is a consulting rule never to go into a situation where the client has not been carefully prepared, and the outcome cannot be managed. His next task is to give the team feedback and prepare for the Friday morning meeting with Flavio.

… WEEK 1

day 2

TOP-DOWN ANALYSES

BEFORE TYPING UP AN UPDATE EMAIL for Alana, Max takes some time to think about helping Alana understand the overall process they will follow. He worries that Alana will fall into the same trap he did as a younger consultant: having to discard extensive analyses after realizing too late that the hypothesis being analysed was inappropriate. This was one of his early mistakes and it could hurt or severely slow down her career should she make the same mistake. Max learned the hard way that just having the right answer was not as important as having the answer the team needed at a specific point in time on the engagement. At the time, Max did not understand the reasoning for how engagements were structured. He was just focused on analyses-analyses-analyses like the forums and younger consultants had advised him to do.

He has also seen many other engagement teams make the same mistake. He fondly, and somewhat anxiously, recalled his first study for a German bank. Max had been with the firm all of two weeks when he was staffed onto the procurement cost-reduction stream. His early sentiments had been largely wrong.

He had thought he was doing well at the time.

He had thought he was a star performer.

He had thought he understood the process perfectly.

In fact, four weeks into the study, Max thought it was going so well and was so easy that he toyed with the idea of leaving the firm to set up his own boutique consultancy focused on procurement work. Max had correctly believed that when he left the firm, he could have recalled most, if not all, the techniques, tools, and methodologies he had used and could easily open up a shop that did the same work, at maybe 1/10th the cost of the firm. He could pass those savings to clients in the form of lower fees and still generate greater profits for himself in the form of a higher salary since his costs would be so low. He would have almost no overhead. Max had somewhat stupendously calculated that he could probably charge about $20,000 to $30,000 a week and would not need to work every week of the year. In fact, he figured he could go as low as $5,000 a week and still come out very profitable since all he needed was to maintain his basic expenses. He could easily pull in between $250,000 and $400,000 per annum based on the relationships he had built.

Retirement seemed within early reach with cold beer in Costa Rica!

This idea gained momentum at a procurement conference in Munich where he had met many family-owned businesses that seemed keen on the idea but could not afford the firm's substantial fees. Max recalls collecting over 50 business cards of which about 15 were serious prospects. The idea of automating the process had also been considered so that Max could serve all 15 clients, and potentially many more, without the need to hire more staff. He had done some research and it seemed he could use websites like Sparehire.com to outsource the labour-intensive analysis to lower-cost countries. He had even found and tested one contractor from India who could perform fairly complex analyses for just $100 and she could convert them into slides! Max had even started doodling a logo and name for this nascent business. He was pumped up and all set to go.

Things changed abruptly during a lunch session at the office on the 6th Friday into that German banking study. On that day, he realized just how little he actually knew about the logic, philosophy, and rationale of problem solving.

A partner from the Charlotte office was visiting and conducting a casual lunch forum/discussion for his office on her recent banking work in the U.S. At first, Max was bored. He had expected a discussion on the detailed analyses she had led but found none of that. The partner, Deepika Sherawat, was talking about how to structure an engagement and the importance of top-down analyses to set direction in a study. To Max, it seemed almost philosophical and he felt the partner was probably not very good at analyses, which is why she was downplaying it.

To Max, this seemed like a wasteful discussion. He already knew how to perform top-down, aka back-of-the-envelope, calculations for all his analyses. How was this new or useful? Then Deepika put up a slide that started the shift in his thinking.

EXHIBIT 4: Overall Analysis Approach

FIRMSCONSULTING.COM & STRATEGYTRAINING.COM

If you look carefully, you will find the same approach behind most strategy and operations studies

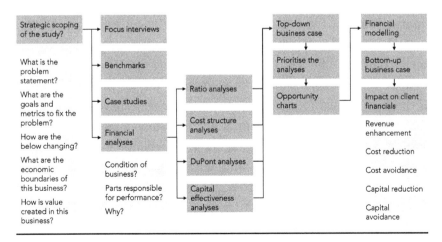

Max had never seen this process outlined in one slide before, but the more he thought about it the more he recognized it from his engagements. It was not done in exactly the same way as presented on the slides, but he recognized the vague structure, especially from the more polished senior partners who were advising on his current engagement.

Deepika was arguing that as computing power had advanced and the firm better integrated its knowledge management systems and sharing of analytic tools, analysis had become too easy to conduct. In fact, it had become commoditized. Like any commodity, it had been abused. Rather than the changes leading to fewer and improved analyses, it had led to too much analysis of questionable quality. This obsession with the complexity of the analysis and volume of analyses was preventing consultants from focusing on solving the client's problems.

She explained how it was possible for many consultants to have done the analyses on an engagement correctly only to add no value to the client since the analyses did not help solve the clients' actual problems. This was money and time spent on the wrong work at the clients' expense. In other cases, the analyses were correct, but the interrogation of their meaning was poor. Having early hypotheses was all fine and well, but the team also needed early validation of their thinking. She was essentially arguing for a way to quickly validate a hypothesis without relying solely on business judgement. If the hypotheses focused on the wrong issues, having to change the direction of an engagement at a later date is difficult to do. The late change creates doubt in the minds of clients, leads to fatigue and stress for the consultants and, ultimately, blame is cast. A study within the firm indicated that engagements where the focus had to change later versus earlier, in the study, led to greater engagement dissatisfaction and more consultants leaving the firm.

Nobody wanted to be on a failing study. In effect, a poor engagement approach was leading to poor performance and this could be mitigated.

And like any individual piece of analysis, such as a market sizing analysis, that had a useful top-down version (in this case, a back-of-the-envelope estimation case) to test if the answer was worth allocating resources to refine and validate, the overall engagement had the same top-down validation. Deepika's point was that it was not being used and the firm could be more successful if they applied this approach consistently.

This was the first time Max had started to understand some of the underlying logic behind engagements. It was clear there was a lot he did not understand.

In any study, especially longer and more complex engagements, the team needed concrete validation that their early hypotheses and focus were correct. So how would they obtain this validation? There are essentially four steps that are common to all well-planned engagements.

Deepika pointed out that engagement managers and partners who avoided these steps were taking great risks. At worst, all the problems listed above would transpire and, at best, they were merely offering cookie-cutter solutions to clients. Neither were good outcomes.

The essence of this approach is that within roughly a week or two at most, the team will have some certainty that the direction of their analysis is correct. Even if at this point they are far from done, and the focus may shift a little, Deepika pointed out that in her experience she found the top-down analyses to be largely accurate. Once the top-down analysis is done, the team is fairly certain they are pursuing the right issues and can focus on more detailed work. And if the top-down analyses indicated different issues to analyse, there is sufficient time to change direction.

She stressed that hypotheses were core to the approach, but a faster check was needed. She also pointed out some limitations of hypotheses.

1. First, the business judgement of the consultant needs to be strong to interpret the initial brief, think about the initial client symptoms, and develop a realistic hypothesis. Not all consultants had this judgement. This had become a greater issue as the firm had expanded hiring into non-traditional fields. She stressed this was not a flaw of the consultant since they could ask for help and should ask for help. Yet, and this was the flaw, many were afraid to do so.

2. Second, the engagement managers and principals need to allocate sufficient time to review the teams' hypotheses. In her experience, this rarely happens since the senior engagement team members tend to be too busy. Therefore, even when consultants asked for help, there was just no time to help them. And it is not realistic for the engagement leadership team to check everything. So, the lack of availability was not at all a critique of their approach to managing engagements.

3. Third, fairly detailed analyses need to be completed before any validation is done. This costs time and money. There are not always simple top-down analyses to test a hypothesis. Consultants were not being taught the philosophy and tools of top-down analyses.

4. Fourth, team members with limited sector/functional experience and judgement are forced to work largely in isolation during this period. This further weakens the quality of the hypotheses and subsequent study results.

So, like any individual analysis, an engagement has a top-down step, consisting of four parts, which solves the problems above.

WEEK 1 - DAY 2: TOP-DOWN ANALYSES

PART 1: Focus Interviews

Focus interviews are a key tool that should be deployed on every engagement. Deepika mentioned that as timelines become tighter, the pressure increases, and overconfident teams think they can bypass the step. Engagements have usually failed to have their maximum impact when they avoided this step. Focus interviews used to be central to the way studies were conducted, but over time they fell away. The benefits are significant, and the firm is trying to encourage their use again.

1. Very early in the study, an update must be presented to the most senior management, usually the CEO and his team, on the initial findings. This happens around Week 2 or 3 on a standard eight-week engagement. Building credibility is always important and is easily one of the top two goals of this update. In that very first update to the CEO, the engagement team must present the findings from the top-down analyses. From a credibility perspective, it is very difficult for the management team to dispute findings from the focus interviews, benchmarks, and financial ratio analyses. These are hard facts with very little interpretation from the consultants. Therefore, in this first update, it is a safe setting for the consultants as they deduce which executives are supportive or not of the engagement. This is a very important psychological logic to ensure progress is made in the first workshop and credibility is attached to the consultants, and the consulting team will not face resistance since nothing they are presenting is their opinion. Resistance, though, could come later when they analyse the implications of their findings, but it should not be a problem right now.

2. The process of developing the interview questions forces the teams to think about whether or not they have the correct hypotheses, and how they could collect the data to test them.

Some hypotheses can be rudimentarily tested with the focus interview feedback. The design of the questions also explicitly forces the team to go broader than their hypotheses to determine if other issues exist. This step is a forced process to ensure that issues are not being overlooked. Without this step, teams tend to focus on perfecting hypotheses versus checking if they are worth analysing in the first place. It is human nature for consultants to pick hypotheses that come to them easily and where the data is easy to collect. She offered the example of a bank where 20 percent of the employees in a regional centre were call centre employees. When reviewing the questions, the team realized no questions looked at opportunities in the call centres. Teams had become narrowly focused on finding the opportunities in other parts of the business, aka perfecting their hypotheses and analyses. The focus interview preparation process highlighted this gap when an associate asked why no one was speaking to the call centre employees. Was there a reason they were excluded?

3. Younger and inexperienced consultants struggle on all studies. This is normal. The more difficult a study and complex the context, the more they struggle. Focus interviews are a safe way for the younger team members to learn about the client and industry. It is a safe setting to improve their knowledge while building relationships with the client employees. It also forces consultants to reconcile their largely theoretical understanding of the problem with the practical considerations shared in the focus interviews. For example, it is one thing to think about a hypothesis to send a call centre to India to lower costs, but it is quite another issue when then subscription retention teams' focus interviews outline the challenges they have convincing customers not to cancel due to accent barriers. This forces the

consultant to think more deeply about their initial solutions. Without focus interviews, many consultants have a tendency to recommend best practices, gleaned from desktop analyses, without thinking through the impact.

4. In another psychology trick, which works the best during difficult engagements, a dynamic is created where the employees appear to be only trusting the consultants to share their thoughts with management, via the focus interviews. Although this is not the case, in situations where there is already tension and mistrust between management and employees, management takes every opportunity to hear unfiltered feedback from employees. The consultants appear to serve this role, although it is far from the case. They seem to have the trust of employees, and management cares about that. In the same situation, and on the flip side, the consultants appear to have the trust of management and employees care about that. This is an ideal outcome in turnaround and implementation engagements.

5. Focus interviews rarely identify the wrong themes to be analysed. Although employees may not clearly articulate the implications of the problem they have seen, when issues are clustered, the theme at the heart of a cluster is fairly accurate. Employees are at the frontline and the frontline is rarely blindsided by market events. Think about this simple example. In the fast-moving retail clothing market, a single clothing boutique store will know by 10 p.m. that night if sales of a highly anticipated new clothing line is not meeting expectations. With better digital tracking, they may even know in real time. The staff in that store will know immediately. That insight, which is crucial, takes its time to wind its way up to the management team. Once it arrives to the management team,

they need to think about the impact, interpret the findings, and set a course of action. This needs to wind its way down to the merchandisers, then designers, then suppliers, and finally the store. It takes time. Yet, the insight is that frontline employees have an unfiltered and uncluttered view of what is happening. They are the organic/non-GMO version of data. Speaking to them offers data in a format that is pure. Access to the frontline staff offers the engagement team a quick list of areas to explore. In many cases, employees can also identify data sources, discuss past efforts to address the problem, and offer assistance. This last part is key since the focus interviews can identify employees who will help the team in the future.

PART 2: Financial Analyses

Financial analyses are scary to an average consultant. Finance is like math. It is generally poorly taught at school and typically by teachers who believe their discipline is superior. They almost create this terrifying rite of passage where one must suffer and earn their right to understand math and finance. The net effect is a majority of students who are treated as collateral damage and remain terrified of the subjects. Yet, they are easy subjects. Due to years of being humiliated when studying, people are naturally unsure of themselves when they are faced with a financial problem. They flounder a little through little fault of their own.

Where do I start?

Where do I end?

What do I analyse?

Deepika mentioned a striking statistic. Done correctly, the average top-down financial analyses across all clients, in all sectors, and irrespective of the client size, can be done in between 24 and 72 hours.

The majority can be done in less than 48 hours. Many consultants and many competitor firms take far too long. They take so long since they do not understand the purpose of a top-down financial analysis. Like the focus interviews, the financial analyses are like a compass. They highlight anomalies, data spikes/dips, patterns, and trends that must be examined further. They set the direction for more work.

Deepika offered four guidelines for top-down financial analyses that seemed counterintuitive, until she explained them.

1. It is not offering a solution.
2. It is not offering a reason for the problem.
3. It is not forecasting nor modelling anything.
4. Financial analyses are not financial modelling.

At first, this seemed ridiculous to Max. What is the point of conducting a top-down financial analysis if it is not offering a solution, not determining the root-cause problem, and not a modelling exercise? Is there anything left that it could do?

Deepika explained that later a model may be needed, but certainly not so early when it is not even clear what problems must be modelled. The aim of the top-down analysis is to find areas where a problem could exist, determine the likely benefit of fixing the problem, and a very rough validation with employees. That is all it does. It is like opening up your child's calendar and saying, "Oh my God, she spent seven hours this week watching *How to Get Away with Murder!* Is she planning my murder?" Then you go into a tizzy and figure out that if your daughter, Stella, cut out the seven hours of television time, she could raise her math scores by 20 percent because your son, Tiberius, did the same and you are using him as a benchmark. So now you need to figure out if it is worth it to validate this, and then implement it. So, if you believe having a grumpy Stella who says "OMG, *you are the worst parent who ever lived!*" storm out of the room and refuse to talk to you for a week is a worthy price to pay for her raising her math scores and getting into a decent college, then you begin the more detailed work. Top-down financial analyses help you understand if everything is worth it. Because if it is not worth it, why do all the detailed work in the first place?

Again, it is hard to dispute the findings because the analyses are not interpreting much. It is simply examining numbers from the clients' own accounts and presenting them in a new way. Like the example above, pulling data from Stella's own calendar is far more credible than saying "*I noticed that you seem to spend too much time watching* ABC." In the latter situation, the integrity of the data is challenged when Stella says, "No, *I am watching the usual amount.*" You want to avoid that. This approach bolsters the credibility of the consultants since not much can be disputed. This credibility will become useful later when the client will want to challenge the consultants' interpretation of things.

Deepika explained that no more than three types of analyses need to be done at this early stage.

1. Ratio analyses: basic calculations of simple profitability, cash flow, and simple balance sheet ratios. There is no point in this being detailed. For example, a profit problem would show up in the net income figure at the corporate level or business unit level. You can dig deeper into which line unit is causing the problem, but there is no point in calculating the net margin by product line and region or examining the cost structure of the problem product line. At this stage, we just want to know if a problem exists, if it is different from what the client thinks is a problem, and where the problem exists. We can then make some basic projections on how the problem may impact the company in the next 12 to 24 months. Later we will determine

and figure out how to fix the root cause of the problems. Why is this valuable? Let's assume this same client wants to increase profits by focusing on growth. This analysis could show the client that reducing costs may be a more urgent problem and could lead to the same results. Naturally, the focus and objectives of the study will change significantly if the client agrees.

2. Cost structure: requires a fairly simple analysis of margins, fixed costs, variable costs, contribution margins, and/or break-even points. Deepika made a very insightful point. The benefit is not in knowing what the cost structure is—it sometimes is too early for that— but in understanding how the business should be run given the cost structure sought by the client, and how it is actually run. For example, she provided the anecdote of a retail banking client trying to increase the volume of transactions in the retail banking side of their business, but the client had cut investments in digitizing many of the approval steps. This meant that their volume-intensive business, which should have had a lower variable cost, was forced to manually approve items and this drove up variable costs, while neglecting the once-off but high fixed automation costs. Helping the client see this disconnect on Week 2 of that study helped the team convince the client that digitizing the back office would become a focus of the study. It changed the focus of the study.

3. DuPont/ROCE analyses: essentially any return ratio would work here. In other words, is the client earning a healthy return for their capital deployed? If not, where are the problems and why is it likely happening? Does the client want to be in a business that destroys so much capital? All are simple analyses to perform using company statements. It is important to realize

that just completing the cost structure and ratio analyses will yield enormous insights. Do not worry if you are not yet ready for DuPont analyses.

Top-down financial analyses operate like a slightly more sophisticated version of a dashboard warning light. It tells the team and client where a problem may exist and provides a little more information. Together with all the top-down analyses, a pattern can emerge. But the rest of the study needs to test the findings, validate the problem, and find a solution.

PART 3: **Benchmarks**

The idea of looking for patterns can be taken further in a simple way requiring little effort, provided the minimal investment is made *ahead of time* on each study to build a proper data capturing system. As Deepika pointed out, she is aware of close to 100 banking strategy studies being done this year alone by the firm. She is involved in seven of them. If each team conducts a top-down analysis of the financials, that is 100 datasets of financial analyses. If the firm is careful about protecting client confidentiality, all this sanitized information can be uploaded to a central financial institution's group database. Any team anywhere in the world can pull up this data to determine if their client is performing roughly the same as other clients in the same stage of rolling out their strategy, with a similar operating environment, cost structure, and business model. If they are not, is it worth examining why? If they are performing as expected, are they in the upper, lower, or middle band of performers and why? How does the performance of other clients generally evolve from the starting point versus the current client?

This is a powerful tool which gives the clients a view they have likely never seen before. It only works if there is consistency in capturing this information. This is actually hard to do and impacts everything about the firm in a number of ways.

1. The calculations must be uniform and consistent. That is, a consultant working in Munich must be calculating ROCE the same way as a consultant in Mumbai. If they use different methods with different assumptions, then comparing the ROCE between both firms is meaningless. This means having a methodology documented somewhere and teaching consultants to access this methodology/data versus pulling information from an unknown source using an unknown method. This requires trust and sharing.

2. Offices must trust other offices and have a central location to collect client data, archive the original data, and only share the sanitized version. If this trust does not exist, the database can never be built. Some firms avoid this problem by having centralized research centres create the benchmarks and databases from public information. Yet, this approach does not solve the trust deficit and that is a far larger problem. Even in these cases, public information needs to always be adjusted with the latest data. An engagement team is working with what is happening on the ground today, and creating the benchmark by using information from the last quarterly filing may not be very helpful. Furthermore, the engagement teams may be using a different method from the data centre and the data centre will usually lack local knowledge to interpret the financial statements across so many different countries.

PART 4: **Case Studies**

Max found the case study discussion most intriguing. His view had always been that a case study was a case study. It meant the same thing in all parts of the firm and the contents/quality/methodology was uniform across the firm. In fact, he had seen many case studies and they tended to look the same. At least the templates did. He also knew of consultants who would push out a case study in a matter of days. In fact, Max had completed a case study on his current engagement in just two days. Had he made a mistake? Max wondered and worried a little.

Deepika had a different view and explained some of the dangers and best practices of using case studies.

1. Case studies help the consultants understand how a problem evolved at another company. They help the clients visualize what did and could happen to them. They are both a visioning and planning tool. They are not a template of best practices to be copied since no two companies are the same and there is a high probability the case study may have been incorrectly interpreted. In other words, when a company says x led to y, is there any certainty that is what happened? What if z led to y and x was actually an impediment? She offered the example of Google's prized idea of allowing employees to spend 10 percent of their time on any pet project. She stressed that Google had not misled anyone about the impact of this initiative, but outsiders had simply assumed the initiative led to Google's success. What if Google's success allowed it to implement this initiative versus the initiative's success leading to Google's overall success? What if Google could have been more successful without the initiative? What if something else had led to Google's success? Did anyone control for the graduating school, part of the business where the employee worked, etc.?

What if the initiative only worked in San Francisco and in one part of the business but failed everywhere else? Deepika mentioned that far too often case studies are used to make an irrelevant point.

2. Case studies are rife with abuse. Any case study can be designed to show anything the consultant wants to show. For example, a case study of company X can show fabulous performance over nine years with slowing growth in that 10th and final year, yet arguing this is a blip not worth analysing further. Another case study of the same company could focus on just the 9th and 10th years to highlight the reasons for the flattening growth in that final year and argue that dark times are ahead. Both are correct, but which insight is appropriate to show?

3. Consultants cherry-pick both the case study to present but also the facts within that case study. Should a case study be selected to support a consultant's pre-existing, but as yet, untested hypothesis or expose the consultant to a new view that disputes their hypothesis? Deepika pointed out that consultants tried too hard to prove a hypothesis with a case study rather than exploring why the data is not fully corroborating their hypothesis, and the implications on the broader study. She felt this was due to a lack of confidence on the part of some consultants. Assuming they found some compelling evidence from the case study to change the direction of the study, many were afraid of the prospect of having to change the minds of their colleagues who had committed time and effort to move their thinking down a pre-agreed-upon path, only to be told they may need to backtrack. The team would naturally challenge the new insights forcing the change and some consultants did not relish the prospect of facing that questioning.

4. Given that it takes an experienced engagement team eight weeks, at a minimum, to understand just one narrow issue at a client where they have full access to the client and data, how can it be possible for a consultant using second- and third-hand information, at best, to know what actually happened at another company to which they have limited to zero access? They cannot. Therefore, a case study should have a very narrow scope, or it is meaningless. Someone developing a case study of an entire company in three to five days is basically conducting a literature search, which is a polite way of saying they are aggregating the views of external reports whose quality is of unknown value. For example, a case study to understand why a bank did not invest in their digital back office is better than a broad case study such as why the retail growth strategy failed. Broad case studies tend to be inaccurate unless they are period case studies.

5. Consultants avoid period case studies since they are harder to do. Doing a case study on Cisco for the 2001 to 2003 period is very challenging, even if it is more relevant, since the client will likely have strong views on what happened. So, consultants tend to pursue new case studies where there is more consensus on the main finding, even if that consensus is inaccurate. A case study about a current event contains data that has not yet had time to be challenged so it is easy to present it as a fact. An example of this is the numerous articles lauding GE as the greatest American company of all time. Around 2000, this was the general sentiment. A case study of GE's success, completed in 2000 and using facts from 2000, would receive little pushback. A period case study of GE outlining an event from 2000, and performed today, would face far greater scrutiny because the market has had time to reassess its view

of GE. Even if the case study of the event about GE in 2000 was actually correct, the negative halo effect of GE's performance today would cloud the discussion the same way the positive halo effect of GE's performance way back in 2000 clouded discussions at that time.

6. Unless the consultant was involved in the company being case-studied, and at a fairly senior level of the discussions with that client, anything they say may lack credibility. For example, how would they know x was the reason that y happened? It is therefore always important to have a partner/consultant in the room who had been involved in the company being case-studied.

7. Case studies generate the least controversy when they lack controversy. Many consultants therefore select case studies that tell the client what they want to hear and avoid controversy. For example, using Google as a case study on innovation will usually work since the company is now seen as innovative. It may not be, but that is irrelevant since that is Google's accepted image in the marketplace. Clients will rarely challenge the case study despite the consultant not really knowing if Google is innovative and, more importantly, why they are so innovative. Taking lessons from a Google case study and directly applying it to a client will gain easy acceptance but may not be the best thing for the client.

BEST-PRACTICE TOP-DOWN ANALYSES

Firmsconsulting Corporate Strategy & Transformation Study: StrategyTraining.com
https://www.firmsconsulting.com/corporate-business-unit-strategy/

Empire International (EI) was a wholly-owned subsidiary of the regulated power utility Empire Energy (EE), which was owned by the government. EI housed all the capabilities EE developed when EE was building power stations decades ago. When EE no longer needed those skills, EI was created to invest in the non-regulated parts of the power sector, building power stations in other parts of the world. The thinking was EI could charge higher fees that could not be capped by a regulator. EI invited the engagement team to develop a strategy to bring about profitable growth since it was losing money. During the top-down analyses, the team looked at the objectives of EI's owner, EE. This is what they found.

Since EI's founding over a decade ago, EE's market had undergone a shift where there was renewed focus on expanding and maintaining the crumbling and outdated infrastructure base to meet surging electricity demand. EE was and is unable to meet electricity demand. Unless EE focused on meeting rapidly growing energy demand, electricity blackouts remained a real threat that would impact the country's productivity and attractiveness for foreign direct investment. Yet EE did not have the skills to do all the construction work after hiving those capabilities off as EI.

Therefore, the team recommended that EI become the in-house construction arm of EE and build new power stations and transmission lines and prepare for a smart grid increasingly powered by wind, solar, and other renewables. The initial idea for this vastly different recommendation came from the top-down analysis. It was not the result of weeks and weeks of analyses. The weeks of analyses only validated this hypothesis developed in Week 0-2 of the study.

As you can see, this is a radically different strategy from why the engagement team was appointed. They only shifted focus once the top-down analyses focused on what EI's owner wanted.

**Firmsconsulting Market Entry Strategy Study:
StrategyTraining.com**
https://www.firmsconsulting.com/market-entry-strategy/#!step-2

A Mexican state-owned bank wanted to create a retail branch network in the U.S. to offer small business loans to Mexican immigrants living in the U.S. This would be their entry into the U.S. market. The engagement team was hired with the specific mandate to create this retail banking strategy to profitably distribute the loans.

The top-down analyses uncovered a host of more pressing issues. First, the bank was not profitable on most loan sizes issued, given their current cost structure. The loan default rate was expected to rise shortly, and the bank did not have sufficient reserves. Most products were destroying value and the existing outsourced distribution network was probably already as efficient as the bank's wholly-owned retail branch network could ever be on its own.

Further analyses from the case studies indicated that no retail bank anywhere in the world had successfully built a large-volume micro-finance business without subsidies of some kind given the large cost footprint of a retail branch network. This was a critical finding that challenged the central argument of micro-finance lending. In other words, micro-finance only worked under very narrow conditions which did not apply to this client.

The study shifted focus from opening a branch network to determining which products should be retained and how to redesign them to increase profits. In other words, the focus went from how to better distribute a weak product portfolio to first improving the product portfolio before focusing on distribution.

Max's thoughts

At the time, Max had come away slightly awed. He felt that too many consultants are analysis-obsessed but never understand the reasoning and logic of why a study is structured as it is. He had been one of them. The idea of a top-down analysis at the beginning of a study makes perfect sense but was never codified before. If one analysis needs a top-down evaluation before it is pursued, it would make sense that a collection of analyses, aka the engagement, would require the same step.

He also felt that the thinking on how to use focus interviews, financial analyses, benchmarks, and case studies makes more sense when viewed in the context of a top-down analysis. It also explains why the detailed analysis is not performed earlier.

Coming back to the present day as his phone reminder beeps, Max makes a note to share these concepts with Alana.

WEEK 1
—

day 2

———

ENGAGEMENT
CHARTER

**AX** types out an email to Alana listing their priorities over the next two weeks:

From   Max Kraus
To   Alana Cruz
Date   Wed, Jun 20 at 2:11 PM
Subject Re: Activities for the week

Alana,

I hope you are settling into the engagement well. I think this will be a very exciting engagement.

This is just a short note listing all the key planning documents and activities we must deliver within the next 2 weeks. The majority could likely be done this week. Have a look at these and let's speak later today.

Complete the stream charter
Complete the model architecture
Complete the model description
Complete the decision tree and data requirements
Complete the work plan
Complete the storyboard
Get the team, engagement manager, and client to agree to the above

Cheers,

Max Kraus

He knows the model architecture may take longer than a week. Yet, he needs to get most of the thinking done this week and actually build the architecture early next week. Although nothing significant on the model can be done until the output from the model is agreed upon, it is hoped that the outline for the financial model can be built in Excel by the end of next week.

With the focus interviews and CFO meetings booked, and team update completed, Max focuses on his first piece of work: the business case charter.

The charter is essentially the business case team's *contract* with the engagement manager. It exists for several reasons:

1. It helps to set expectations from both sides. The engagement manager uses the charter to understand the work the team will do, and the team can tell the manager what they intend to do. The charter ensures that no one can claim ignorance about the way forward. Both sides can then proceed, having a good idea of what to expect.

2. The manager uses the charter to manage client expectations and the rest of the engagement team.

3. The charter becomes an important tool to manage the performance and performance review of consultants both during and after the engagement. If expectations are written down, it is much easier to measure performance.

4. From a legal perspective, if the client agrees to the charter, it is much more difficult to claim the work was not done or they misunderstood what they would receive.

The charter is not just there to protect Max and Alana from the client. It is also there to protect them from the pressure cooker environment of a typical engagement. With really aggressive timelines, an unpredictable client, daily challenges, and data problems, it is easy for the team to lose focus on their priorities. The charter can serve as a necessary reminder of the objectives, ensure they understand why they are on the engagement, and what they need to accomplish. It is very common for consultants to use the charter as their primary reference document throughout the engagement. While everything else may change, the charter should never change unless the scope of the engagement officially changes. *The charter should be only one page.*

EXHIBIT 5: Charter Template

Charter Template: Business Case – 21 June

Objectives	Key Activities	Deliverables
Scope		Critical Success Factors

The consultant needs to write clearly and focus on outcomes. The charter must be written so that the rest of the engagement team can clearly understand the purpose and boundaries of the work. If the charter is more than a page in length, it is a fair indication that the consultant is struggling to understand what is needed on the engagement. Most charters are done on a PowerPoint slide so that they may be presented. For the moment, Max simply writes out his charter in a Word document and will convert it to PowerPoint when it is finalized. The charter has five components:

1. OBJECTIVES

The objectives are the reasons why the business case team exists in the engagement. In this engagement, the team has three objectives:

1. Determine the benefits for the shortlisted options to improve production value.
2. Guide the recommendation of an option.
3. Explain the trade-offs of the preferred option.

2. SCOPE

Determining the scope is important. It creates the boundaries for the business case team. Many engagements become difficult to manage because the scope is not clear. If it isn't, the engagement continues to increase in size since the client can request more work to be done or the consultant may keep adding superfluous analyses. Unclear boundaries make it difficult for the engagement team to know when a request for work falls outside the agreed-upon boundaries. The scope could be described along such dimensions as geography, level of detail, value chain, or parts of the company analysed. The scope should also outline the depth of analysis required. Max has set the following boundaries for the engagement:

1. Only examine options related to the core gold mining and processing business.
2. Options for value creation that can lead to more than a 10 percent increase in value will be analysed in detail.
3. Only one mining hub will be analysed in this phase. The other hubs will be analysed in subsequent phases of the engagement.

Although more detail can always be included, the aim is to follow the 80/20 rule. Focus on those 20 percent of items that will comprise the majority of the work.

3. KEY ACTIVITIES

Many activities will be required to complete the work. This section lists the main clusters of activities that are critical to reaching the objectives above. This is the critical path for this team. These are the activities that must be done to generate the deliverables. No matter what happens, the team must complete these activities.

1. Expectations exchange with the CFO to agree on the approach and deliverables.
2. Develop framework (architecture) for the business case model and obtain buy-in.[5]
3. Identify key information requirements to build the model.
4. Understand the existing financial baseline performance of the business and performance drivers and levers. Complete benchmarking.
5. Source/facilitate the finding of information.

---

[5] Buy-in means getting the client's acceptance and understanding.

6. Guide other work streams.
7. Assist in identifying key stakeholder groups:
    a. Assist in the development of focus interviews
    b. Help to conduct interviews, if required
8. Guide the strategic decision-making process.
    a. Help to develop key decision criteria for option selection
9. Build a model with key inputs and assumptions highlighted.
10. Develop recommendations on the best way to improve production value.

4. DELIVERABLES

If the objectives of a work stream are defined as what the team wants to accomplish at the end of the engagement, the deliverables are the work and insights to be provided to the client at the end of the eight-week engagement. They tend to be more tangible in nature. Max and Alana have decided on the following deliverables:

1. A business case for each option and the preferred option.
2. A flexible model to simulate revenues, decrease costs, and enhance value created for each of the options.
3. Consolidated view of whether or not Goldy can execute the preferred option and its financial health[6] in pursuing the preferred option.
4. Overview of the drivers and levers of production value.

---

[6] The financial health and performance of a business are different. A business can post impressive results while still having poor financial health and vice versa. Performance and health should be examined together. Enron and WorldCom were well-known examples of companies performing well but with unhealthy business practices.

Note the language. Consulting firms never present solutions/answers. They always present the implications of various options, and it is up to the board to decide the way forward. A consulting firm cannot and should not try to make a decision for the board of directors. This is a critical and subtle choice of language.

5. CRITICAL SUCCESS FACTORS

The critical success factors (CSFs) are important. Most consultants forget to write down what *they* need to make this engagement successful. If Max does not explicitly state his requirements, he may not get them. Should this happen, it is difficult to blame anyone since they did not know the business case team's requirements. Therefore, CSFs are the business case team's requirements from the client and the broader team to ensure they can meet their expectations.

1. Client commitment
   a. Timely access to key personnel within Goldy and access to the CFO
   b. Timely access to key external stakeholders
2. Timely access to information
3. Accurate data
4. Clear, open, and honest communication between the engagement manager, consultants, and client

Max is not naive. He knows that not everything they need to be successful will come their way. By carefully listing his requirements, however, the engagement manager, client, and his team can regularly check to ensure they are on track and receiving the support they need. Should the direction of the engagement change or scope increase, they can always revert to the charter and understand how the changes will affect their ability to deliver. If the proposed changes distract the team from their objectives, they can use the charter to reject such changes.

A good charter is not just written to create the impression of control. It is also created to help manage the work stream. In the first week, it is usually tweaked and updated every day. The charter is shared with other consultants on the engagement for feedback but not discussed with the client until approved by the engagement manager.

After the draft of the charter is completed, Max leaves for a meeting with the operations improvement team and will thereafter spend the evening preparing the remaining Week 1 documents.

WEEK 1

—

day 2

———

WORK PLAN

MAX AND ALANA have seven critical tasks to complete in the first two weeks. Thus far, they have only completed the draft stream charter.

Max needs to think carefully about the time he has available and how he can complete the work. He arranges a meeting with the engagement manager, Luther, and talks him through his initial thinking. Max explains that he feels comfortable this will be a typical business case engagement, and he thinks the charter is a fair reflection of what to expect. Luther cautions Max about several peculiarities/issues of the industry, which must be carefully analysed and built into the timeline. These are unusual items that Max will need to address to demonstrate that the consultants have a grasp of gold mining industry economics:

Consideration 1:

The gold mining industry strongly believes in the existence of a gold premium. The gold premium is an "extra" valuation of 15 to 30 percent, which supposedly exists for gold mining companies purely because they exist in the sector. Basically, this means that irrespective of the valuation techniques used, the pure gold companies typically have a valuation of 15 to 30 percent higher than calculated—at least that is what the gold companies claim. The approach must understand the implications of and on the gold premium, as the client's executive committee will specifically want to understand how this may be affected by the recommendations. Luther is not sure if this will be an issue or not. That is for Max to determine.

Consideration 2:

Most of Goldy's operations are in emerging economies. Luther advises developing an approach that specifically caters to determining production value in emerging markets.

Consideration 3:

The client has its own views of what drives production value, which may not necessarily align with the correct principles of value creation. Therefore, the business case stream must be able to educate the client about how to think about production value. Everyone needs to agree on a consistent definition of production value. Luther mentions that in four client meetings thus far he has come across three different definitions used.

Consideration 4:

Luther also cautions Max on the differences between production, productivity, and production value. They are different. There must be clear distinctions between them. The client must accept the distinction, and everyone must be using the same definitions. He thinks the business case team must take ownership for defining production value and develop drafts for the team to review.

Consideration 5:

Goldy's board would like an update after the engagement, so the engagement is actually going to be extended by four days into

WEEK 1 - DAY 2: WORK PLAN

Week 9. There are rumours in the press that the board is extremely unhappy with the sagging share price, and this session could lead to any number of changes. Luther cautions Max to stay focused on being rigorous on the business case. Given the enormous attention that Goldy is receiving in the press, any recommendations put forward will be carefully scrutinised. The engagement team must not make a populist recommendation but must have exhaustively debated the options and proof for their recommendations.

After the meeting, Max and Alana head for a coffee break. They start jotting down the principles for designing the work plan:

1. The first four weeks of the engagement (50 percent of the overall engagement) must be focused on collecting all the input for the analyses and building the high-level framework.

2. Within this time, the baseline financial analyses of the business must be completed. They need to know the performance and health of the business. In other words, they need to determine the baseline against which all improvements will be measured.

3. The next four weeks will be dedicated to completing the model, generating the preferred option, assisting with the focus interviews, and analysing the trade-offs.

4. A top-down model will be built using the firm's extensive benchmark database to estimate the possible scope of improvement for Mino 1's ROCE. This should also be done in the first four weeks.

5. Although a bottom-up model will be built to simulate some of the operating conditions and test the opportunities, it will not be an extensive bottom-up calculation of mining costs, contractor's fees, and more. It will simply model the volume of ore produced. This will be completed between Weeks 4 and 6.

6. They will need to use workshops to ensure the executive and management teams understand the definition of production value and what drives value in the business.

With these principles in mind, Luther's advice, and the draft charter, Max and Alana develop the draft work plan. This is still subject to change after the planning documents are done and both Luther and Marcus, the engagement partner, provide their feedback.

Comfortable with the charter and work plan, the team heads off to the hotel. Max will spend the night tackling the decision/value tree and data requirements. Alana will continue working on the Week 1 planning documents. This will leave them the entire day on Wednesday to think about the model architecture and description.

EXHIBIT 6: Draft Work Plan

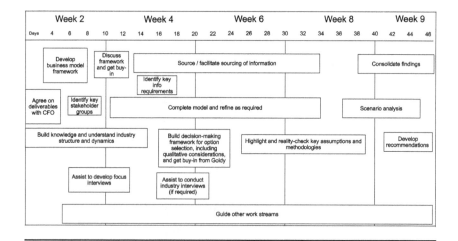

WEEK 1

—

day 3

———

THINKING ABOUT
THE VALUE TREE

ON TUESDAY NIGHT, over in-room dining, Max thinks through the events of the past week and a half. Clearly, this is an exciting engagement at one of the most prolific and high-profile emerging-market companies. Successfully helping Goldy would be a significant breakthrough for the firm in the important Brazilian market. Despite being in the Brazilian market for the last nine years, the firm initially struggled to build the office, attract talented consultants from sister offices, and break into major Brazilian companies. That changed four years ago when Marcus Capple, a talented director from the London office, was persuaded to bring his successful resources sector and organisational improvement skills to Brazil. Born in Brazil to an English expatriate father and Brazilian mother, Marcus had been schooled in Brazil, understood the culture, and spoke the language. He fit in well. The Goldy engagement was an outcome of his perseverance.

Now it was up to the engagement team to take Marcus's strategy to the next level. In the closed Brazilian business culture, personal referrals between business leaders are paramount, and everyone would be watching Goldy after the WSJ article. Much depended on the business case team's ability to deliver an exceptional analysis and set of recommendations. It was clear that while the client was tough and would not tolerate mediocrity, Max felt that a relationship could be built with the CFO, provided they could deliver real value. Determining the drivers of value in the gold mining industry, however, would not be as easy as he had initially thought. The industry and Goldy were clearly influenced by their own interpretation of what drove value creation, and the engagement team would have to work harder to educate the client.

WHAT IS PRODUCTION VALUE?

Like any good associate, Max knew that it would be foolish to take heavily marketed and hyped approaches and push them on the client. The firm believes in developing bespoke solutions specifically addressing individual client issues. While EVA and Holt analyses were popular, the team needed to start from first principles and design the approach from the bottom up. If the outcome of the bottom-up approach was the need to use EVA, they would recommend Goldy do so.

Starting from the first principles, Max writes down several "truisms" about increasing value:

1. Goldy must produce growth in revenue.

2. If Goldy did not produce growth in revenue, it needed to slash costs. This is not a long-term answer since the company cannot diet to a higher valuation, i.e., the company could not perpetually increase value by cutting costs. Yet, being lean was a condition of benefiting from strong revenue growth since a leaner operation meant lower costs and higher profit margins.

3. Goldy must get a return for the cash they are putting into the operations.

WEEK 1 - DAY 3: THINKING ABOUT THE VALUE TREE

4. To be more highly valued than its peers, the return must exceed the cost of capital and the return of its peers.
5. The P/E ratio could serve as the proxy for valuation.
   a. Since they are analysing just one of Goldy's operations, they would need to determine that particular operation's contribution to Goldy's overall P/E ratio.
   b. This could certainly be done, but it was not an intuitive measure to use. It was also difficult to measure.
   c. It would be difficult to measure the operation's contribution to the Goldy P/E ratio continuously and track it over time, as there was significant subjectivity in the process.

Max knows that he needs to use an approach that will be easy to explain to the board. While the logic of working out the contribution to the P/E ratio made sense to the engagement team, he is not convinced that this was the best metric for measurement. It was difficult for him to see how the management team could galvanise the organisation around such a measure. It was not intuitive and difficult to understand.

He decides to keep his notes and speak to Luther and Alana tomorrow before building a definition for production value.

MORNING MEETING

Hendrik, a director of the firm, is visiting Goldy's head office the next morning. While Hendrik waits for his session with Selgado, he joins Max and Luther during their coffee meeting. Hendrik patiently listens to Max. He asks questions about the approach and makes some suggestions. It is quickly apparent that he has a completely different approach in mind. It is a good thing that Max discussed his thoughts before proceeding. Hendrik thinks Max's thinking on value is correct but is too focused on corporate valuation. Hendrik thinks this particular engagement is an operations issue, which ultimately affects the corporate valuation of Goldy. Accordingly, the engagement must be focused on the operating issues. Mino 1 is a division of Goldy. He agrees that a corporate value-based management programme is needed, but that would be a separate issue driven from the CEO's office, and it is actually the purpose for Hendrik's meeting this morning. For this engagement, he offers the following advice:

1. "Value" needs to be quickly defined and agreed on with the client. At a company level, the fundamental drivers of economic value are the rate at which the company can grow its revenues and profits and its return on invested capital (ROIC) relative to cost of capital (WACC). At the mining site level, value is driven both by the tonnage produced and the economic spread (ROIC – WACC). Yet, the operations will have no control over the cost of capital though they may indirectly influence it.

2. For this study, ROCE, relative to cost of capital, will be used to determine "value," a measure similar to ROIC but more suitable to determine the value created at a mining site level. ROCE is equal to EBIT (earnings before interest and taxes) divided by capital employed, a sum of fixed assets, and working capital. This is versus ROIC, a similar performance measure, calculated as net operating profit less adjusted taxes divided by capital employed.

3. To create value, a mining site must increase both the tonnes of ore mined (for example, by removing bottlenecks and gaps) *and* improve the return on the tonnage produced after considering the assets required to produce the ore. In other words, Mino 1 must produce more *ore* and thereafter produce more *gold* from the ore without an equivalent increase in costs.

4. Mines built in extreme and isolated terrain usually have large support services. Since very few external companies are willing to build a facility in these extreme locations, the mine will do so itself. Over time, these support services become expensive and entrenched parts of the business. The team needs to determine if this is the case and if it needs to be factored into the engagement.

5. It is important to keep in mind that managers are often under pressure to deliver short-term results, especially in mature companies, such as Goldy. Such short-term results are often achieved at the expense of long-term value creation. Moreover, ROCE and other accounting measures can be manipulated to pump up returns in the short term. To encourage focus on long-term value creation and make value creation a part of a company's culture, key operating and strategic drivers should be included to measure and monitor the health and performance of the business. Examples of such drivers include the ability to meet delivery deadlines and quality measures. Moreover, the company's day-to-day processes, such as performance management and compensation systems, should be aligned with long-term value creation.

6. To recap:
   a. Production is the amount of gold or ore refined/mined and usually measured in ounces/tonnes.
   b. Production value is the dollar value of the gold output.
   c. Productivity is basically output value of refined gold / cost of all inputs to produce the refined gold.
   d. Therefore, production value can increase while productivity drops if the cost to produce more gold grows at a faster rate than the value of the gold produced. In another example,

production value can drop while production increases if there is less gold in the increased amount of ore mined.

e. A mine wants to increase all three measures.

Hendrik has now effectively split the engagement into three parts:

1. Operational improvement
2. Business case
3. A possible third part would be the analyses of the service functions. Until this time, only the initial two areas above comprised the engagement team. The services issue did come up during the decision tree analyses, but the team felt it was out of scope. Luther will need to determine if the service functions needs to be incorporated into the analyses and, if so, how.

After Hendrik leaves to meet with the client, Luther and Max both agree it was a good idea to share their thinking with Hendrik early on. His comments were extremely valuable, and the new direction he has recommended certainly makes more sense. Having the meeting on a Wednesday morning means they still have sufficient time to incorporate the changes. They realise an early lesson learned is that they should be much more focused on the question they are trying to solve rather than the solution to that question. It is all too common for teams to go ahead and do considerable work without carefully thinking through the problem statement. The idea of dedicating a week to planning and planning reviews is again shown to be a wise way to set up engagements.

Before he joined the firm, Max served as a summer intern at another consulting company that was not known for its rigorous analytical skills. That was ultimately the reason why Max left. He recalled serving on an engagement where each person on the team broke up into their mini-engagements and did their work with very little collaboration. The financial modellers built complex models that did not address some of the key challenges facing the client. Quality standards within the team were vastly different, and there was constant bickering and tension. There was little focus on trying to understand the root cause of the problems, and the key question was vague. Consultants simply went off and looked for interesting analyses. A lot of time was spent on Google, and no time was spent on hypotheses and decision trees. No one had ever heard of MECE. The company also brought in senior advisors with 30 years' experience in the sector. The advisors typically pointed out the problems, and the recommendations were built around these ideas. Most of it was opinion, and there was little substance to the recommendations. The company believed that these experienced advisors already knew the problems and solutions. This was the wrong way to do the analyses and led to incorrect recommendations.

Max was glad he left. Despite this radical change in direction from Hendrik, it makes perfect sense. Moreover, outside the firm, it is very rare for a senior partner to patiently listen to an associate's ideas, reflect on them, and incorporate them into his thinking to build a better approach for the client. Accessibility to the firm's best-known partners was another reason he joined. After all, in how many companies could a relatively young MBA graduate sit down over coffee and have a meaningful discussion with a partner who the *Harvard Business Review* once called "one of the most influential thinkers in business"?

WEEK 1

day 3

OPERATIONS STRATEGY & PRODUCTIVITY

'**SHOULDN'T YOU** *be raising our productivity versus our production volume?*' asked the chairman of the Goldy board as he thumped down the firm's recent U.S. country study extolling the importance of productivity. It seemed clear to Marcus why production volume should be the goal along with cost reduction, but it was clearly not obvious to everyone else. And that is because the concepts are similar, and productivity is a well-used term but poorly defined. The engagement manager and other team members had asked the very same question. Marcus thought it would be a good idea to gather his thoughts on the subject so he could properly explain his thinking. He needed to do so in a way that everyone understood.

So, he went back to first principles.

WHAT IS PRODUCTIVITY AND WHY DOES IT MATTER?

Let's assume Viviana ran a lemonade stand. It was a basic stand outside her home composed of some old apple boxes. Viviana had the most basic ingredients, no branding, no marketing, and no real understanding of the market. She was 5 years old after all. She plucked some lemons from the scrawny-looking lemon tree in her backyard, used tap water and sugar she could find in her pantry. The sugar was so old it had settled into crystalline blocks in the packages and needed to be broken apart with a spoon. Let's assume Viviana sold 20 cups in that day for $1 each, but her total cost of running this operation was $10 (her initial investment to set up everything) and there was no opportunity cost. That means if she did anything else with the $10 investment, she could not make more than $20.

So, her profit was $10.

Let's assume her friend, Elena, a few blocks away decides to do the same thing. Obviously, Elena is competitive. Again, assume she is far enough away that she does not impact Viviana's business in any way. She figures out a way to use riper lemons, so they are naturally sweeter. So, she cuts down on sugar costs. She also sells 20 cups at $1 but makes a profit of $14 off a cost base of $8. She takes the $4 additional profit (versus the $10 Viviana made) and invests in better branding for her cups. She prints out a photo of herself with her dog and sticks them on the cups. Due to this, her profits rise to $20 the next day. She now has $10 additional profits (versus the $10 Viviana is making) which she invests in better lemons, sparkling San Pellegrino water and setting up another stand.

Her profits rise to $30 a day.

What does all of this mean? Productivity is measured as the output value / input. There is no other definition of productivity. It is erroneous to assume productivity is how fast one completes a task, or the number of tasks completed in a year. Completing a task quickly that is of little value or completing many tasks that add little value will actually lower productivity. Completing just one task over an entire year that is very valuable means one is actually very productive. Understanding productivity is important. It will change your life if you manage your schedule by this definition.

So why does productivity matter? Elena is more productive than Viviana. Her ratio of output value / input costs is higher since Elena's profits are higher off the same cost base. Assuming Elena wisely invests this additional profit, she will slowly but surely grow and become more and more profitable than Viviana. Elena starts with changing the branding on the first day. By the second day, she has changed the lemons, water, and opened a new location. Imagine the impact of the improvements if she makes 20 such improvements in each month. This is why productivity matters. A more productive enterprise, versus its competitors, generates incrementally more value which can be reinvested in the business to keep growing. An unproductive enterprise, relative to its peers, cannot make the necessary investments to grow, fight in the market, introduce new products, block competitors, attract talented employees, etc. A productive business can do so, and the most productive enterprise can do the most. It will have a major advantage in the market. Crucially, unless Viviana raises her productivity or finds investor(s), she will never have sufficient excess cash to compete with Elena. And as Viviana expands, this becomes harder for Elena to do. So, coming from behind is hard to do with the same business and/or business model.

Productivity is always a relative measure. There is no such thing as a productive or unproductive business/person. A business can only be less or more productive relative to some comparison business. So, when someone says, "I am very productive," the response should always be, "Relative to whom?" This is because competition is always between two or more companies/people and if productivity is essential to competing, it can only be measured relative to competitors. The next question should be, "Why are you comparing yourself to this person/company?"

The principle of productivity clearly applies to people, their lives, and/or careers. In a manner of speaking, we all have the same cost base, only 24 hours in a day. Someone who invests in themselves to study, build relationships, understand clients, etc., will likely earn a higher salary than someone who does not do much of the above and, partly as a result, earns a lower salary. The high-income earner is typically left with greater cash on hand at the end of the year to further invest in their development. Provided the investments are made wisely, their productivity ratio (total output value / total input costs) should rise. That is, their productivity should keep rising. It is a virtuous cycle. And they will have incrementally larger and larger excess funds to reinvest to sustain earning higher and higher returns. Yet, it does not matter where you start. Even if you start at the lowest possible career path, as long as you keep earning some excess value and continue wisely reinvesting this excess in your development, you will benefit significantly in the long term. It adds up like compounding interest. This is compounding productivity. It's a term invented for this book.

The very same principle applies to a country. A country is productive if it is producing incrementally more value relative to other countries. It does not matter how poor it is. Provided it keeps investing the money wisely to increase productivity (raise output value at a faster rate than input costs relative to competing countries), it will end up with more funds to invest. And since a country's total productivity is the aggregate of the productivity of all the individual businesses, people, organizations, etc., we can look at one business to explain country productivity.

For example, a factory in a relatively poor country may have a total input cost of $20 to produce one product item and let's assume it takes a full work day to produce that one item and it takes only one worker to make that item. Of the $20, let's assume $13 is labour costs and $7 is all other costs. If we assume the factory is paid $22 for the product, it generates $2 of profits. Assume $0.50 is invested in better production, $0.50 in R&D, and $0.50 to increase salaries, the factory takes a $0.50 profit on each product. That may not seem like much. That is only a ($0.5/$13) percent increase in salary for the worker. That is 3.85 percent. Assuming the investments are made wisely, the factory can grow, and two things happen. First, more people who never earned much start earning this base salary as the factory hires them. They are naturally better off, can consume more, save, and pay taxes. Second, over time, their salaries increase due to inflation, improvement in skills, and demand for skills. Over 30 to 50 years. the changes can be dramatic.

Look at China, Singapore, and South Korea. This is essentially what they did. The key is to be consistent. Countries, like people, sometimes start with unfair disadvantages. Provided you are earning even a little excess cash that can be redeployed, and provided it is redeployed into the business wisely, things will improve.

A person, company, and country must be productive. The point of being competitive is to drive up productivity. Without greater productivity, you cannot hope to win. And one cannot be competitive unless one is productive. They reinforce each other.

HOW IS PRODUCTIVITY LINKED TO COMPETITIVE ADVANTAGE?

A person, organization, or country must be productive to succeed in the long term. Competitive advantage is how one will go about being productive. We know that productivity is total output value divided by total input costs. Competitive advantage is knowing whether the company will *mostly* differentiate itself on the numerator or denominator and *how* it will differentiate itself to be productive. See the two exhibits below.

EXHIBIT 7: Productivity Definition - Output Lever

FIRMSCONSULTING.COM & STRATEGYTRAINING.COM

Operations strategy is about enabling a company's competitive advantage while increasing the output value / input cost ratio
Output value levers

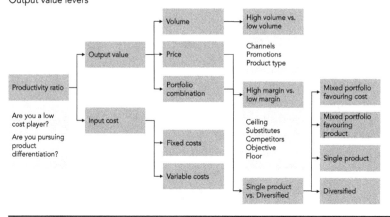

EXHIBIT 8: Productivity Definition - Input Lever

FIRMSCONSULTING.COM & STRATEGYTRAINING.COM

The goal is to stake out a competitive advantage and determine if the output/input lever must be pulled and how far
Input cost levers

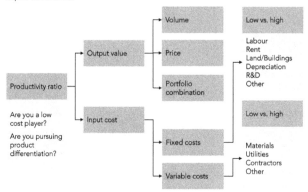

WEEK 1 - DAY 3: OPERATIONS STRATEGY & PRODUCTIVITY

There is no other reason to be competitive nor way to be competitive. We say *mostly* since you have to do both but truly excel at one. To make this point, let's step outside the lemonade example and think about the luxury auto sector.

Let's assume an Italian sports car maker has a productivity ratio of 2.7. The company manufactures cars in Italy that are also designed and largely handmade in the country. Most of the suppliers are domestic and it launches two new models a year in very limited volumes of about 5,000 total vehicle sales per year across all models. All the cars are sold in company-owned showrooms or through select prestige online distributors. Broadly speaking, the input costs are driven by five areas:

1. Handcrafted/assembled (Labour costs)
2. Manufactured in Italy (Production costs)
3. Domestic suppliers (Raw materials costs)
4. Two new models (R&D costs)
5. Private showrooms (Distribution costs)

The CEO and board want to keep the company in the high-end luxury performance vehicles space. They have defined the positioning of the car as such. The job of the COO is to maintain this position, but he has quite a lot of freedom in *how* he manages the production process to achieve this goal. At the highest level, and in aggregate, a person, organization, or country is either trying to raise productivity by competing primarily by raising output value or lowering input costs. While they will pursue a combination of both, only one lever is the goal that cannot be compromised. This company is clearly competing on the output value side. They incur steep costs to produce a car that sells for the highest possible output value. That is not to say they ignore input costs, but it is not their point of differentiation. If they have to spend more to manufacture the car, they will do it provided the return is very high as evidenced in the sales price and margin.

Now this is where it gets interesting. *It is possible to raise productivity significantly by hurting the company.* That is a counterintuitive yet common strategy and operations mistake made in business. And this is why it is not sufficient to just raise productivity. One has to raise productivity by pursuing the right competitive strategy. Let's look at some of the things the COO could do to increase productivity to illustrate this point.

First, he could keep the status quo. That seems plausible since they are very profitable. In this option, he runs everything as it is but does it better. Same production line, same suppliers, same components, same factories, same configurations, etc.

Second, he could focus on the value output lever but change things to improve the car. Leather crafting would move to France for the seats and interior. Design would move to Germany or the UK. He may find some cheaper suppliers and have different dates for the rollout of the sedans and SUVs. He may allow test drives in the showrooms. The changes are not radical but since Germany, the UK, and France have higher labour costs than Italy, total input costs will rise at a faster rate than output value in the short term and the productivity ratio drops to 1.9 from 2.7. However, the positioning remains the same and it is believed in the long term, as more production moves to France and Germany, the cost savings and better quality reflected in higher prices will lead to rising productivity that will eventually exceed 2.7.

Third, he could really vault the productivity up to 8.7. Who wouldn't want that? That is essentially a tripling of the productivity. To accomplish this, he would radically lower the costs. He would shift all design and R&D work to Bulgaria, knowing that the skill level and track record of this new team is inferior to the previous design and

R&D team. Assembly would shut down in Italy and move to a less advanced facility in Hungary. For the components of the car hidden from consumers, they would use suppliers who supply cheaper rival passenger vehicles. SUVs would be rolled out first and sports car rollouts would be pushed back since the latter requires more costly development. Online sales would be prioritized across all viable platforms versus high-end sites, and glitzy showrooms would close.

EXHIBIT 9: Operations Strategy Options

As you can see, the third option would be a disaster. While productivity rises steeply due to dramatically lowering the cost base, they are no longer making a luxury car and that will lead to a steep and sustainable drop in revenue over time. The COO is also competing on the cost lever versus the required value lever. Initially, sales will rise as the volume of cars produced rises in Hungary. Yet, over time, the car will lose its appeal for two reasons. First, it is no longer exclusive since more people own the car. Second, customers will notice the poorer quality and cheaper parts. That will drive down demand and prices. Over time, productivity will suffer and drop far below 2.7. As this example shows, it is not enough to increase productivity in the short term, one has to do it by focusing on the competitive advantage that is appropriate to the company's strategy and think how actions taken now will impact productivity in the long term.

A resources company can be analysed in the same way. Its productivity is a ratio of total output value to total input costs. As a commodity business, almost all resources are commodities, a resources company automatically struggles to compete at the output value level. It can do a few things to increase output value but not much. First, it can improve mining techniques to extract more valuable ore from a ton of rock. For example, rather than extracting 1 ounce of gold from a ton of rock, it could try to extract 1.2 or 1.5 ounces from the same weight of rock using better crushing and chemistry. Second, it can operate in commodities with higher prices and lower extraction costs. There is not much else it can do. The prices are set by the market and attempts to manipulate the market generally do not go down well with the U.S. Justice Department.

EXHIBIT 10: Commodity Company Strategy

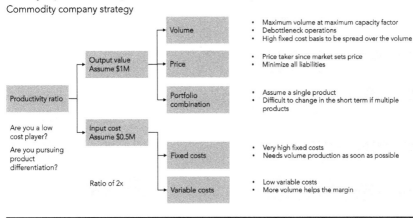

That leaves the total input costs side. Fixed costs tend to be very high in mining. It takes years to bring a mine to the point of production and even highly automated mines have high costs. Even so, this is the only lever the company can manipulate. It must find ways to lower fixed and variable costs. So, a COO at a resources company will try to raise total output value by increasing production volume and the quality of the ore mined, but much remains out of his control since prices are set in the market. He really needs to focus on driving down costs at all times, even when he is trying to increase production volume.

EXHIBIT 11: Saudi Oil Example

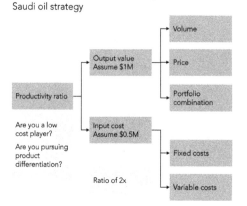

Given the cyclical[7] nature of resources, having the lowest cost position is key. And this is hard to achieve. When demand is rising, and prices for commodities subsequently surge, companies ignore lowering costs since high prices can mask poor cost containment. Under pressure to benefit from the higher commodity prices, management typically focuses on output versus cost containment. So as prices climb with demand, companies tend to score big profits but on the back of creeping costs. When prices fall, those with a high cost base suffer. It is not easy to quickly lower costs. In fact, as prices fall, demand typically falls, and companies must fight for market share just to stay in business. One way to do this is to charge clients less for the commodity. This is hard to do when you are a high-cost producer but easier to do if you are the lowest-cost producer. The lowest-

---

[7] Cyclical means that changes in demand are not predictable. They do not follow patterns like seasons or calendars. The beginning, end, and length of occurrence is not fixed.

cost producer can offer prices that are lower than the production costs of competitors but higher than their own production costs. They, therefore, lower their profit per ton/ounce/barrel but offset this with high market share gains. Eventually, the higher-cost players close facilities, shut down, or are acquired.

We can take this example further. As the COO in a resources company, we know that both the total output value lever and total input cost lever must be managed. Yet, we need to be best on the total input cost side and volume production side. So, we can take the costs and break them down into fixed and variable costs. We can keep breaking it down and then identify the tools like strategic sourcing, gold platting, service operations management, just-in-time delivery, etc., that can be used to lower the costs. These tasks are then assigned to the various operating teams to execute. This is, in effect, how the COO should be pushing down priorities to his teams.

EXHIBIT 12:
From an Operations Strategy to an Operations Plan

FIRMSCONSULTING.COM & STRATEGYTRAINING.COM

Every single operations tool in the world can fit into this approach, which provides often ignored direction

Raise productivity.....by pulling the output or input lever.................through a tool

Productivity ratio
- Are you a low cost player?
- Are you pursuing product differentiation?

Output value
- Volume
- Price
- Portfolio combination

Input cost
- Fixed costs
- Variable costs

- Six Sigma
- Lean manufacturing
- De-gold plating
- Product development
- Procurement
- Strategic sourcing
- Service operations
- Just-in-time

Operations strategy is about:
- Increasing productivity
- Knowing your competitive advantage
- Knowing the lever which maximizes the advantage
- Knowing which tool to use to pull the lever
- Knowing if the advantage is maximized
- Knowing the trade-offs when you begin maximizing your advantage

IMPLICATIONS FOR GOLDY

The team is correct in looking at raising production volume and lowering costs. Raising volume costs money. It is not free to increase the output value side of productivity. As the team looks at raising production volume from the existing operations, they will naturally do so with the following objectives in mind:

1. Raise output value of the ore such that the output value rises at a faster rate than the accompanying input costs to raise production volume.

2. The ratio between output value and input costs after the engagement should be higher than before the engagement. That is, productivity should rise.

Some common mistakes consultants make is to assume that productivity should first be increased on the new production and then the focus should shift to the existing production. That is, if the mine is producing 20,000 ounces of gold and wants to raise output to 24,000 ounces of gold, the team should first look at increasing productivity on the additional 4,000 ounces. Once this is done, the lessons should be applied to the existing output. This is erroneously positioned as a pilot to the client. This is illogical since the additional 4,000 ounces of gold originates from the same facilities as the existing production. That facility needs to be fixed and the changes will affect both existing and new production.

Note that the other mistake is assuming moving from 20,000 to 24,000 ounces of gold production by itself raises productivity. This is not the case if the ratio of total output to total input costs to produce the additional 4,000 ounces is the same or less than the ratio of total output to total input costs to produce the existing 20,000 ounces.

So, the engagement team is correct in their focus. Focusing on raising production volume can increase productivity provided it is done with the correct definition of productivity in mind. Max decides not to type up his thoughts. It is better to explain this in person to the Chairman and the team.

WEEK 1

day 3

DEVELOPING THE VALUE TREE

S**ITTING DOWN WITH ALANA**, Max explains the firm's approach to management consulting. After a two-year career with the firm, he knows that management consultants have their own disciplined way of conducting research, and new joiners often simply assume their university training will equip them for the rigors of consulting analyses. It does not.

When consultants talk about business cases, they refer to the quantifiable and financial impact of implementing a set of recommendations. This is a very specific definition that carefully shapes the work that will be done. And the work that will not be done. Although Max has spent much of the last week and a half explaining the process to Alana, only practice will allow her to understand the approach.

A central part of building business cases and economic models is the value tree. In simple terms, a value tree takes the value creation metric and breaks it down into its constituent parts. For example, if the business case team needed to build a value tree for the metric "profit," the value tree for profit would have two legs: one for revenue and another for costs. Costs can be further broken down into fixed and variable costs. This process continues until the team can understand the different parts of the operation that drive profit.

WHY BUILD A VALUE TREE FIRST?

This is the question posed by Alana. She is an eager and exceptionally smart physics undergraduate. She sailed through her studies with a 4.00 GPA and performed very well on her case interviews. This is her first engagement, and she is eager to get on with the work. Max knows he needs to find a way to channel her enthusiasm and intellect into a structured approach so that they can solve the problem without undertaking work that is irrelevant and frustrating for her. If the latter occurs, even high-potential consultants can become disappointed, and this frustration affects their work. The analyst is of the view that since she attended the weeklong MBA training in Barcelona and knows how to build an economic model, she is ready to go! She is not.

Max begins the session by discussing the economic model they will need to build:

1. Every economic model has a core calculation engine that *produces* the data around which all the calculations will be performed.

2. The core engine, sometimes called an activity model, itself must be driven by a set of primary data. The model determines how key metrics (such as ROCE) change as the primary data is altered. In this case, the primary data will likely be the variables to determine the amount of ore mined. The primary data is different in every engagement. It is really up to the business case team to design the model and ensure it performs the task required. The business case team needs to make this decision.

3. Built around the core engine, the model will have several options that must be tested. An option is a different route for management to fix the business. Different options usually lead to different results. In other words, they are the different paths available to management. The ability to test the options must be built into the engine or around the engine.

a. One example of an option may be keeping production constant *while* increasing productivity.
   b. Another option may be keeping productivity constant *while* increasing production volume.
   c. Another option may be keeping production volume and productivity constant *while* cutting costs.
   d. There may be other options or derivations of the three above.
4. The model should be able to test all the options that have a significant impact on production value. At this early stage of the engagement, the team will not have determined all likely options, though they would have identified the main options. No more than two to four options should be modelled.
5. The model must be explicit about what will be assumed, what will be measured and included, and what is simply taken from industry benchmarks. Benchmarks are critical. How will Goldy know it can or should improve productivity? Benchmarks help indicate how much better or worse Goldy is performing against its peers. Although benchmarks are useful, the team must be able to explain why there are differences. Sometimes there are legitimate reasons for the differences.
6. Not everything in the model is variable/flexible. The amount of variability/flexibility in the model is determined by the following:
   a. Options to be tested
   b. The economic environment to be simulated (we term the economic environment a scenario while the decision/path management can take is termed an option)
   c. Insights the team wants to extract from the model
   d. Other analyses they need to run

7. The output of the model is just as important as the input. What metrics and measures do they want the model to generate? Is the approach to generate these figures in the model comparable to the approach used internally at Goldy to generate benchmarks? If not, how will comparisons be made? Financial models should never be generic. The top-down financial analyses will indicate what must be analysed further with the financial model.

8. The economic model must be simple and specifically answer the questions to be answered. Too many consulting firms offer clients the model as part of the deliverable. These firms have a vested interest[8] in building complex models to impress the client. Max's previous employer was such a consulting company. The firm does not operate in this way. Their value is to analyse the output of the model and produce insights. They are not model developers. They are management consultants.

Alana admits that this thought pattern to building economic models is very different from her university studies, and she says it was covered during the quick overview she received in the training programmes. Since everything stems from the core business value, she now understands the importance of breaking down the core business value into its different components.

Max agrees that is a good place to start. He steps up to a whiteboard and writes down the definition of ROCE, which essentially measures the return on capital from the mining operations.

---

[8] A distinction must be made when a consulting firm has expressly been appointed to build a model **and** present recommendations. In this case, a model is one of the primary deliverables.

WEEK 1 - DAY 3: DEVELOPING THE VALUE TREE

Max explains to Alana that earlier in the planning week the team used a quick definition of production value to determine the drivers of value creation. Given the early stage of the engagement, the rough breakdown made sense and would work just fine. The earlier breakdown was also not incorrect; it was just not specific. Going forward, they would need to be much more specific to guide the rest of the team. ROCE will be the measure with which they will work.

Max knows that breaking down ROCE into the various parts is not easy to do without a detailed knowledge of the mining site and its operations. As they go further and further into the detail, they will reach a roadblock since they have limited knowledge of a gold mining operation.

To avoid this problem, Max invited the financial manager to join the session. The financial manager, Sergio, had been recommended by Flavio and has been with Goldy for 48 years. He joined as a pit cleaner when Goldy was a single shaft in Brazil and rose in the company through all the acquisitions and consolidations that created the current mining giant. He studied part-time through night school to complete an accountancy degree and is regarded as the *most* knowledgeable person about Goldy's operating finance issues. Flavio had warned Max that Sergio tends to like details and can become stuck on an issue if it remains unsolved. The importance of the issue is apparently irrelevant to Sergio.

Max has already met and briefed Sergio about the approach and meeting. Max has politely asked that Sergio follow the process and work with the team. On Friday, they would have a full meeting to address any concerns Sergio may have about the meeting and broader engagement.

Sergio arrives punctually at 3 p.m. He only speaks Brazilian Portuguese and a little Spanish. Max thanks him for attending and gives him a 10-minute update on the conversation thus far. The conversation tends to be slower than planned since Max needs to switch between Portuguese and English for Alana's benefit (Alana does not have a perfect grasp of the Portuguese language, although she can read Portuguese). Sergio *seems* happy and mentions that he can only spend an hour before he needs to leave. Max decides to gain maximum value from this initial group meeting. It is usual for clients to be more attentive and willing to learn new ideas at the start of the engagement. He wants to use this opportunity to ensure that Sergio understands the process used to deconstruct value creation. They will use this time to build a proper value tree at least four to five levels in detail so that everyone understands the process.

BUILDING THE VALUE TREE

Max splits the whiteboard into six columns of equal width. He leaves an equal space at the top of each column for a label/headline. He labels each column as follows:

1. Headline 1–Core Measure
2. Headline 2–Level 2
3. Headline 3–Level 3
4. Headline 4–Level 4
5. Headline 5–Level 5
6. Bs/Cs[9] and Next Steps

---

[9] Bs/Cs are an acronym for benefits and concerns. This is a process that usually ends all meetings and workshops. The attendees discuss the benefits of the sessions and concerns. All concerns must be acted on through next steps. Concerns must never be left as unaddressed items without a clear next step, a person accountable for the next step, and a deadline.

WEEK 1 - DAY 3: DEVELOPING THE VALUE TREE

In the middle of column 1, he writes "ROCE." Working with Alana and Sergio, he proceeds to break down ROCE by writing the following information inside the columns:

1. Column 1 – "ROCE"
2. Column 2
   a. "EBIT" near the top of the column and
   b. "Capital Employed" near the bottom of the column.
3. Column 3
   a. "Revenue," "variable costs," and "fixed costs" aligned to "EBIT," and
   b. "Working capital" and "fixed assets" aligned to "Capital Employed."
4. Column 4 – Each of the five branches in column three are split even further.
   a. For example, aligned to "revenue," he writes "price of gold" and "volume produced."
   b. Aligned to "variable costs," he writes "mining," "processing," "transportation," "royalties," and "labour."
5. Column 5 – Each of the branches in column four are broken down even further.
   a. For example, aligned to "mining," he writes "waste removal," "vamping (cleaning)," "mining," and "mining overheads."

He then connects each of the branches.

EXHIBIT 13: Building Value Trees

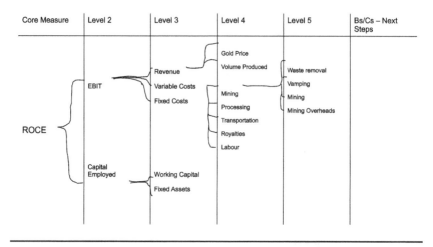

At the end of the meeting, the hand-drawn tree above has been fully developed and completely covers the whiteboard. The team ensures they have adhered to MECE principles throughout the session. The value tree emerges.

At the end of the meeting, when they have completed all the branches, Max asks both Alana and Sergio if they see any value from the process.

Alana says:

1. "Overall model building approach is very logical."

2. "Everything has been reduced to an equation. For example, Revenue = Gold Price x Amount of Gold Produced. Using this approach, we have actually worked out the relationships to use in the Excel model."

WEEK 1 - DAY 3: DEVELOPING THE VALUE TREE

3. "Value trees present a great overview of what needs to happen."
4. "Easy to zone in on potential problem areas."
5. "Glad Sergio attended the meeting."

Sergio:

1. "Good process and overview."
2. "I did not notice the part about the equations, but I see it now, and it is really easy to understand and use."
3. "I have never seen this before, but it is very useful."
4. "Shows the complexity of the mining site."
5. "Will we get a copy of the model once you are done?"

Max then asks both Alana and Sergio to list their concerns about the meeting and process:

Alana:

1. "There is a lot of detail and a requirement to be focused. This process definitely helps focus all the thinking."
2. "We need to start data collection early."

Sergio:

1. "How will this be used to increase production value?"
2. "I am still confused about the role of the business case team. How will the work be done, the objectives, and deliverables?"
3. "What is my role?"

Max must wrap up the meeting by capturing and addressing each concern. If he does not do so effectively, Sergio may feel that Max is simply following a consulting process and the consultants are insincere about discussing and attending to potential problems. He is careful to write points raised, on the whiteboard, using the same words used by Sergio and Alana. He does this to show Sergio that the engagement team will address the concerns as they are stated by Sergio. For each potential problem raised, a next-step item is listed to address the issue. Max suggests to Alana that she take over and work with Goldy financial analysts to get to a level 8–10 amount of detail in the value tree. They will address the data requirements once he has spent some time thinking through the modelling approach.

Walking Sergio to his office, Max suggests they meet on Thursday at around 4 or 5 p.m. He will need about an hour to explain the overall process and will specifically address Sergio's concerns raised. Sergio thanks Max and asks for a clean copy of the value tree when it is finished. He thinks it can serve as a useful guide for some of the younger financial analysts on his team.

Max and Alana have a five-minute debriefing after the meeting. This is standard consulting protocol to ensure they have achieved their objectives and that there are no "loose ends" that must be addressed. It is critical that the agreements, decisions, and next steps from the meeting are captured in an email and circulated among attendees. The person who writes the next steps has lots of power. They get to interpret all the agreements and propose the way forward. Alana volunteers to produce this and send it to Max for review.

Max is pleased with the day. The team achieved their objectives:

1. Introduce everyone to the proper approach to build economic models.
2. Work with Sergio to build a value tree and ensure he understands the process.
3. Ensure Sergio is a part of the early development stages of the engagement.

WEEK 1 · DAY 3: DEVELOPING THE VALUE TREE

"Everything has been reduced to an equation. For example, Revenue = Gold Price x Amount of Gold Produced. Using this approach, we have actually worked out the relationships to use in the Excel model."

Max is very pleased that Alana made this observation. It is a critical requirement of effective value trees. Essentially, an effective value tree involves layers of equations. What does that mean? All of the level 2 branches can be added, subtracted, divided, or multiplied to obtain the level 1 question. This relationship applies to all branches in the value tree. Done correctly, the value tree essentially determines the relationships to be used when building the Excel model. The reader can imagine the addition or multiplication symbols being used above to show the branches coming together.

However, not all decision trees can be broken down into these neat equations. In many engagements, particularly organisational design and organisational issues, there are no equations as such. Max recalls an engagement done for a Chinese client to design their optimal organisational structure. The decision tree created could not be broken down into perfect formulas, but it did meet the requirements of MECE. Max makes a note to explain this to Alana. It is important for her to understand that not all decision trees have such mathematical precision, although all of them are logical and follow the MECE rule.

Max is particularly pleased since Sergio did not find any gaps in their value tree. Max takes out his notebook and starts thinking through how the economic model should be structured.

WEEK 1

day 3

DEVELOPING THE
MODEL ARCHITECTURE

MAX IS NOW FAIRLY CONFIDENT that if he can produce a very good draft of the model architecture and description, the business case team would have a tremendous first week on the engagement. He is aware that it is important to start the engagement in the right way. If the client and engagement manager believe that the business case team is organised, prepared, and logical in their thinking and operating well with the broader team, then the business case team is likely to find it easier throughout the engagement. Their early successes and organizational skills *may* allow them to get the benefit of the doubt in future discussions.

Building the model architecture this early does not mean that it must be perfect. It just needs to have sufficient information so that his colleagues can understand his thinking and provide feedback. Putting down ideas on paper is a good way to build on concepts that work, discard those that do not, and consider different architecture frameworks.

Max quickly ticks off the planning documents they will likely have by Thursday midday:

1. Complete the stream charter ✓
2. Complete the model architecture ✓

3. Complete the model description ✓
4. Complete the decision tree and data requirements ✓
5. Complete his work plan ✓
6. Complete his storyboard

Typically, developing the model architecture can take up to one week or more. It is essential to also first have the completed value tree to understand the levers and drivers of value for Goldy's mining operations. These form the basis for the model architecture. He will have to wait for the value tree as Alana completes the final branches.

Max was recently assigned in Vietnam on a coal mining engagement and led the business case team in that engagement. Although gold and coal mining are vastly different, he knows enough about mining to make the necessary adjustments to produce the architecture early. So, he feels confident about his ability to produce a high-level architecture in a few days. As soon as Alana provides the value tree, he can compare the model architecture to the value tree and make the necessary corrections.

The architecture is not an overly detailed layout of the economic model. It does not consist of many pages of drawings and notes. It is actually a one-page diagram. The architecture explains the conceptual logic behind how the model will work. It visually indicates how the different blocks of analyses will link together to produce the final results. If the conceptual logic makes sense, the team can then go ahead and figure out how to actually build the model. Having the architecture does not mean that all the questions about the model have been answered. Far from it! It just means the team knows what they are building, how it will likely work, and what it will produce. They will still need to actually build the model, overcome data challenges, and even make changes to the way the data is used in the model.

The model architecture is somewhat similar to the early design mock-ups produced by architectural firms to demonstrate early concepts to a client. These mock-ups are usually paper or wood models built to scale. They are far from perfect and lack the technical accuracy of the actual building that will be constructed. Yet, they convey the overall concept. As they are very early versions, the architecture firm usually does not have the detailed designs prepared. Architects create these mock-ups because it is very difficult to explain in words how the building will look. Only by seeing a mock-up can the client decide if it fulfils their requirements. After the client agrees on the overall concept, the architect then builds a new mock-up and the detailed designs.

The same principle applies in a management consulting engagement. Only by seeing the model architecture can the team decide if the model is conceptually correct. Thereafter, it is up to the business case team to plan and build the model architecture.

WRITING THE PURPOSE OF THE MODEL

Max writes down the purpose of the model:

1. Calculate ROCE.

2. Analyse the existing operations to generate the base case. This is the operation's current performance. (The baseline performance is required for the team to measure the impact of the recommendations. The baseline analyses are both an assessment of the current performance and a benchmarking exercise.)

3. Produce the business case for each option. Although the options are not yet known, Max makes educated guesses about what they are likely to be:

a. Improving productivity
   b. Improving production
      i. Reducing bottlenecks
      ii. Removing gaps in production
   c. Reducing costs
      i. Procurement costs
      ii. Supply chain costs
4. The business case must answer the following:
   a. The expected dollar size of the opportunities from the recommendations.
   b. The expected return generated from the opportunities.
   c. The expected cost to achieve the returns.
   d. The expected payback period and cash flow.
   e. Determine if the funding for the recommendations would be operating expenditure or capital expenditure or both.
   f. Determine if the improvement can be implemented given company constraints, legislation, and similar barriers.
   g. Will it be easy to implement?
   h. Who can do the implementation (consultants or employees or both, since this drives labour costs and the implementation timelines)?

Max emails the list to the engagement team for feedback. He then calls each team member to ensure that he is capturing all their areas of focus. It is particularly important that the business case team can assess all the options the operations team will pursue. Through the calls, he realises that the operations team is specifically looking at opportunities to reduce costs. They believe the supply chain and procurement costs can be dramatically cut. Max realises that although his initial notes captured these costs, they would need

WEEK 1 - DAY 3: DEVELOPING THE MODEL ARCHITECTURE

greater attention in the model. He goes back to his notes and includes the details on cost reduction (in italics above).

He opens a Word document and writes out a half-page draft description of what the model will do. The aim is to create a simple description of what the model should accomplish. Things left out of the description will not be in the model.

"A flexible model, with a 10-year projection was built, to better understand the mining operations at a global average basis with a focus on different mining types and geographic regions. We subsequently tested the feasibility of operating with a geographic focus.

The model can be adapted to test three types of options: changes in production (debottlenecking and removing production gaps), productivity, and cost reduction by changing the key inputs and assumptions accordingly. These three types of options are related since production value (output) divided by cost (input) equals productivity. Key outputs from the model include ROCE, costs, and asset base size and evolution."

Max decides to have a coffee break and think through how this description will work in practice. In particular, he focuses on the following challenges that the description above presents:

1. Given the changing nature of the industry, is a 10-year projection feasible?

2. Goldy has at least 18 operations using over six different mining techniques and at least seven different operating and cost structures. Should one model have the capability to be applicable to all the operations? Should he not simply build a model specific to Mino 1?

3. Are these all the possible options for analyses that should be included in the model?

4. Are these the right outputs?

After thinking it through and discussing it with Alana and several team members, Max makes the following changes:

1. A 10-year projection is not possible. It will take about two to three years to fully implement the recommendations and embed them in the operations. Moreover, much has happened in the sector in the last six to seven years. There is no reason to expect the next 10 years will produce any less change. Therefore, a five-year projection is as far as the model can go while generating realistic output.

2. Modelling such complexity into one model means that too many assumptions will have to be made. The one model will need to be able to incorporate different mining techniques, operating environments, cost structures, operating models, and mine structures. The model becomes too generic. Max will recommend to Luther that the model should only simulate one mining site. Thereafter, the recommendations should be rolled out in this site, and then the model can be refined for use in other sites based on what they have learned. Building one global model now is not wise since they have no idea what to expect on the other sites.

3. Max seems comfortable with the scenarios, but he makes a note to ask the rest of the engagement team to share their hypotheses in the team meeting on Friday evening. This will give Max and Alana an indication of whether or not they are on the right track.

4. The outputs are consistent and make sense.

WEEK 1 - DAY 3: DEVELOPING THE MODEL ARCHITECTURE

Max now changes the model description to reflect the improvements (changes in bold):

*A **flexible** model with a five-year projection was built to better understand the mining operations at a **site** average basis with a focus on the **operating structure. Production volume will be modelled.** We subsequently tested the feasibility of operating under **different macroeconomic environments (scenarios) by changing the following variables: currency exchange rate, inflation rate, and the gold price.***

*The model can be adapted to test three **broad** types of options available to **Goldy management:** changes in production (debottlenecking and removing production gaps), productivity changes, and cost reduction changes by changing the key inputs and assumptions accordingly. Key outputs from the model include ROCE, costs, cash flows, and **financial and operating trade-offs between all options and the recommended option.***

Max is more pleased with this description due to its clarity. It is more precise and leaves little open to interpretation:

1. The scope is clear: five-year timeline, one mining site, and analysing only the operations. Non-core businesses like the support functions have been excluded unless they directly impact the core business.
2. External (macroeconomic) shocks tested will be limited to currency, inflation rate, and gold price fluctuations.
3. The primary data (variables to alter production volume) to drive the core engine is listed as well as how it will be calculated (it will be modelled).
4. All three types of options are listed. The actual options may vary, but they will likely be a subset of this list.
5. Outputs are listed.

Using this description, Max sketches out the model architecture on paper with a pencil. When he is comfortable it matches the description above, he converts it to a strawman slide for further improvements.

EXHIBIT 14: Draft Financial Model Architecture

Draft Model Architecture: Business Case – 21 June

- EXISTING PRODUCTION FIGURE BASELINE → FACE ADVANCE & BLASTING CYCLES → OPENING DEVELOPMENT TUNNELS TO MINE FACE → GENERATES TONNES MINED
- IMPROVEMENT OPTIONS
  1. TBD
- RESOURCES REQUIRED FOR MINING
- LABOUR FOR MINING
  1. Labor
  2. Contractors
- PRODUCTION VARIABLES
  1. TBD
- OPEX
- REMUNERATION
- WORKING CAPITAL
- CAPEX
- OTHER OPEX → TOTAL OPEX
- BENCHMARKS
  1. Best Practice
  2. Gap
  3. Business case to close the gap
- CALCULATING PRIMARY DATA
- FIXED ASSETS
- PROFIT & LOSS STATEMENT
- ROCE

Max knows it is critical for the engagement team to understand the logic of the economic model. He also knows just how difficult it is to do this. In his experience, engagements where the team is not absolutely clear about the outputs of the business case stream are usually problematic. In some cases, the business case team has been known to generate a business case without including some of the key recommendations from the rest of the engagement team. Clear, consistent, and frequent communication is therefore essential.

WEEK 1 - DAY 3: DEVELOPING THE MODEL ARCHITECTURE

Max writes down the logic of the model and emails it to the engagement team:

From	Max Kraus
To	Engagement Team_M2212
Date	Sat, Jun 23 at 10:15 PM
Subject	Re: Activities for the week

Colleagues,

See my early thoughts on the model. Please read this so that you will have the background when we discuss the model later in the week.

1. All business metrics will change as the production volume changes AND the means to change the production volume changes. Everything is dependent on volume and the means to change volume.
2. Therefore, calculating production volume is central as this drives the model.
3. To calculate production, the model will do the following:
   1. Calculate changes in volume of tonnes mined by modelling the number of mining faces mined and the number of new mining faces opened (from development tunnels to mining faces).
4. Changes in variable costs will be directly driven by changes in volume of ore mined:
   1. We will work out the existing and historical relationship between costs, productivity, and volume. This will act as the baseline against which all improvements will be made.
   2. Using the existing relationship between costs, productivity, and volume, we will estimate the future changes in cost, revenue, and ROCE.
5. Labour costs are the largest cost driver, and the entire mining operation will be split into a value chain, with labour requirements calculated per a segment of the value chain. Opportunities to improve processes, which in turn impact the labour number, can then be assessed with the model. Full-time-equivalents (FTEs) will be estimated for each part of the value chain and the amount of ore produced. Therefore, labour will partly be a fixed and variable cost.

Cheers,

Max Kraus

Max makes a note to build the value chain for the mining operations. At least 60 percent of operating costs are driven by labour. Labour costs will be modelled according to their use along the value chain. Therefore, the value chain will be needed to build the economic model.

In the description above, it is not important to outline all the details about the model. It is too early in the engagement for the business case team to have this information. It is also unnecessary. The rest of the engagement team must simply understand how the model will work and ensure they are comfortable with this approach and the flexibility or lack of flexibility this will create.

It is like driving a car. The engagement team simply needs to know that if they press the brake, the car will stop. The calculations behind the hydraulics, whether to use a 7 percent or 9 percent gradient on the brakes as well as the design, designing the brake, and so on is the responsibility of the engineering team. It is their responsibility to solve this problem. It is the same on this engagement. The engagement team needs to know what will happen and why. The "how" lies with the business case team to solve and share at an appropriate time. In this example, the business case team is like the engineering team building the car's braking system.

While Max knows his team will understand the reasons for a summary, he is aware the client likely expected pages and pages of information when they initially read about the charter, model architecture, and model description. Max will need to manage Sergio's and Flavio's expectations.

Before he leaves the office, Max clears his diary to spend at least three hours tomorrow completing all the outstanding documents for Week 1. Although the high-level model architecture and description were produced in a day, he knows it will take at least another week to finalize the documents. Nonetheless, he is pleased with the start thus far.

WEEK 1

—

day 4

———

DRAFTS OF
WEEK 1
PLANNING
DOCUMENTS

UST FOUR DAYS into the engagement, the team has started to develop good momentum on the engagement. Max, of course, is tired. He worked until 3 a.m. the previous night to get out the top-down analyses. The results were as expected, and that is a great finding to have this early since the team is now confident of the direction they are taking. Max recalls working on a prior engagement where the team had to change direction with 70 percent of the study time completed. It was a cathartic and troubling experience. Everyone who worked on that study with Max suffered burnout and depression. All had eventually left that firm and many had received negative reviews.

Luther commences each day with a 7:30 a.m. planning meeting. Each stream of work, operations improvement, business case, services, and the overall strategy (led by the engagement manager), has seven minutes to deliver their update in the following format:

1. Key insights and findings
2. Things useful to the other teams
3. Help needed

Luther follows this up with a nine-minute discussion by summing up what he has heard, where he thinks the team should focus, feedback from the client, and the plan for the week.

After the planning meeting, Max has arranged a one-hour working session with Alana to review progress to date. This is an important pre-meeting to arrange all the documentation for the next 24 hours. Later in the day, Max will meet Sergio; on Friday morning, he will meet Flavio; and on Friday afternoon, he will meet Luther and Marcus. From this planning meeting, Max and Alana will need to produce final working drafts of the following documents:

1. Stream charter
2. Model architecture
3. Model description
4. Value tree and data requirements
5. Work plan
6. Storyboard

Max thinks it may be unlikely to get everyone to agree to the drafts in Week 1. It is unlikely he will himself be comfortable with the documents. If he is not comfortable, there is no point in getting an approval. He has decided that the objective for Week 1 must be for Luther, Sergio, and Flavio to review and provide guidance on the early working drafts. The new milestone will be to sign off these planning documents by the end of Week 2 of the engagement.

The session starts promptly, and each document is reviewed. Max explains to Alana why it is important to present all this planning information as one package and so early in the engagement. Luther is ultimately responsible for delivering the engagement, while the engagement partner and senior partner will be held accountable by the CEO. They are both very experienced partners of the firm, but they cannot know everything. Max and Alana need to help the partners to help them. *Only* by providing the appropriate material for review can the partners provide guidance. Max outlines the principles for preparing these planning documents:

1. The documents help the business case team in requesting assistance. By reviewing the documents, the partners can determine if a work stream is on the right track, if they understand the problem, and if they need more help.

2. Many documents discussing the same work stream allows for the planning to be viewed from different perspectives. This is critical. If viewed from just one perspective, for example, only the work plan document, it is possible that gaps or misunderstandings may not show up. Many different viewpoints minimize the chance of this happening. The same gaps/misunderstandings are not likely to be missed in all the documents.

3. Many consultants want help and simply expect the partners to know what to do to help them. This is inappropriate because they do not have all the answers. To get quality feedback, these documents must be provided for review.

4. This process creates a paper trail. It is there to protect the consultant, engagement management, partners, and client. With transparent communication and sign-off, no party can claim to have had limited information and be unaware of any activities.

STREAM CHARTER

Max and Alana are happy with the draft work stream charter. They make a few changes based on the model architecture and comments from the senior partner:

EXHIBIT 15: Draft Charter

FIRMSCONSULTING.COM & STRATEGYTRAINING.COM

Draft Charter: Business Case

Objectives	Key Activities	Deliverables

1. Determine the benefits case for the shortlisted options to improve production value and better manage the service functions
2. Recommend an option to improve production value
	1. Expectations exchange with CFO to agree on deliverables
	2. Develop framework for the business case model and get buy-in
	3. Identify key information requirements to build the model
	4. Conduct baseline analyses, and advise the engagement team
	5. Understand existing financial baseline and benchmark performance of the business. Understand performance drivers and levers
	6. Source / facilitate the finding of information
	7. Guide other work streams
	8. Assist in identifying key stakeholder groups:
	   1. Assist in development of focus interviews
	   2. Help to conduct interviews if required
	9. Guide the strategic decision-making process
	   1. Help develop key decision criteria for option selection
	10. Build model with key inputs and assumptions highlighted
	11. Develop recommendations on optimal route to improving production value
		1. Baseline assessment
		2. A business case for each option and the preferred option
		3. A flexible model to simulate revenues, costs, and value created for each of the options
		4. Consolidated view of whether or not Goldy can execute the preferred option(s) and its financial health in pursuing the preferred option

Scope		**Critical Success Factors**

1. Producing mines and development shafts
2. Options for value creation, which can lead to more than a 10% increase in value will be analysed in depth
3. Only currency and gold price's external drivers will be analysed
		1. Client commitment
		   1. Timely access to key personnel within Goldy, including the CFO
		   2. Timely access to key external stakeholders
		2. Timely access to information
		3. Adhering to the scope around the services function
		4. Accurate data
		5. Clear, open, and honest communication between engagement manager, consultants, and client

MODEL DESCRIPTION

Max talks Alana through the model description. She raises some questions that he feels will be addressed in the architecture:

EXHIBIT 16: Draft Financial Model Description

FIRMSCONSULTING.COM & STRATEGYTRAINING.COM

Draft Model Description: Business Case – 22 June

A flexible model with a five-year projection was built to better understand the mining operations at a site average basis with a focus on the operating structure. Production volume will be modelled. We subsequently tested the feasibility of operating under different macroeconomic environments (scenarios) by changing the variables: currency exchange rate, inflation rate, and the gold price.

The model can be adapted to test three broad types of options available to Goldy management: changes in production (debottlenecking and removing production gaps), productivity changes, and cost reduction changes by changing the key inputs and assumptions accordingly. Key outputs from the model include ROCE, costs, cash flows, and financial and operating trade-offs between all options and the recommended option.

MODEL ARCHITECTURE

Max is both impressed and pleased with the probing questions Alana asks of the model architecture. It is clear she has thought about this very carefully. She raises some valid issues that Luther is already reviewing. A decision will likely be reached soon:

1. Goldy owns its gold refinery, and opportunities may be available. They have been excluded from the modelling.

2. Goldy's Brazilian, Venezuelan, and South African mining operations are self-sufficient entities. They own hospitals, schools, power plants, municipalities, and more. Excluding

them from the analyses presents a skewed data set. The idea of removing them unless they affect the core operations does not make too much sense. For example, the hotel does not affect the core operations but does impact the hub's finances. Adding in all the other service functions that did not affect the core operations will lead to a significant impact on the hub's finances. This rule of excluding non-core activity, for the business case scope of work, may need to be refined.

Max decides to present the model architecture as is but to raise the two points above with Luther. Including them will require a significant change in scope and may be outside the engagement boundaries. However, he does believe a decision will need to be made on them.

EXHIBIT 17: 2nd Draft Financial Model Architecture

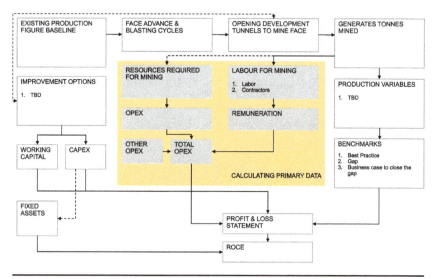

WORK PLAN

Both Max and Alana agree that the work plan is fine as it currently stands. Max asks Alana to spend more time with the planning documents before they assign roles and responsibilities for the activities.

EXHIBIT 18: Draft Work Plan

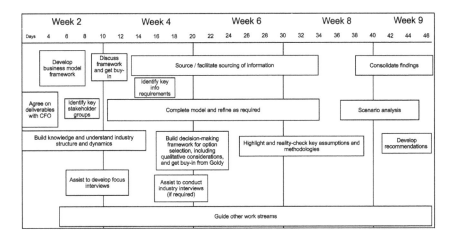

VALUE TREE

Given the size and complexity of the final value tree eventually developed by Alana and the Goldy financial analysts, they decide to present the tree in two formats:

1. A simplified concept view
2. Detailed branches presented in the appendices

The simplified concept view will simply show the overall concept. This is done to ensure that both the client and engagement team understand the overall concept. This is shown below:

EXHIBIT 19: ROCE Value Tree

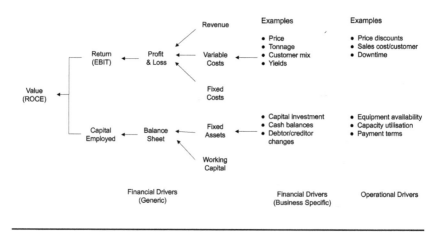

They both think about different ways to present the detailed tree. Given the size of the value tree, they decide to split the tree into its three main arms/branches:

1. Revenue
2. Costs
3. Net Assets

Presenting even one of the branches above is too confusing. They decide to split each of the arms above and present just part of the branch to explain the concept. Anyone requiring more information can easily refer to the appendices in the final study. Each arm or branch is referred to as a lever.

In the appendices, they have included the more detailed value tree branches. In total, they have over 40 such detailed value tree branches. They will use them with Sergio's team to check the accuracy of their calculations and approach. This does not mean they will model all 40 branches. They will apply the 80/20 principle and only model the 20 percent of the value tree that impacts 80 percent of the ROCE. Together, they review one of the detailed value tree branches.

Max has seen some firms arm their teams with detailed value tree branches for different sectors and sub-sectors. Therefore, a young consultant could go onto a study and use the value tree as a blueprint off which to discuss potential issues with a client. While there is nothing wrong with this approach, and it could add tremendous value, Max had also observed some consultants being too dependent on the value trees and not developing the skills to build the trees or interrogate the meaning once an area of the tree was prioritized. Max would not have minded having such a value tree in this case pre-built, but he felt the process of teaching Alana how to do the work from first principles would be extremely useful for her in the future. That is the value of a slower learning process on a younger consultant's very first study.

EXHIBIT 20: ROCE Detail

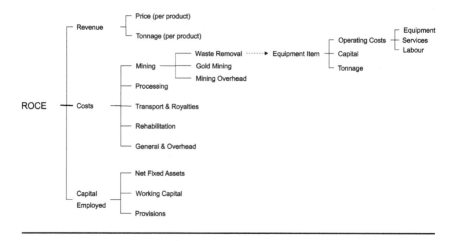

Before Alana leaves, they agree she will spend Friday morning working with the financial analysts to develop a value chain of the overall gold mining operation. She will work with some of the mine planners before they can take this map to Sergio for review.

MEETING WITH LUTHER

Max calls Luther, who agrees they can review the team's planning documents over lunch. Luther asks for copies in advance so that he may review them before they meet. To save time, they have lunch at the client's cafeteria. Since they are working on client premises, they have shed their typical crisp suits and ties for chinos and plaid shirts.

WEEK 1 - DAY 4: DRAFTS OF WEEK 1 PLANNING DOCUMENTS

Even so, they barely fit into the culture, as most of the employees are dressed in old blue jeans and short-sleeve shirts. It is important for the consultants to blend into the culture of the firm. "Sticking out" only creates more difficulty for the engagement team to build relationships with the client. The irony is that the head office has two cultures, and they barely fit in irrespective of the way they dress. The Goldy executive office is all suit-and-tie, while the rest of the head-office building is quite casual. If they try to match the dress style of one, they automatically do not fit into the other. They decided to compromise and dress smart casual.

Luther has carefully reviewed the emails from the previous night, the planning documents, and spoken to the other team members. Overall, he is very comfortable with the work done thus far. He feels the business case team is moving fast but keeping everyone updated. Both Sergio and Flavio have not raised any concerns after Max's meetings with them.

Luther suggests that Max consider the following and build it into his approach and objectives for the study:

1. Luther needs to see the storyboard. While the planning documents all make sense, Luther urgently needs to review the storyboard and determine if the direction is correct. The storyboard is the most important initial output to review. He asks Max to try to get this out as soon as he possibly can.

2. Alana is very smart and learns very quickly but is still very inexperienced. Max needs to ensure he provides enough "air cover" for her to fulfil her potential that is apparent to everyone on the team. Luther asks Max to think about a stretch[10] role

---

[10] A stretch role is one that forces consultants to move outside their comfort zone by learning new skills, operating in a new environment, or doing work they have never done before. Stretch roles help develop consultants.

for her where she can take guided ownership of part of the engagement. Luther points out that if Max does this, Alana will want to continue working for him since he is helping with her development. Luther explains that is how one gets ahead at the firm: *the principle of "followship"*. If Max sincerely invests in the development of his colleagues, these smart and capable people in the firm will support him, he will progress rapidly, and have a strong support base.

3. Luther mentions that he, Luther, will not be the main relationship contact with Flavio. He wants to leave this responsibility to Max. He believes Max can effectively manage this, but he stresses that a sign of leadership weakness is *not* asking for help. He expects Max to ask for help when needed.

4. The model and business case are very complex, and Alana is correct: more complexity will need to be added. The hospitals and schools will need to be analysed in the study. Hendrik has discussed this with the client, and additions to the engagement team will be made. A new associate will be brought in to lead this analysis, but the refineries are not within the scope of the study since they are leased and not owned.

5. Luther indicates that IT costs do not seem to be covered and wants to know if they are critical. He is not sure but thinks Max should look into it.

6. Luther's final comment is for Max to take proper ownership of the work and deliver the quality Max has come to be known for within the firm. They need to trust and support each other.

Before leaving, Luther also points out how important the baseline analyses will be to the engagement. The baseline analyses are the calculations of Mino 1's current financial and operating performance.

There have been rumours that Goldy has had problems aggregating its accounts and cost structures. From what they have seen thus far, there are strong indications that this is true. The financial analyses for Mino 1 (the first mining site to be analysed) will need to be carefully validated and analysed. To make matters worse, the economic model developed by the business case team will not have a peer model within Goldy because Mino 1 does not have a strong handle on its finances, and it is unlikely the internal financial model will be accurate. Testing the model outputs will be much tougher but not impossible.

With this information, Max prepares to meet Sergio later that afternoon.

WEEK 1

—

day 4 & 5

———

WRAPPING UP
WEEK 1

AX KNOWS this meeting with Sergio, a key operations finance manager, is crucial. The basis of a client-consultant relationship is usually set over the first one or two meetings. Unless something radical happens to alter the basis of the relationship, this meeting will determine the ongoing working relationship.

This meeting is important for other reasons as well. The engagement team is unlikely to get much access to Flavio. Hendrik, the senior partner, provided feedback from a meeting with the CEO who mentioned that Flavio was opposed to bringing in the firm. He felt that proper operations consultants were needed and did not believe the firm could handle the problem. The CEO did not feel Flavio would immediately support the consultants or give them sufficient time. This is why a relationship with Sergio becomes important:

1. Without much access to Flavio, Max would need to work more closely with Sergio and only take decisions and findings to Flavio.
2. Flavio is likely to heavily rely on Sergio's opinion of the consultants and their abilities.

Understanding the importance of this relationship, Max has developed a strategy for the sessions with Sergio. He will follow three simple principles in developing the relationship:

1. Consistently impress Sergio and present an image of an engagement team that is organised, understands the business, and meets deadlines. To be successful, Max will only present work that has been checked and is logical. Incomplete parts of the analyses or errors will be checked by Goldy financial analysts before discussing with Sergio.

2. Build both a professional and personal relationship. Next week, Max intends to invite Sergio and some of his senior analysts for dinner in their hometown. Max has heard the grumbles about consultants who want to only work out of the Rio office and are unwilling to spend the weekend in the mining towns. Max plans to take them out on a Friday and spend the weekend in the mining town.

3. Raise Sergio's profile. It is apparent that while Sergio is respected, not many people see him as the authoritative right arm of Flavio. He is seen more as a walking encyclopaedia. Max wants to help raise Sergio's profile and, hence, build an ally.

Arriving at Sergio's office, Max is surprised to see a very tidy office unlike that of his colleagues down the hall. Sitting on his desk is only one noticeable personal item: an autographed football. Trying to break the ice and build a relationship, Max asks Sergio about the football. That lights up Sergio. Over the next 20 minutes, they discuss football and Sergio's favourite team, Flamengo FC. Sergio is very pleased that Max also likes football and knows the statistics, transfer fees, and so on. Of course, as a German national, Max is more familiar with the Bundesliga. This helps Max to connect with Sergio on a personal level and set a less formal tone for the meeting. After the first 20 minutes, the conversation naturally progresses into discussing the engagement and business case work stream.

Max asks Sergio if he can first present the planning documents before answering the questions from the previous value tree meeting. Sergio agrees. Max ensures that for each document, Sergio understands the one or two key points that are essential for the success of the business case team. Given that only about 40 minutes remain in the meeting, there is no time for more detail:

Stream charter:

1. This is an overview of the business case scope of work.
2. If it is not in the charter, it will not be done.
3. Flavio must approve the charter.

Value tree and data requirements:

1. This document explains the key metric to be measured.
2. It breaks down the metric into drivers.
3. The value tree will form the basis for how the relationships between outputs, such as costs and revenue, will be modelled.

Model architecture:

1. This is a conceptual overview of the overall economic model.
2. If it is not in the architecture, there must be a compelling reason to include it.
3. The architecture must be decided before the details can be developed.

Model description:

1. The description summarises the model architecture in words using no more than half a page.

Work plan:

1. The work plan is a high-level guide to key targets and activities.
2. It is meant to guide everyone's expectations regarding data requirements and deliverables.

As expected, Sergio is happy with what he sees but is unable to comment because he has not seen the detailed model. He thinks that it is best to see a detailed model plan before giving his sign-off. Max explains to him why this will not work. The details can only be developed once the high-level approach is approved. They need to know what they are building before it is built. Furthermore, signing off the charter and other documents does not mean that Sergio is approving the final results. Signing them only means he agrees with the objectives and plans of the business case team. As their work is done, he can always check to see if they have stuck to their plan.

Max follows this up with an analogy of building a house. He says that the planning documents are like the early sketches an architect will develop for the owner. Before the architect can start any detailed work, the owner must agree to the type of building they want to see.

If the architect does not interpret the owner's vision correctly or makes mistakes, the owner can always come back and point this out. For the architect to work accurately, though, he needs for the owners to approve the overall concept before he begins, i.e., do they want a large Spanish-style home or a modern home? Should the house be one level or several levels? Is a pool required? What about a large garden? Do the owners want one or two carports? The homeowner does not review and decide the exact specifications to be used. The owner simply sets the outcome he seeks. The same principle applies here. Sergio should agree on the outcomes or objectives of this team. The team will be responsible for deciding how to conduct the study.

This analogy works with Sergio, and he asks for the weekend to review the planning documents and provide his comments. Then Max covers the concerns raised by Sergio in the value tree meeting:

"Still confused about the role of the business case team, how the work will be done, the objectives and deliverables."

Sergio agrees that he now better understands the objectives and deliverables. Yet, he is still unclear about how this team's work will fit into the rest of the engagement team's activities.

Max talks him through the role of each part of the engagement:

Engagement Manager–The engagement manager must guide the team and bring together the findings from the operations improvement, services, and business case teams. The engagement manager must also ensure that the approach is robust enough to deal with any changes to Mino 1's and Goldy's business or operating environment. He is responsible for the overall study.

Operations Improvement–The objective of this team is to find ways to raise production value for the core mining operations. They will likely generate many small opportunities, several medium-sized opportunities, and a few large opportunities.

Service Functions–The services team will analyse all the service functions in the Mino 1 hub. They will need to determine what impact this is having on the performance of the business and recommend a set of actions to manage services. The services team will analyse all service functions, including hospitals, hotels, sports facilities, and internal support services, such as maintenance engineering.

While the teams above can calculate the increase in production and impact in just their part of the analyses, they will not have an overall viewpoint to answer the following questions:

1. If capital is limited, which opportunities should be pursued and in which order?
2. Given the options available to management, which should they pursue and why?
3. What are the costs, payback period, and returns from the opportunities/options?
4. Are opportunities being double-counted?
5. What is the impact on the mine's overall returns?
6. How can the opportunities be implemented?

These are all questions for the business case team.

"How will this be used to increase production value?"

Referring back to the first question, Max explains that all this work, the model, value tree, and so on helps prepare the business case team to analyse each option to improve production value. They serve as the internal check on the engagement.

Max also tempers Sergio's expectations. He mentions that three steps are required to fix the problem:

1. First, they must confirm the correct problem. Sometimes what looks like a problem is not the real problem at all; it may be just a symptom.
2. Second, they must diagnose the problem (identify its cause) and develop options to address the problem.
3. To finally correct the problems, the recommendations must be implemented.

WEEK 1 - DAY 4 & 5: WRAPPING UP WEEK 1

This eight-week engagement will only confirm the problem, diagnose the problem, and develop a range of options to address the problem. Another engagement will be needed for implementation. Sergio enquires if the firm has been retained for the implementation. Max mentions that there may be discussions about this matter, but he is not aware of any. He recommends a weekly meeting so that Sergio can see how all the different activities of work come together.

"What is my role?"

Max understands that Sergio must not see his role as purely administrative. He must see it as something important if he is to be excited and contribute to the engagement. Max lists four roles for Sergio to serve:

1. Serve as the operating point of contact for the business case team and sounding board for ideas and findings.
2. Help open doors and find data.
3. Serve as a key channel to Flavio. (Max does not intend for Sergio to be the only channel or the gatekeeper to Flavio, but he expects him to be another route to the CFO.)
4. Ensure the process is not seen as separate from the finance function but is slowly taken over by the finance team once the consultants depart.

Sergio seems happy with this but again asks for more time until the next meeting so that he can review the work. They both agree that a 7 a.m. Thursday meeting is the best time for a weekly update.

Max leaves thinking that the meeting went well:

1. There was genuine interest from Sergio.

2. There were no objections.
3. They both seemed to connect on a personal level around football.

Max makes a mental note to ensure that Sergio gets what he wants from the engagement from a career perspective. It was premature to ask this in the first meeting, but it will be a good topic for next week.

Checking his iPhone, he sees that Luther has cancelled the Friday meeting, and Flavio has postponed their review meeting to next Tuesday. He accepts Luther's invite for a mining site visit scheduled for Monday. The team will have to be at the site by 6 a.m. on Monday. It's going to be an early morning!

That means he can continue working on wrapping up the planning documents all of Friday. Given the scale of the engagement, this time will be put to good use. Alana is visiting the operations centre on Friday, so it is unlikely the process map will be ready. Despite the delays in the storyboard, Max still thinks it is a good start to the week. He knows that storyboards are typically one of the first items developed, but with Alana, a new business analyst, on the engagement, the slightly different approach will help her understand the process much better. She needs to learn the basics and then be taught the storyboarding.

WEEK 2

day 1

MINE SITE VISIT

*A*FTER A FLIGHT FROM RIO DE JANEIRO on a hot and humid Sunday afternoon, the team arrives in Minas Gerais' city of Belo Horizonte. Traditionally, the firm tries as much as possible to not have consultants work on weekends. Given the long working hours on a weekday, weekends are reserved for personal time. In this case, the flight times were inflexible, and the team had little choice. They could not secure a charter flight to the mine from Rio, and Belo Horizonte was the only available option. They spent the night in Belo Horizonte since it is the departure location for their very early flight the next morning. At 4 a.m. on Monday, everyone is at the company airstrip and boarding a chartered flight to Goldy's massive Mino 1 complex deep in the Amazon rainforest. The one-hour flight passes straight over the jungle. The engagement team cannot see much given the limited light in the early hours of the morning.

Appearing from behind a hill, the Mino 1 mining complex is the world's largest gold mine. Over 60,000 mine workers toil in this self-sustaining facility deep in the Amazon jungle. Given the size of the complex and its isolation, it was built as a fully enclosed and self-contained "city." The complex has its own hospital (rated as one of the best hospitals in Latin America), housing facilities, recreational facilities, school, hotel, shopping centre, theatre, pharmacy, airport, and more. All of this exists within a facility under 24-hour armed surveillance.

Mino 1 is Goldy's flagship operation. It contributes 18 percent of all gold ounces produced and approximately 15 percent of Goldy's EBIT. It was originally built in 1972 and reached its peak in 1996. Production has dropped since then, but the mining complex is still expected to be viable for the next 12 to 15 years. Mino 1 currently consists of one shaft at 2.8 km in depth linking seven different mines. On any given day, about 45,000 men work underground.

The team will have a safety induction for 15 minutes, followed by 15 minutes to change into protective gear. They will go down with the morning shift at 6 a.m. and stay underground until noon when they will return with the same shift. They will then tour the above-ground facilities. Later in the day, the team will have an early dinner with the Executive Vice-President (EVP) of the Mino 1 complex, Gavrilo Pinto, and his executive team. They will return to Rio on Tuesday morning to complete the planning phase of the engagement. They will return to Mino 1 at the start of Week 3 and will be based there for the majority of the engagement thereon.

WHY MINO 1

Picking Mino 1 as the first mining hub to be studied was not an easy or popular choice. Gavrilo Pinto was reluctant to have external consultants visiting his operations and reviewing his team. Goldy's culture has always been to treat each major complex as a separate company. The concept of the CEO sending in consultants to help a mining hub was unusual and not well received.

Mino 1 encapsulates Goldy's tough and independent culture. The complex was developed in the 1970s after the Brazilian President

WEEK 2 - DAY 1: MINE SITE VISIT

decided to move Brazil's capital from Rio de Janeiro to Brasilia. This was partially done to promote the development of the interior. Goldy was the first local mining company to push into the interior. Supporting the Brazilian president gained it favour when it was time to negotiate mineral and resource rights. The mine was built and commissioned a full five years before proper roads and supply lines were established. The complex battled terrorist attacks, activists, and flooding to consistently exceed its targets in the early years. The consultants knew that Mino 1 was central to understanding Goldy's culture.

The CEO has decided that Mino 1 will be the pilot of the consulting study. He felt that tackling a complex as large and entrenched as Mino 1 would demonstrate to the company that he was serious about changing the business. The consultants would need to analyse this hub first before rolling out the programme to the remaining hubs and regions.

CONTEXT FOR THE TRIP

The best management consultants understand that it is impossible to properly advise a client without understanding the environment, culture, history, and challenges within the location where the solution will be implemented. This first trip is a fact-finding mission to help the engagement team understand the culture before they return in Week 3 for an extended stay. They need to understand the working conditions, size of the facility, location, and operations.

More important than anything else, they want to understand Gavrilo and his management team. Gavrilo and his team will need to embrace the recommendations and work with the opportunities to improve production value.

UNDERGROUND

After putting on proper safety gear, the engagement team boards a carrier (elevator) with 30 other miners and prepares for a 10-minute ride down to the bottom of the shaft. The team is quick to note that despite Goldy's claims of "safety first," they only received an eight-minute safety lecture before putting on their gear.

Arriving at the bottom of the shaft, the team walks out into a cavernous chamber with strobe lights. They are now in the main shaft. It is possible to access all the surrounding mines from this one location. They will visit Mino, which is the main mine in the Mino 1 complex. To get to the actual mining operations, the team needs to travel another 3.2 kilometres horizontally. In their case, the mine has arranged a tram to take them. Employees of Mino 1 do not have this luxury. They have to walk to the mine face and back every single day. It was not always this way. When the shaft was first sunk in 1970, it was in the perfect location. Over time, the face of each mine moved farther and farther away from the shaft as they were mined. Mino is the newest mine and is closest to the shaft. Some mining faces are 6 kilometres away.

As the team proceeds, they make some observations:

1. Despite being the youngest mine, Mino is pretty dilapidated. Most ore tram crossing lights do not work. Large parts of the underground complex are dark or flooded.
2. Workers are poorly protected and most remove their heavy gear to survive the 40 to 50 degree centigrade temperatures.
3. Most workers are darker Brazilians, while supervisors and other senior staff are of a lighter complexion.
4. Safety does not seem to be a priority. At least 20 different safety hazards were passed during the 40-minute ride.

WEEK 2 - DAY 1: MINE SITE VISIT

Once they get to the end of the ride, they notice that many workers are still walking through. The engagement team is briefed on what they will find. From here on, the mine visit will be more treacherous, so they need to be more careful. To reduce wastage, costs, and time, the mining follows the seam of the gold through the rock. In some cases, the seam can be 2 metres in width and in others 2 cm. Where it is 2 metres, they can drill and blast out at least 2 metres of rock. Therefore, there is a comfortable space for the workers. Where the seam is 2 cm, they drill and blast out just 80 cm, which means the workers essentially work in a space just 80 cm in height. This is the minimum amount of space needed for a worker to drill and blast. Removing just 80 cm dramatically reduces the amount of rock removed that does not contain gold. Since the miners are chasing just a 2-cm seam, removing any more rock than the 2 cm is extra work that creates no revenue, slows the process, and raises costs. This particular mining face has a 4-cm seam, so the area they will enter will be claustrophobic, noisy, humid, loud, busy, and just 80 cm in height. They need to be careful and follow the instructions received.

As the consultants enter the drilling space, they are shocked by the conditions. The mine face is not a small room 80 cm in height. It is a massive space with many tunnels and corridors but just 80 cm to 120 cm in height. It is dark and noisy, and they need to crouch on their knees and hands. Some workers spend at least six hours here before taking a break. The ground is uneven. Sharp rocks and boulders lie everywhere, and the ceiling is also uneven. Pillars of wood are stacked up against the ceiling to prevent a mine roof collapse. It is a scary sight. There is dust and water in the air. Close by, at least six drillers are crouched on their knees and working this section of the mine face. Peering around, the team can see many more teams crouched and working around the chamber.

Not all workers have communication equipment; only the work foreman and some of the workers carry walkie-talkies. Equipment and supplies are passed along in little buckets carried by a conveyor attached to the roof. It does not look very reliable.

While they are watching the workers, a huge machine that looks like a ship's anchor is pulled along a conveyor belt on the ceiling and scoops all the loose rocks and boulders. Apparently, this is the ore collector. It does not do a very good job. Moreover, it has no flashing lights or sound alerts. It is a safety hazard.

The engagement team follows the cleaner until it deposits all the material at the bottom of a pit. As more cleaners deposit material, the ore accumulates and is tipped into a hole in the pit. Each mine is layered above the other, so the ore is falling to another level, where it accumulates again and collects until it tips over again to a lower level. This process repeats itself until the ore collects at the bottom of the lowest shaft, is washed, and taken out for crushing. The pits are unmanned, and their guide mentions that safety "incidents" have occurred, without elaborating.

The team then takes a tour of the underground supply rooms, clinics, and training centres. All of them look unused and are in pretty poor condition. Lunch is arranged with the other mineworkers. The traditional dish is served, which is a mixture of dark beans and meat that is based on the dishes eaten by the African slaves who came to Brazil over 100 years ago. Most of the workers are very friendly and try to speak to the consultants. The workers do not speak the traditional Brazilian Portuguese but rather a dialect developed at some of the mines.

The trip ends when the guide takes them to the edge of a shaft and indicates that this is the boundary between Goldy's operations and pirate mining. Apparently, due to the complexity of the mine shafts, unknown corridors, and demand, criminal gangs run their own mining operations underground. They usually mine, smelt, and prepare the gold underground. Various reports have placed the losses at between 5 percent and 10 percent of total legitimate production for all of Brazil. Goldy once tried to remove the illegal miners, but a violent response from the armed gangs forced them to simply place a wooden barrier between their operations and that of the illegal miners. The guide did not venture any information on whether or not the flimsy wooden demarcation was honoured.

The consultants beat a hasty retreat.

ABOVE-GROUND VISIT

The facilities above ground are much more impressive—all the way from two fully equipped football fields to a fully outfitted shopping centre. Goldy's above-ground facilities can best be described as those of a middle-class small town in the USA. There is even a Starbucks, KFC, and McDonald's in the complex.

DEBRIEF

The team decides to have a shower and get together to debrief an hour before the dinner with Gavrilo and his team. They are pretty shocked by the working conditions at the mine. While they expected things to be worse than conditions of mining operations in Canada and Australia, they did not expect large parts of the mine to rival the worst mines they had seen in South Africa, Borneo, and the Democratic Republic of the Congo. They are definitely worse than other Brazilian mines the team has seen.

The reality is all the more jarring since their only previous exposure to Mino 1 had been the glossy annual report descriptions and the sparkling infotainment videos played on a continuous loop at the head office. Luther is convinced that cultural issues and getting the basics right will likely generate significant results for Mino 1. Marcus will join the team for dinner with Gavrilo, and they will discuss this with him tomorrow at breakfast before they leave.

DINNER

Dinner was a grand affair held in Gavrilo's company-sponsored estate in the complex. Over a meal of traditional Brazilian meat and drink, Gavrilo was a gracious host who spent lots of time discussing the history, heritage, and legacy of Mino 1. Gavrilo firmly believed that Mino 1 was at the peak of its performance, and nothing more could be done. Nonetheless, he is open to having the consultants see what is possible. Thus far, he has not had many discussions with the CEO about the process and how the pilot will work.

Marcus intends to keep the dinner a social event and offers to discuss the complete engagement details with Gavrilo and his management team either tomorrow morning or in the third week when the engagement team relocates to Mino 1. The exhausted engagement team leaves at 10 p.m. and were in bed by 11 p.m.

WEEK 2

—

day 2

———

CONTEXT AFTER
THE SITE VISIT

tHE MINO 1 VISIT had more than one benefit. Since the charter flight out could only leave at 10 the next morning, the team had an opportunity to have an unusually long breakfast. The other benefit was the presence of the engagement partner, Marcus, and the ensuing discussion.

Marcus actually developed the engagement principles with Goldy's CEO, Carlos Selgado, and guided his thinking to change the performance of the business. Marcus's comments are very interesting since they provide further context for the engagement. While Hendrik had previously summarised most of this information, it was still useful to hear the detailed background.

As Marcus recounted, his first discussions with Selgado took place about nine months ago when he, Selgado, was being wooed by the chairman of the board to come across and run the business. At the time, Selgado was running a Brazilian electricity utility. He had done an excellent job at the utility and was not particularly keen to go into a new industry and turn around one of Brazil's floundering mining giants, especially when the giant did not consider itself to be in trouble. To Selgado, on the one hand, he had the opportunity of exiting the business world on a high note, and on the other, he would be going into a very uncertain situation at Goldy. After numerous and persistent requests from the chairman, he agreed to conduct his own due diligence on Goldy. Then he would make his decision, which could still very well be a polite decline of the offer.

He contacted colleagues to find mining specialists who could talk him though the changes in the sector. Through referrals, Selgado arrived at the firm and Marcus in particular. Over several dinners, they sketched out the challenges facing the mining sector, gold mining companies, and Goldy in particular:

1. The traditional gold mining centres are dying. Famous deep (over 2 km underground) mining centres in Brazil, South Africa, Venezuela, and Asia are becoming more expensive and difficult to mine. The deeper they go, the tougher the job.

2. Sweeping activism among shareholders is starting to hold gold miners accountable for safety and mining deaths. Safety is a major issue and, until recently, most miners have avoided scandals. It is every gold mining CEO's nightmare that a campaign will start similar to the *"blood diamonds"* campaign, which had cost the diamond industry millions of dollars. Increased safety costs money.

3. Due to the older, inefficient equipment and techniques, production volumes were dropping.

4. Gold mining is moving to new centres in Canada, Mexico, and Asia, which require new mining techniques that the established companies do not necessarily have. They are not comfortable transferring their core mining knowledge since it does not always work in these new locations. Many of the established miners lack mechanized mining know-how. Bringing in new mining technology and mining partners costs money.

5. The need for more capital is forcing gold mining companies to go to the capital markets. They are doing this at a time when

they have been performing relatively poorly due to rising costs, and the capital markets are forcing them to undergo greater scrutiny—something they have tried to avoid. Moreover, given all the uncertainty in the markets, access to capital is coming at a high cost.

6. Given the location of mines, the sites need to be self-sustaining with their own hospitals, schools, and housing. Mines are now saddled with these assets, which add little if any value and often destroy value.

7. For the same reason as above, activities that could be outsourced were done in-house.

8. Gold exchange-traded funds have allowed investors' exposure to increases in the gold price by bypassing gold stocks. No one is yet sure of the impact on gold companies, but it is likely that it will affect the existing business models.

9. Gold mining companies are struggling to grow and want to expand into adjacent sectors, such as uranium and platinum. For example, the vast slimes dams holding ore residue and chemicals contain minerals. They now lie dormant, and gold miners want to mine them, but investors are unhappy since they want pure gold stocks. Investors can diversify by themselves and require access to pure gold equity. If gold mining companies diversify, investors lose access to pure gold equity, which has created tension between the investors and gold companies.

10. The conditions of gold mining in Brazil, South Africa, the DRC, and Indonesia have typically attracted low-skilled workers. Poor education and poor working conditions have led to major health problems. This has created huge insurance liabilities for the companies as well as potential lawsuits.

11. Gold mining companies have tried to make money in all market conditions and held all types of mines, e.g., those that consistently made money, even at a low ROCE, those that only made money during high gold prices, and those that made money at high tonnages. This model is not sustainable, and gold miners have been thinking about specialisation.
12. In Brazil, the government will soon grant licenses to foreign companies and allow them to own and operate local facilities.
13. Goldy still has the government of Brazil as a major shareholder. This is unlikely to change and creates a huge barrier to change.
14. Cheap labour has meant that mines have never mechanised. They are struggling to extract efficiencies from their operations.

Based on all these issues, the CEO felt he could only accept the offer and fix Goldy if he could:

1. Change the culture to a performance-based system.
2. Slim down the company and refocus on gold.
3. Wring out efficiency by sharing services.
4. Choose a new business model and shed assets.

Even though the board was willing to allow such a drastic possibility, the CEO initially declined. It took some high-level pleas before he accepted the position.

Marcus confidentially mentions that the CEO is going to implement this four-pronged plan across the business, but rather than proclaiming this in the annual report, internal communication, and press releases, he is finding reasons to implement the process first where there is the greatest need and in the most critical centres. Marcus and the

CEO have also been careful not to use this description for the current engagement at Mino 1. That would create too much resistance. They felt that a proper consulting study would naturally test if these four focus areas were the correct ones. In some ways, this engagement serves as a check on the CEO's thinking.

This engagement team has to help the CEO turn Mino 1 back into an effective, efficient, and productive mining operation. The CEO can then use this success at the largest centre to drive improvement across the business. Marcus mentions that the firm is already preparing initial study packs to roll out this approach in the administrative areas and corporate offices of Goldy, which could become one of the firm's most important clients in the next few months, provided this team could successfully show the CEO a viable turnaround plan for Mino 1 when adopting the four-pronged strategy.

In the breakfast discussion, several other important decisions were reconfirmed:

1. Another associate arrived at the Goldy head office a few hours ago and is working on the service functions analyses.

2. The team is correct to focus on the cultural issues, but they should not worry too much. That is the CEO's job to manage, and they should simply guide him.

3. The business case team needs to re-create Mino 1's finances due to the numerous finance system issues.

Although it remains unsaid, Max and Alana know that the engagement team is heavily dependent on the business case team delivering a credible, validated, and accepted business case.

WEEK 2

day 2

DEBATING METRICS WITH THE CFO

THE TEAM is back at the office by noon on Tuesday. The working conditions, state of the mine, viewpoint of Gavrilo, and information from Marcus were extremely beneficial and helped frame the engagement and clarify the context of the study. The Week 1 planning was certainly useful, but at least now the team knows the type of corporate environment within which they operate. Looking around the Goldy head office with its modern finishes and decorated offices only reinforces the difference between the company's culture for the 1,000 people at the head office and the 120,000 employees in the mines.

Max wonders if his priorities should change based on all the new information received in the last few days:

1. Goldy will likely go through some dramatic changes in its organisational structure, business model, and operating model. This engagement is a smaller version of such a corporate-wide initiative.

2. Despite the eventual and far-reaching corporate overhaul, the business case team needs to focus on delivering the business case for just Mino 1. The more he thinks about it, the more challenging this seems to be unless it is carefully managed. The engagement has not yet settled down, and the arrival of the new associate will increase the changes.

3. The analyses of the services assets will likely generate new opportunities. The business case team must make modifications to their work to analyse these opportunities.

The bottom line is clear: the business case team needs to quickly sign off on their approach and lay the groundwork for the analyses. Max is also thinking through a decision that could save his team a lot of time in the long term or create numerous delays if he is incorrect.

This is the trade-off he needs to consider. It is clear that a financial baseline assessment of Mino 1 must be done soon. There are two possible ways to do this:

1. The first option is to complete the baseline analyses in a separate and simple Excel spreadsheet. After this is done, the business case model can be built in another Excel spreadsheet, which will result in two financial models: a simple model for the baseline assessment and the main model to evaluate the options. This is a faster approach that could yield a baseline result within a week at most. The downside is that the main model building will be pushed back, and the baseline data will need to be reinserted into the complete model.

2. The second option is to develop the full model and populate it with "best guess" data simply to test the model and make sure it works. This will be a fully functional model. Once the model is working, the team will insert the current and past actual financial data to generate the baseline. In this option, there is only one model, which is designed to perform the financial baseline analyses and evaluate the options. This will take longer but allocates more time to the model building. This creates more flexibility and reduces the number of errors that occur when two models are used.

From previous experience, Max realises that no matter how smart or diligent the team is, errors will likely occur if different models are used:

1. Since the models will likely be constructed in different ways, making the same assumption in both will have to be done in different ways. Each way will need to be recorded and checked regularly.

2. Both models will need to be updated. Verification becomes a problem, as the person validating the model needs to understand two modelling approaches and remember to carry through updates in one model to the other.

All of this simply creates too many problems, so Max decides to build the complete model framework in Excel and only then complete the baseline analyses. Just one model will be built. Despite all the pressure for the baseline analyses, he feels this is the right decision. He decides to speak to Luther to get approval for this decision.

LUTHER'S OPINION

Luther disagrees. He explains that the entire team is trying to understand the scale of the problem and likely location of the opportunities. At the moment, they are working according to focus interviews, external data, and direction from the client, which may not be very accurate. Any delay in getting out the baseline analyses is setting the team back by a few days. This is time the team cannot afford to lose—valuable time they need given the size of Mino 1's operations and the tight timeline.

Max expected this pushback. He also realises the hallmark of a great management consultant is one who can see an argument from both points of view and do what is best for the team and the client. If Max still believes he is correct, he needs to convince Luther. That is the responsibility of a good team player.

Max points out that with Luther's recommendation the team may move rapidly in the first two weeks, but having two models will create so many delays that the gains may have disappeared at the end of the engagement. Luther's approach creates momentum at the beginning but more delays at the end.

Luther still insists that this is needed, especially for a client where the finance department data is not at all accurate. After 30 minutes of discussion, Max thinks of a compromise. What if Max did the following?

1. Builds the full model framework and just one model.

2. Yet, the model will be built in isolated and distinct modules, which might be divided according to parts of the value chain.

3. To test the model, the team will use the data required to generate the financial baseline analyses. The output will be about 90 percent accurate in the third week and will only be validated by Week 4.

4. Each module will be completed one at a time. Once a module is built and analysed, the business case team could advise the rest of the team about the potential size of the opportunity and if it is worth examining further.

5. Rather than waiting for the entire model to be completed before results can be generated, the engagement team will receive results as each module is completed.

6. Everyone wins in this approach. The business case team can focus more time on building one robust analyses platform, while the overall engagement team will receive updates faster.

Basically, Max is offering a completed part of a portion of the overall analyses earlier rather than all of the analyses much later. Luther accepts this as a fair compromise and asks Max to update the team in the meeting tomorrow morning.

MEETING WITH THE CFO

Max prints and binds two copies of the planning documents. Although he has updated the documents, he decides to take along the version everyone has already seen. This will allow him to make like-for-like comparisons between the comments he has received and Flavio's feedback.

Flavio only has about 25 minutes for the meeting, but the meeting took a direction Max did not expect, although he should have. Flavio was absolutely focused on trying to understand why the consulting team is measuring ROCE. According to Flavio, there is no use in approving the approach unless the correct measure is used. Based on Flavio's passing comment about an update with Sergio, it is likely this line of question originates from Sergio or as a result of an update meeting they have had. Flavio raises the following points:

1. Before any work can be done, the correct business measure must be chosen.
2. He cannot understand why ROCE is chosen over EVA.
3. He points out that a highly respected rival firm ran a workshop last year to evaluate implementing EVA, and he has tasked some of the analysts to look into this. To him, EVA seems like a good measure.
4. Flavio indicates that unless people understand ROCE, why it was chosen, and why it is a superior measure for this

engagement, it is unlikely anyone will manage their business to optimise this measure.

5. Lastly, Flavio raises one other critical point. For the last six years, Goldy has invested in explaining to the investment community the importance of pursuing a net profit margin strategy. How can he go back and tell them this has changed? He needs to present a very compelling reason for the change and how it will impact the business and shareholders.

Max reverts to his core training and probes further to understand if these are the real concerns facing Flavio. It is pointless and time consuming to address these issues only to find out they are not the real reasons for the pushback from Flavio. Should that happen, even more time and effort will be required to finally address Flavio's true concerns.

Max first asks Flavio if he has any other concerns. Flavio says no. For him, these are the main issues to be settled before they can proceed. The financial analysts and Sergio can worry about the details of the financial analyses.

Next, Max paraphrases Flavio's feedback and reflects his comments back to him. Paraphrasing is important. Sometimes clients miscommunicate or their perfectly communicated ideas are misunderstood by the consultant. Paraphrasing distils the discussion into the key elements and forces the client to think about the most important elements. If the client disagrees with the interpretation, he can explain his original thoughts. Clarity in communication is important.

"I am going to repeat your concerns in my own language to ensure I have understood them all.

You have listed the following concerns:

WEEK 2 - DAY 2: DEBATING METRICS WITH THE CFO

1. What is the reason for measuring ROCE versus other measures available?
2. How do we ensure that everyone else understands this reason and how it will impact them?
3. What does ROCE mean in operating terms and on a day-to-day decision-making basis?
4. How do you justify this new measure to the analyst and investment community?"

Flavio agrees that those are his main concerns.

Max asks if, assuming he could correctly and adequately address these concerns, Flavio would approve the ROCE metric and approach taken. Flavio agrees and says that he raises these questions purely because these are the challenges both the consultants and management would face in attempting something new.

Max decides not to answer the questions in the meeting. There is not enough time. He offers to come back with a proper response to each question. With just five minutes left for the meeting, the discussion shifts to the mine visit and upcoming focus interviews.

A huge mistake many consultants make is to try to answer immediately or without adequate reflection. Any perceived time saved is squandered by the fact that a poorly constructed response will discredit the consultant. It is far better to take the time to respond. Under pressure in a tough study, this may be hard to do but is essential.

After the meeting, Max feels a little frustrated that he did not anticipate the questions. In hindsight, this should have been expected. Clients almost always raise concerns about the approach used. More time should have been spent ensuring that they understood what was happening. Max worries about having meetings where no decisions are made. He is a little concerned that the targets of the work plan for the week may not be fully met. This could become a big problem if the value creation metric remains unresolved. He commits to spending the rest of the week completing all the outstanding planning documents and thinking through the analyses. He hopes to start the model building as well. He needs to be prepared to handle any potential distractions as they arise. He pulls out his mobile phone and calls Luther to update him.

WEEK 2

—

day 4

———

ALL THE PLANNING
IS DONE

MAX ARRIVES at Goldy's head office at 6 a.m. On a typical day, he usually arrives at 7:20 a.m., and no parking can be found. On those days, he needs to park about 200 metres from the entrance. Today, he has his choice of parking spots. As he crosses the foyer and goes through the security scanners, he thinks about the final planning he has completed over the last two days. Despite the delay yesterday, he feels good about the week: Alana has done a great job of preparing a useful value chain analysis, and all the planning documents are ready for his final review.

Max is more pleased because he believes *he* understands what needs to happen, is driving the process, and not relying too much on Luther, Marcus, or Hendrik. In his experience, he knows that despite all the assistance partners and team members offer on an engagement, unless the associate or business analyst responsible for the work takes full ownership and understands the problem in its entirety, it will never be a successful engagement for that consultant. Ownership of the problem *and* solution is a prerequisite for success. Attitude is just as important as skill. Ownership implies taking charge of the process and pulling in help as needed. Max has thought through the model architecture and determined how to build the model and how to include most of the changes discussed over the past few days.

He is especially pleased because his solution to analyse the service functions (e.g., hospitals, schools) is simple and effective.

Arriving at 6 a.m. gives Max a full 90 minutes to print and review the documents before the engagement team meeting. So far, the days have been very busy, and the best time to complete the work is in the early mornings and late afternoons. He hopes to free up time in the evening to review documents by starting some days a little earlier than usual. Max reviews the final planning documents for the last time.

WORK PLAN

Max has altered the work plan to emphasize the following:

1. Tasks in white are important only to the business case team because they are necessary to complete the development of the business case. They support the development of the final deliverables but are not the final deliverables themselves.

2. Shaded tasks are important to the engagement, engagement team, and client. These have been shaded to ensure clarity on when the deliverables will be completed.

3. The model building and financial analyses have been segmented. More milestones are added so that they may receive earlier warnings should they fall behind their schedule.

EXHIBIT 21: Final Work Plan

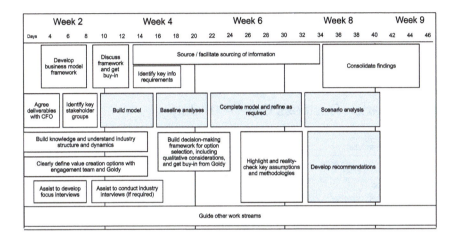

CHARTER

Max is most concerned about the focus on the service functions. Analyses of the service functions (e.g., hospitals, schools, facilities) will likely create value if they are managed well, but it is not clear how this relates to the core mining and extraction problems. There is also the danger of the entire engagement becoming too focused on the service functions, resulting in resources being pulled away from the operations issues. To prevent this from happening, Max has decided to build the following condition into the charter for the business case team.

1. Opportunities affecting the ROCE of Mino 1 through the core mining and extraction activities will be prioritised. The remaining opportunities will only be analysed once the production activities are analysed or the engagement team makes a decision to change the prioritisation order.

EXHIBIT 22: Final Charter

Final Charter: Business Case – 07 July

Objectives	Key Activities	Deliverables

1. Determine the benefits case for the shortlisted options to improve production value and better manage the service functions
2. Recommend an option to improve production value
3. Explain the trade-offs in the preferred option
	1. Expectations exchange with CFO to agree on deliverables
	2. Develop framework for the business case model and get buy-in
	3. Identify key information requirements to build the model
	4. Conduct baseline analyses and advise engagement team
	5. Understand existing financial baseline performance of the business and performance drivers and levers
	6. Source / facilitate the finding of information
	7. Guide other work streams
	8. Assist in identifying key stakeholder groups:
	   1. Assist in development of focus interviews
	   2. Help to conduct interviews if required
	9. Guide the strategic decision-making process
	   1. Help to develop key decision criteria for option selection
	10. Build model with key inputs and assumptions highlighted
	11. Develop recommendations on optimal route to improving production value
		1. Baseline assessment
		2. A business case for each option and the preferred option
		3. A flexible model to simulate revenues, costs, and value created for each of the options
		4. Consolidated view of whether or not Goldy can execute the preferred option/s and its financial health in pursuing the preferred option.
		5. Identify drivers and levers

Scope		**Critical Success Factors**

1. Only examine options related to the core gold mining and processing business, and the service functions, should they impact the core business
2. Producing mines and development shafts
3. Options for value creation, which can lead to more than a 10% increase in value will be analysed in depth
4. Only currency and gold price external drivers will be analysed
		1. Client commitment
		   1. Timely access to key personnel within Goldy and the CFO
		   2. Timely access to key external stakeholders
		2. Timely access to information
		3. Adhering to the scope around the service functions
		4. Accurate data
		5. Clear, open, and honest communication between engagement manager, consultants, and client

MODEL ARCHITECTURE AND DESCRIPTION

Max makes changes to both documents to finalise the inclusion of the service functions analyses.

EXHIBIT 23: Final Model Architecture

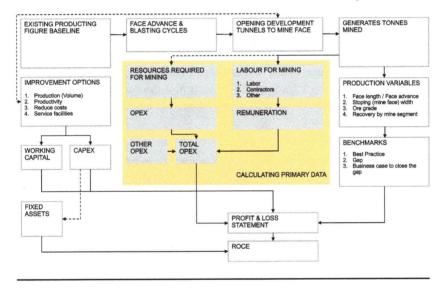

EXHIBIT 24: Final Model Description

FIRMSCONSULTING.COM & STRATEGYTRAINING.COM

Final Model Description: Business Case – 07 July

A flexible model with a five-year projection was built to better understand the mining operations at a site average basis with a focus on the operating structure. Production volume will be modelled. We subsequently tested the feasibility of operating under different macroeconomic environments (scenarios), by changing the variables: currency exchange rate, inflation rate, and the gold price.

The model can be adapted to test three broad types of options available to Goldy management: changes in production (debottlenecking and removing production gaps), productivity changes, and cost reduction changes, by changing the key inputs and assumptions accordingly. Key outputs from the model include ROCE, costs, cash flows, and financial and operating trade-offs between all options and the recommended option.

VALUE TREE

The value tree is completed, and Max includes samples in the main presentation. He carefully checks to ensure the appendices contain all the remaining value trees. It is important that he can refer to these when discussing key ideas and data requirements with the financial analysts and Goldy employees.

EXHIBIT 25: Final ROCE Value Tree

The impact of lower-level financial and operational drivers on ROCE will be established

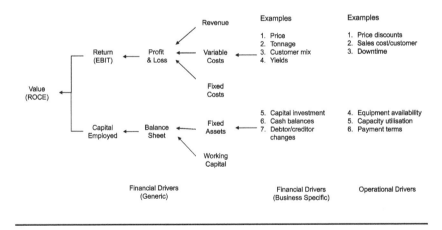

EXHIBIT 26: Final ROCE Detail

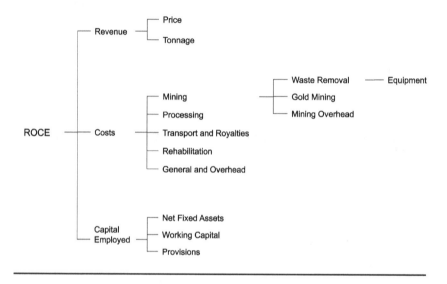

Value Tree showing the link from ROCE to total costs to mining to waste to equipment costs

VALUE CHAIN

In briefing Alana about the process map/value chain, Max cautioned against a mistake many new business analysts make. When new business analysts hear the words "process" and "map," they assume a detailed flow chart is required that lists every single pipeline, valve, chamber, vessel, and channel in the mining operation. That is not required. Early in a management consulting engagement of this nature, the process map is more like a more detailed value chain. Max is still not sure how all the parts of the model will be built. He wants a process map to help him understand the major processes. As he builds the model, he will need to develop further detail to understand how each part of the process map works. For now, however, a higher-level map will do.

As he explained to Alana, it is important to collect *just enough* data and information to answer the primary question of the engagement and work stream. Anything more is not useful to the engagement. Not everything needs to be correct to two decimal places. In fact, it is better to first do a back-of-the-envelope calculation to see if something makes sense before doing the detailed calculations.

Max is happy with the process flow developed by Alana:

1. It outlines the overall process well.
2. It is at a high enough level to see the overall production process but segmented into logical changes in the production process.
3. The annotations and descriptions are intuitive.

This is more than sufficient to guide him in the early stages of finding data. It points him in the right direction to ask questions and find information. Over the course of the model building, this process flow may become more detailed.

EXHIBIT 27: Draft Value Chain

Draft Value Chain: Business Case – 07 July

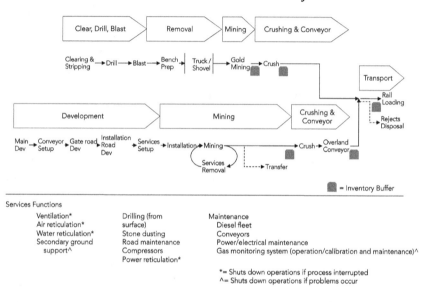

ADDITIONAL QUERIES

Finally, Max gets around to addressing the concerns raised by Flavio about the type of business metric used. He chooses not to convert these to slides. Max does not want to create the impression that the engagement team needs support slides to explain their rationale. He decides to write down the rationale and email it to the team. Everyone on the team should understand this and be able to explain it. This also demonstrates to the client that the consultants understand their material well and builds the credibility of the team.

Max also feels this approach will better suit the Goldy employees and executives who have already started complaining about the excessive presentations they have to read and review. From previous experience, Max understands that to decisively end the debate about the business measures, the team must address the root concern directly and as quickly as possible. He types out a note for the engagement team.

"What is the reason for measuring ROCE versus other measures?"

1. Calculating EVA (economic value added) for Goldy is possible but is a complicated process that does not help Mino 1 improve its operating performance more than using ROCE.
    a. Calculating the EVA for Mino 1, which is not a separate legal entity, is difficult to do, especially given the poor recordkeeping and short duration of the study.
    b. It will require a more involved calculation, and complex adjustments will need to be made to estimate Goldy's and, thereafter, Mino 1's WACC. None of these calculations will have any impact on improving Mino 1's operating performance. As a result, using this measure is not optimal for this study. The team does not have sufficient time to use EVA as a performance measure for this engagement.
    c. EVA is difficult to benchmark across companies since they use different adjustments. **In other words, using EVA means Mino 1 cannot be easily compared with any other Goldy operation or competitor unless we go out and calculate those EVA numbers as well, which widely increases the scope of the study.**
    d. On the other hand, the engagement team can create estimates of ROCE for Goldy's other mining operations and for competitors. They would need to be improved if the engagement is rolled out to other sites, but for now, they will provide a reasonable set of data for internal and external benchmarking.

e. Overall, given the above, we have chosen to use one measure for this study. That measure is ROCE.

   f. However, ROCE and other accounting measures can be manipulated to pump up returns in the short term. We need to ensure proper checks and balances are suggested to the client to prevent this from happening.

"How do we ensure that everyone else understands this reason and how it will impact them?"

1. Not everyone needs to understand the financial logic. This calculation only needs to be understood by the executive and management teams.

2. The ROCE metric will be broken down into levers that are applicable and appropriate to each level of employee. For example, if we trace the value tree for ROCE down to the transportation team, their metrics may change from the number of hours uptime for the conveyor belt to the number of hours uptime for the conveyor belt multiplied by the percentage capacity utilisation of the belt. This drives volume and is the measure they need to understand and drive. They need not understand ROCE.

3. It is not important for everyone to understand ROCE. It is more important for employees to understand their contribution to increasing production value in their own part of the business, even if they have never heard of ROCE.

"What does ROCE mean in operating terms and on a day-to-day decision-making basis?"

1. Same as above. It should not be a topic of conversation for front-line staff even though it may change their metrics and targets.

"How do you justify this new measure to the analyst and investment community?"

1. The analyst community is interested in the overall value creation at Goldy and how Goldy means to sustain this creation of value.

2. ROCE does not replace the overall corporate value creation measure. ROCE is simply used because it is an appropriate measure to determine the value created at a mining site level.

3. Every financial analyst understands that ROIC drives share appreciation. Measuring ROCE is very similar to ROIC, and ROCE does encourage activities that create value in the long term, provided key operating and strategic drivers are included to monitor and measure the health and performance of the business and to drive a focus on long-term value creation and ensure that a company's day-to-day processes, such as performance management, are aligned with long-term value creation

Max is glad that the planning is done. He attaches a copy of the final planning documents and sends it with the email. He also stores a copy in the engagement team's main online folder.

He presses send just as the 7:30 a.m. team meeting is about to begin. He feels excited about the next few days as the team starts the focus interviews, maps key processes, and builds the overall business case model.

WEEK 2

day 4 & 5

DESIGNING &
CONDUCTING
FOCUS
INTERVIEWS

"**GIVEN ALL THE CHANGES** to the business case in the last few days and the need to get my head around the services analyses, I think we should just focus on the business case.

I think we should not do any of the focus interviews. It's not that I do not want to help the other team members. I just really believe we need to be focused on what is most important to the task at hand and the client's needs."

When Alana mentioned this to Max after the morning team meeting, he realises how frequently new business analysts misunderstand the importance of the focus interviews and the purpose of a business case. It is apparent that Alana probably sees the business case team's objective and way of operating as simply building a model, crunching the numbers, and handing this over to the rest of the engagement team.

Too many young business analysts think the business case team's work is done once the model is built and ready; little do they know that this is just the beginning. The real work starts once the model is ready, and it must be used to analyse the various options and guide the development of the final recommendations. The latter part requires building client relationships, understanding all the issues, and being able to communicate clearly. Business case development is not about model building. It is about understanding the business. The model and analyses are the means to the end, not the end itself.

It is also apparent that Alana may not fully understand how the business case team collects information and influences the engagement. The business case team does not simply work with reams and reams of data. They need to think carefully about the questions the model will answer, design techniques to collect the data, and find ways to verify their initial hypotheses. For the business case team:

1. The focus interview is a critical tool to collect valuable data and test hypotheses.

2. It is known as one of the four primary top-down analysis tools completed at the start of an engagement. The other three are case studies, benchmarking gaps, and financial ratio analysis of the client. In this study, we have referred to the financial ratio analyses as the baseline analyses.

3. The client will almost certainly know more than the consultants. The client can outline what has been tried, what has failed, and what has worked. The client may also indicate opportunities the engagement team has not considered. The business case team must use the focus interview feedback to confirm, change, or reprioritise their work.

4. Thus far, all the information has been coming through from the finance department. The focus interview levels the playing field by allowing every level of the organisation to comment on an issue or raise new issues. It allows the consultants to view the problem from multiple angles.

5. A good business case consultant must be able to use many soft skills to produce a business case that is accepted by the client. The ability to design, conduct, and analyse a focus interview is one such soft skill.

6. The business case team cannot work in isolation. It is not a data processing centre. They need to be just as engaged as the rest of the teams. The focus interview provides them an opportunity to develop client relationships and look for clues in the body language of interviewees as they deliver feedback. The team must engage clients directly; otherwise, they run the risk of receiving "translated" messages and could miss key signals.

PREPARING FOR THE FOCUS INTERVIEWS

Max decides to involve Alana as much as possible in the process, knowing that she will come to appreciate its value only through her direct involvement. Together, they decide with the rest of the team how they want to conduct the focus interviews. The overall engagement team has the following objectives for the focus interviews:

1. Build relationships with key employees and executives.
2. Understand where the likely problems lie.
3. Understand previous/current efforts to address these problems.

Within these broad objectives, the business case team has a very specific set of objectives:

1. Build key relationships with employees who can supply data and those who can test the team's assumptions and outputs.
2. Understand Mino 1's finances.
3. Isolate and describe potential opportunities.
4. Educate the interviewees about ROCE.

With this in mind, the business case team agrees to interview those employees whom they think can help them collect this data and support the development of the business case. They will conduct 16 formal interviews followed by several follow-up sessions:

1. CFO
2. Finance Manager
3. EVP – Mino 1
4. Ore Reserve Manager – Mino 1
5. Services Manager – Goldy
6. Services Leaders x 2
7. HR Manager – Mino 1
8. COO
9. Financial Analysts x 2
10. Shift Supervisors—in different sections of the mine x 3
11. Mine Managers x 2

The business case team decides to build two types of focus interviews. One type will be used for the executives and the other for the operating staff and mine workers. Questions about the finances and collection of data will be reserved for the operating staff. Creating specific focus interviews ensures the questions are not generic and can focus on issues and problems relevant to the level of the interviewee.

For the executive group of interviews, Max decides to keep the interview short. They prepare over 30 questions but prioritise them. In each section of the interview, the top three questions are the ones they most want answered. Should they run into time constraints, they will simply focus on these top three questions.

WEEK 2 - DAY 4 & 5: DESIGNING & CONDUCTING FOCUS INTERVIEWS

From their experience, executives tend to prefer elaborating on the initial information, and they need to set aside time for this. Forcing the executive to complete a long list of questions without pausing to explore issues creates the impression that the consultants are more interested in completing the focus interview rather than understanding the issues. They need to allow sufficient time for this, but they still need to ensure the interviews provide the information they seek and do not veer off in the wrong direction. They must control the interviews.

Focus interviews must *always* begin with the interviewer providing the background and details. It is best to have two people conducting the interviews: one person to manage the discussion and the other to take detailed notes. Several important messages must be delivered during this short introduction:

1. Introduce the engagement and interviewers.
2. Confirm the time commitment.
3. Confirm the interviewee's name and title.
4. Explain to the interviewee the complete confidentiality of the information provided.
5. Explain that the interviewee is not being assessed in any way, and no information will be shared with his or her superiors. Summaries of the interviews will be shared with Goldy management, but it will not be possible to identify the source of the comments.

These are the questions Max and Alana develop for the focus interview:

1. Overview
    a. Is performance between Goldy's operations consistent? Why?

b. What is the management model of Goldy and Mino 1?
   c. How do the two management models interact?
   d. What is your perception of the current state of the gold mining sector?
   e. Does this differ between countries? How does Brazil compare?
   f. How has Goldy performed in the last two years? Why?
2. Perceptions
   a. What has been done to improve operating performance at Mino 1? What have been the results?
   b. Do you believe Mino 1 can do more? Why or how?
   c. Can you name the initiatives Mino 1 has undertaken to improve performance? What were the results of such initiatives?
   d. Are any initiatives planned but not yet undertaken?
   e. Can you list the issues affecting Mino 1 performance?
   f. How would you rank these issues in importance to improving operating performance, 5 being the most important and 1 being the least important?
3. Data
   a. How do you measure the performance of Mino 1?
   b. Can we have access to the data?
   c. Whom would you recommend that we contact to understand the data?
4. Operating Environment
   a. Does Mino 1 have a different operating environment from other comparable mining hubs? If yes, in what way?
   b. How does this difference affect its performance?

- c. How would you rank the importance of the differences on Mino 1's operating performance, 5 being the most important and 1 being the least important?
- d. Please list the different stages in the production process, from mining all the way to the point when the ore reaches the refinery (ask the interviewee to draw it out).
- e. How does Mino 1 perform in each part of the process? Please explain.
- f. Which areas are underperforming? Why?
- g. Which areas are exceeding the performance of peers and expectations of management? How?
- h. How did you answer the two questions above? Are benchmarks available? Can we have them?
- i. For the different stages, which are outsourced?
- j. What are morale and culture like at the mine?
- k. Is the culture an asset to the mine? What improvements to the culture do you believe will benefit business performance?

5. Services
   a. Could you please list the different services offered?
   b. Why are they needed?
   c. What is the value of keeping them in-house?
   d. Will outsourcing these services affect production in a material way?
   e. Where can we obtain data and finances for the services?

6. Other
   a. Is there anything else you would like to add?

In preparing these focus interviews, Max and Alana have adhered to the following best practice principles:

1. Use the interview responses to test their initial hypotheses/ideas
2. Have an objective for holding the focus interviews.
3. Use the interviews as an opportunity to build allies for the engagement team.
4. Build the questionnaire around extracting the data/information needed to answer the primary question for the work stream and build the model.
5. The primary data focus is on the mining operations, and they have built the largest part of the questionnaire around this subject.
6. Include ranking questions so that comparisons can be made between interviewees. Focus on collecting data for comparisons.
7. Order the questionnaire so that the critical questions are asked before the time limit is reached.

Max discusses the interview questions with Luther, who cautions him that these are quite long, and it is unlikely they will get more than 60 minutes to do the interview.

As the team will be working from Mino 1 all of Weeks 3, 4, 5, 6, and 7, Max decides he needs to conduct the focus interviews with Sergio, Flavio, Heinze, and the services manager over the next two days. They are all based in the Rio office, and it is the only chance to see them in the next four weeks, but he cannot arrange the interviews just yet. Luther will need to have the CEO send out a notice indicating that the consultants are working on an engagement and will need to conduct interviews. Then the team can arrange the interviews.

WEEK 2

day 5

FEEDBACK FROM THE FOCUS INTERVIEWS

MAX AND ALANA sit down at a Goldy employee cafeteria table after an exhausting Thursday evening and Friday morning spent conducting focus interviews. In all, they have conducted four such interviews: CFO, COO, Services Manager, and Finance Manager. All went well over their allotted time schedules, as the interviewees were keen to provide their feedback and ask many questions regarding the engagement. The good news is that all the concerns about the ROCE metric and role of the business case team have disappeared.

Sitting in the corner table out of hearing range of Goldy employees, the team members sift through their handwritten notes and prepare their focus interview summaries. Although the complete write-up can be done in the evening, it is important to provide feedback in the form of summaries as quickly as possible to the rest of the team. Feedback from focus interviews is only effective if circulated immediately and shared by everyone to build a more complete picture of the organisation. Moreover, information from one interview may require the questions in a subsequent interview to be changed. Rapid sharing of information is critical.

For each interviewee, they capture the five most important findings or observations to shoot off as an email.

Flavio, CFO

1. "Mino 1 is too independent, and you will likely find many more problems."
2. "Mino 1's production has dropped due to negligence and poor management."
3. "It is likely that other mines have the same problem."
4. "The culture is a huge problem. In fact, it's probably the biggest problem. There is little accountability in the culture."
5. "Neither Mino 1 nor any of the other mines can compare their performance due to a lack of benchmarks."

Sergio, Finance Manager

1. "The head office does not seem interested in operations. It is all about deals, deals, and more deals."
2. "Production failed when they adopted a new mine management model."
3. "Mino 1 is not the only problem. Mines in South Africa and Russia are probably worse."
4. "Goldy is sitting on huge uranium and platinum reserves, which should be exploited."
5. "There is a problem with the SAP costing database, and no one wants to fix the problem."

Heinze, COO

1. "Mino 1 is aware of its problems and has tried many different things to fix these problems: supply chain optimisation, cost reduction, production improvements, changing contractors, and more."

2. "The problem is getting the head office to pay for these things and the challenges of execution. All the initiatives failed about six to nine months after the launch of the pilot."
3. "Talent is a significant problem. Almost all of Goldy's competitors have poached Goldy executives. Goldy trains people very well but cannot retain them. That is one reason why the initiatives fail. They start well, but the champion leaves, and they fall apart."
4. "The regional mines still have too much power. It is very difficult to coordinate activities between mines. For example, the shared services initiative was started 18 months ago, and no progress has been made."
5. "Goldy's culture needs to change. The board acts as though the company is still a star. It is dying from within, and tough steps must be taken. It is hoped that the new CEO can do this."

Paulo, Services Manager

1. "I am not sure what I must do. There are too many barriers to my work. Each mine is too independent and cannot be centrally managed. My coordinating role cannot be done. None of the services people report to me, and I do not set their compensation. They will not listen."
2. "It is impossible to drive a central initiative. Each mine replicates its own support and service functions. I hope you are looking at that."
3. "Culture is a tremendous problem. It needs to change, but a bigger problem is the former CEO who allowed this to continue. No one talks about the failure of the former CEO to bring order. Unless Goldy is centrally managed, nothing will change."

4. "Mino 1 is performing poorly? Yes, but the other mines are just as bad."
5. "Fixing Mino 1 will be tough. No one really knows what is happening at the mine."

The themes virtually jump off the paper. It is apparent that senior management thinks the CEO needs to bring order and control to the company. He faces a tough and independent culture but needs to do this for the good of the company. It is intriguing that Mino 1 has tried so many initiatives, and all have failed. The operations team will need to understand what happened to all these initiatives. Loss of talented implementers may be one reason, but there are likely to be many, many more.

Max and Alana capture opportunities from the interviews and split the opportunities into two lists. One includes opportunities that can be quantified and tested, and the other involves opportunities that are more difficult to quantify:

LIST 1: **Quantifiable and can be tested:**

1. M&A focus at the expense of operational improvement.
2. New management model affecting performance.
3. No benchmarks.
4. SAP database problems.
5. Problems in South Africa and Russia.
6. Prior Mino 1 failed improvement initiatives.
7. Loss of skilled employees.
8. Poor aggregation of performance data.

LIST 2: **Nonquantifiable and more difficult to test:**

1. Cultural roadblocks.
2. Negligence.
3. Poor management.
4. Opportunities in platinum and uranium (though quantifiable, added to this list since it may be outside the scope of the engagement).
5. Effect of the decentralised structure.
6. Weak former CEO.

Alana pulls out her laptop and types out an email with the summary and list of opportunities. She will send this to the operations team and services team. While the business case team will investigate these further, they will do so merely to understand how to test the production value impact. It will be the responsibility of the other teams to dig in and understand these issues.

As the study progresses, the business case team will calculate the benefit of a recommendation; yet, it is still the purview of the stream analysing the recommendation to ensure it is viable and correctly modelled by the business case team. If the work stream arrives at the conclusion that a benefit is not feasible, the business case team must adjust/remove the benefit. In most cases, the benefit is not removed entirely but is given a 5 percent to 10 percent probability of occurring or a 5 percent to 10 percent weighting in the final benefits case.

This is the relationship between the streams. These balances and checks work well when they are used.

GUIDING THE TEAMS

Although the other team members will need to analyse the services and mining operations, it is still the responsibility of Max and Alana to guide them and ensure that all the thinking can be pulled together to show the overall impact on Mino 1. The earlier the guidance is given, the better it is for the engagement. Guidance received too late cannot be effectively incorporated into the engagement. A key technique used by the business case team to provide guidance is the opportunity chart.

Over Friday evening, Max and Alana prepare their opportunity charts and tracking tools. The charts will be sent to the operations improvement, services, and engagement management work streams. The business case team will use the charts in the following manner:

1. Either Max or Alana will meet with each work stream over the next three days to understand their list of potential opportunities. The opportunities do not need to be completed, although any extra detail does help. This allows the business case team to determine if their model can assess all likely opportunities.

2. Based on the details provided, they will test each opportunity, pull it apart, and ensure it can withstand the likely scrutiny it will receive from the client.

3. Ensure there is no duplication of benefits or double counting. This usually happens on engagements, and the team must ensure that all opportunities are mutually exclusive and collectively exhaustive.

4. Determine which opportunities are quantifiable and nonquantifiable. For both quantifiable and nonquantifiable opportunities, determine which are financial and which are nonfinancial in nature. For example:

WEEK 2 - DAY 5: FEEDBACK FROM THE FOCUS INTERVIEWS

    a. Reducing transport costs by 5 percent as a result of changing suppliers is a benefit that can be measured in financial terms and is clearly quantifiable.

    b. Improving Goldy's investor profile can be measured in financial terms but is nonquantifiable (at least not in this engagement).

    c. Improving morale is a benefit that is difficult to measure in financial terms. It is nonfinancial and quantifiable through surveys. Yet, outside the scope of the business case stream since it is not a financial metric.

5. Thereafter, the 80/20 rule will be applied to determine which opportunities have the greatest impact on ROCE. Only these opportunities will be modelled.

6. In the fourth or fifth week, they will go back to the work teams for their completed opportunity charts.

7. Develop key metrics and indicators to measure capturing the opportunity.

8. Start validating the opportunities in the sixth week. Validation involves working with Goldy and Mino 1 finance and operations employees to determine if they agree the opportunities are viable, they can be implemented, and the assumptions and the benefits are reasonable.

Alana attaches the following two slides and note before sending off another email to the team:

"Max, Luther, and I conducted several focus interviews over the last 24 hours. I have included the summaries in this email. We have also included a list of opportunities that may be worth investigating. Please review these and send us any questions you have. The transcribed interviews will be archived later today.

I am also attaching the opportunity chart templates. For those who have already sent me their draft templates, thank you. For the rest, please use these templates or feel free to come see me if you need any further information."

EXHIBIT 28: Opportunity Chart Template

FIRMSCONSULTING.COM & STRATEGYTRAINING.COM

The first part of an opportunity chart provides a description of the opportunity and KPIs, aka top-down

	Opportunity:		Created by:	
1.	What is not working / could be improved?	Describe the opportunity?	What must we change?	
2.	How do we know it is not working?	How is the process *currently* measured?	How good/bad is it today?	
		Measure 1 /KPI	Quantify	
		Measure 2 /KPI	Quantify	
3.	If I change x, y and z the opportunity can be captured by the client			
4.	How good could/should the process be? (Lead: How will we know we eventually hit our target? Lag: How do we know it worked?)	How *could/should* "we measure success for this opportunity? Lead/Lag KPI Measure 1 Lead/Lag KPI Measure 2 Lead/Lag KPI Measure 1	Targets: High Confidence → Stretch Quantify Quantify Quantify	
5.	Opportunity Sheet Developed With:			
	Name:	Dept./Title:	Completed:	
	Name:	Dept./Title:	Completed:	

EXHIBIT 29: Benefits Calculation Template

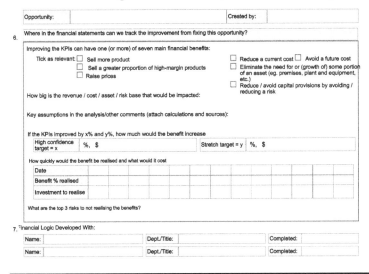

Next week, the engagement team arrives on-site at Mino 1. The number one objective of the business case team will be to understand the financial accounting system and ensure the issues can be simulated in their model. Then they will need to complete the financial baseline analyses.

WEEK 3

day 1

PREPARING
THE DRAFT
STORYBOARD

MONDAY MORNING is a difficult time for the engagement team. Mino 1 is not ready for the team. The morning is spent scrambling to find proper office space to use. Having private office space is crucial. It must be secure so that the team can discuss confidential aspects of the engagement and, if needed, review previous consulting material without divulging the details to Goldy employees. Sharing an open space with Goldy employees compromises confidential information.

Mino 1 can only find proper facilities out in the operations centre, which is about 1 kilometre from the executive offices. Although it is not close to Gavrilo and his management committee, it does mean the team will have more space and can work more closely with the operations team. Given that most of the data will reside with the operations team, Luther feels this may not be such a bad arrangement for the engagement.

The business case team takes over one corner of the large office. They immediately print out large poster-size copies of their planning documents and put them up on the wall. This gives everyone a clear view of what needs to be done and progress made to date. Providing this visual transparency is critical and avoids any bottlenecks in sharing information. Even when the business case team is away, their colleagues can walk up to the charts to see their progress or the latest analyses. Comments can be left with post-it notes.

Despite the rapid progress of the team, Max has been criticised for not yet producing his storyboard. Typically, the storyboard should have been done at the end of the planning week and no later than the start of the second week. Max feels Alana has settled into the engagement well enough for him to teach her the concept. He sits down with Alana and explains the concept of a storyboard.

STORYBOARDING

Storyboarding is one of the most powerful tools used by management consultants, and the ability to produce and use a storyboard is one of the most critical skills needed. Max needs to take his time to ensure that Alana understands the process. In his experience, he finds that many business analysts learn how to produce an average storyboard without really understanding why it needs to be done and how it can be used. He wants to make sure Alana does not become one of them.

To explain the concept, Max uses an example from the animation industry. He asks Alana to name the most original, most creative, and entertaining animated movie she has seen. Alana picks *Finding Nemo*. Max asks her the following questions to illustrate the concept of storyboarding and its importance:

1. "Given that the movie had little or no precedence, how did the producers get their own teams to understand the concept?

2. Movie executives needed to sign off on the movie before it was made. How did they do this without seeing the movie? How did they understand its uniqueness without first incurring the costs of producing the final movie?

3. *Animated movies sometimes employ up to a thousand people spread across different countries. How do they all stay focused on the development of the movie and on developing plot?"*

Max explains that storyboarding helps with each of these problems.

1. Before producing detailed animations and more, the team must first agree on the story. Animation teams gather together in a room and take blank pieces of A4 paper, write out a short 10-word description of a scene on the top of the page, and produce a very rough 15-second pencil sketch to outline the animation that could go into this part of the movie. In all, they may produce about 30 to 120 such A4 pages, stick them on a wall in sequence, and everyone can follow the story. This allows the animation team to debate the story and messaging without expensive animation work, which would definitely change as the process continues. Changes can be made in the meeting since the sketches are very basic. It is a little bit like a simple comic book.

2. Once everyone agrees with the storyboard, the movie executives will receive a slightly "prettier" version of it. At this stage, no animation has been done. It is still a set of A4 pages with the story on top and an image below. The producers and directors will usually act out part of the storyboard to help the executives visualise the movie. The "acting" allows the movie executive to visualise the story.

3. Thousands of people can visualise the same movie since everyone is looking at and developing the same storyboard. There is only one master storyboard. If the director makes a change, he simply puts up the new A4 page and highlights it with a coloured post-it so that everyone can see a change has occurred.

Max extends this analogy to a management consulting storyboard. The business case team needs to prepare a story of their message so that everyone in the team can understand their thinking and provide feedback. Max explains the concept using four slides:

EXHIBIT 30: Overall Presentation

FIRMSCONSULTING.COM & STRATEGYTRAINING.COM

Your title page needs a few basic elements

- Name of target audience

- An active title that generates interest:
  - Begin with a verb form (e.g., Developing, Evaluating, Understanding, Assessing)

- Subtitle:
  - An option that allows you to elaborate on the title

- Author and/or Office

- Date delivered

EXHIBIT 31: Headlines

FIRMSCONSULTING.COM & STRATEGYTRAINING.COM

Headline (usually a sentence)

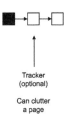

Tracker (optional)

Can clutter a page

Head (optional)

- Bullet:
  - Sub-bullet (as needed):
    - Sub-sub-bullet (as needed)

"Kicker" (optional)

EXHIBIT 32: Where Are We in the Story?

FIRMSCONSULTING.COM & STRATEGYTRAINING.COM

What this page is about

A key category or idea

- A main point:
  - A sub-point
  - A second

- A second main point:
  - A sub-point
  - A second

Implications: "So what?"

EXHIBIT 33: Writing Headlines

FIRMSCONSULTING.COM & STRATEGYTRAINING.COM

Good headlines focus attention on the page's main idea

- Usually a brief sentence:
    - One line is best
    - Two lines maximum
- Say something meaningful that directs attention to the page's important point, e.g.:
    - "ROCE varies greatly across businesses"
- Avoid empty statements, e.g.,
    - "The next step of the analysis is as follows"
- Use headlines as the "storyboard" of your document
    - Reading only the headlines should tell a coherent story

---

Once Alana is comfortable with the concept of slide decks and storyboarding, they discuss the principles of putting together their storyboard. The principles will guide them as they develop the storyboard today and make changes throughout the rest of the engagement.

The preparation and presentation of the storyboard must follow several principles:

1. The storyboard must go up on their working space walls.

2. Initially, the storyboards will just be pencil sketches on A4 sheets of paper, but over time, each page will gradually be replaced with a draft slide prepared with PowerPoint. Over time, this draft slide will be updated.

3. The business case team must write out their proposed story so that everyone on the team can understand their progress and thinking. If their thinking changes, this must be immediately reflected in the storyboard by taking down a page and replacing it with a new page.
4. There should be a story! The story should flow horizontally across headlines *and* vertically down an individual slide from the headline to the content and finally the kicker.
5. Colour-coded post-it notes must be placed on the lower left corner of each A4 sheet so that they do not obscure the information and also provide a key for the reader.
   a. Red note: The slide is seriously flawed and needs to be redone.
   b. Orange note: Data needs verification.
   c. Yellow note: Findings do not reconcile with findings by other members of the engagement team.
   d. Pink note: Data verified internally and with the client.
   e. Green note: Slide is completed.
6. Anyone can leave comments using post-it notes.
7. The storyboard should *never ever* be a diary of the work done or analyses completed. Not everything done needs to appear in the storyboard. Only the most important insights should appear, and the best storyboards are simple and logical to follow. They are also short.

   If an analysis was important in disproving a key option and required weeks of work, it should only be included if it contributes to the final story. If it does not contribute to the final story, it should be excluded from the storyboard and rather included in the appendices. Like all things, however, discretion must be applied here as well. If the disproved idea was important to the CEO and his team, it would make sense to explain why it has been removed from the analyses. The importance of the concept being analysed should determine how it is presented.

8. The story must stand by itself. By reading the story, the rest of the team must be able to understand the details. No further explanation should be needed. If a storyboard needs a verbal explanation for the reader to understand the meaning, it is incorrectly designed.

9. The storyboard must be created before the data is ready:

    The hypotheses and value trees outline the data *needed* to prove or disprove them. Accordingly, the storyboard should be constructed before the data is ready, by assuming the results of testing the hypotheses, and not conveniently developed based on the data the consultant can find. Poorly constructed storyboards are built after the data is collected. Consultants simply find interesting information and thereafter develop a presentation, which means that consultants are building their story based on the data they *have* and not on the data they *need*. The storyboard should not be designed around interesting data. It must always be designed around telling a story based on the required analyses to test hypotheses in the engagement.

10. Only the headlines of the panels comprise the storyboard. No data and graphs should be added at this point, but the consultant could think about the data that will be used.

11. Kickers ("so what" statements) at the end of the slide may also be added.

WEEK 3 - DAY 1: PREPARING THE DRAFT STORYBOARD

12. The business case team will use a deficit model to design the business case. This type of model describes the approach the team will use to deliver their findings. It is one whereby the first feedback session to the client shows that the situation is very bad and likely to get worse before things improve. The objective of this style of business case development is to create a "burning platform" for change. The client must see how bad things are before they will change. Change must start immediately or the business situation could get much worse or even lead to a closure of the business. Each subsequent presentation takes the client on a journey out of the hole (deficit) and shows them how to improve performance.

EXHIBIT 34: Deficit Communication Approach

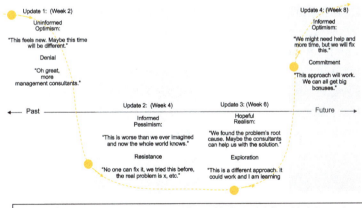

13. The alternative is to use an aspirational model where the business case team shows the client how good things *could be*. The immediate poor performance is indicated but is not the central point or reason for change. The potential of the business and subsequent value creation in fulfilling this potential is the reason for change. Aspirational models are used for clients who understand the reason for change and are trying to move forward with their businesses. CEOs and executive committee members who see themselves as visionaries tend to like this model. Given the culture of Goldy, Max and Alana believe that the deficit model is likely to result in the best chance of a change to the business. Besides the CEO who understands the performance problems, the rest of the business needs to see just how bad things are before they will embrace the case for change.

14. Deciding between the deficit and aspirational models is a critical step. It will have a significant impact on the engagement and must be agreed to with Luther before the team can proceed. If one work stream uses the deficit model, everyone needs to use the deficit model. Luckily for Max, this does not mean much rework for the other teams. The business case team will produce most of the material for the first steering committee[11] session, so any change they make will not immediately affect the other teams. Nonetheless, this should have been a decision made much earlier in the engagement.

---

[11] A steering committee is a temporary committee assembled to provide governance for the engagement. It primarily consists of the client and the consulting firm, usually just the engagement partner and director. The engagement reports into the steering committee, and decisions about the engagement are made by the steering committee.

WEEK 3 - DAY 1: PREPARING THE DRAFT STORYBOARD

EXHIBIT 35: Aspirational Communication Approach

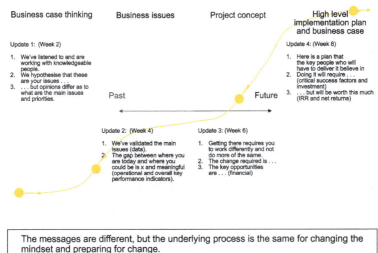

BUSINESS CASE STORYBOARD

Max picks up a blank A4 sheet of paper and writes down the gist of the storyboard–the most important findings the business case team expects to generate over the next eight weeks. He is essentially writing down the likely findings from testing each hypothesis. Writing the gist first forces them to think through their overall message without getting lost in the detail. The gist can be thought of as the *most* important slides to be presented. Only about five to 10 slides make up the gist, and the entire story should be captured in them:

1. Mino 1 is destroying value by earning less than its cost of capital and is a bottom-to-mid-tier performer when benchmarked.

2. Poor cost tracking and allocation have made it difficult for Mino 1 to calculate its true value creation position.

3. If Mino 1 continues on its present course, it could lose $1.4bn over the next three years.

4. Mino 1 can reverse this problem by engaging in a series of capital and operational improvement programmes costing $780 million but generating 4 percent more than the cost of capital.

5. The improvement opportunities will take nine months to implement and require substantial changes to the operating and management model.

6. Mino 1 must sell and outsource most of its services operations.

The numbers above are purely best guesses at this stage.

During the first steering committee meeting with the client, points 1,2, and 3 of the gist will be presented and comprise the bulk of the presentation, usually with focus interview data. The client will not see the rest of the presentation until much later. For a period of time, the client will only see the most negative news. Then the engagement team will work with the client to find opportunities for improvement, and over time, the client moves through the deficit model explained earlier.

As the analyses are completed and the model is built, the headlines above will be tested, verified, and altered if necessary. For now, they provide direction for the rest of the team.

Max takes the gist and expands it into a full story. The gist above allows them to test the overall message, and they can add layers if they feel comfortable. Max explains that producing a good storyboard will only happen if they have done the initial research and value tree analyses well. These activities enable the team to gain a very good understanding of the business. Although data or results may change, it is unlikely that the overall storyboard will change. It is their responsibility to find the data to support the headlines. If the data presents a different message, the headline and story may change. They continue developing the complete storyboard based on what they think the analyses will show them:

1. Mino 1 is destroying value by earning less than its cost of capital and is a mid-tier performer when benchmarked.
    a. Over the last six years, Mino 1's ROCE has steadily decreased, and it has destroyed value in the last three years.
    b. During this time, production and productivity have decreased.
    c. Costs have increased 58 percent as the mines have become deeper, salaries have increased, and support costs have increased.
    d. Costs are poorly tracked and allocated, making it difficult to measure real profit.
    e. Mino 1 is now a bottom-to-mid-tier mine when benchmarked against international gold mines.
    f. The new mine management model is unpopular and difficult to measure.
    g. The services function is a significant drain on Mino 1's cash flow.
    h. Services accounts for 32 percent of operating costs and 7 percent of capital expenditure, while peer gold mines achieve lower expenditures.
    i. At least 67 percent of the services portfolio is no longer critical to be done in-house and could be outsourced.

2. Poor cost control and management are reducing the amount of capital Mino 1 can invest in its core business.
    a. Mino 1 only spends 48 percent of Opex and 67 percent of Capex on its core business.
    b. Key debottlenecking initiatives are starved for capital and de-prioritised.
    c. It is not clear how capital allocation is made to initiatives.
    d. This has led to a direct loss in revenue.
    e. Costs have increased 58 percent, driven primarily by labour costs. (Duplicated above and should be removed.)
    f. Mino 1 has a higher cost structure on every benchmarked category.
    g. It is very difficult to allocate and account for at least 12 percent of the rise in overall costs and 18 percent of yearly Opex.
    h. A contract for $20 million/annum has never been audited, and no performance benchmarks are in place.
    i. This situation appears to be the norm for six contracts valued at $183.5 million/annum.
    j. We have identified 18 opportunities to reduce costs by 43 percent over the next four years.
3. Mino 1 can reverse this problem by engaging in a series of capital and operational improvement programmes.
    a. Mino 1 is a bottom-to-mid-tier performer against all production benchmarks.
    b. Simply moving Mino 1 to the middle of the tier 1 pack would allow it to create value.
    c. We have identified five key opportunities to increase production value:

    i. Stop development on the Mino 12a shaft and allocate resources to the Mino 71a production line.
    ii. Change the tramline to allow offloading in all directions.
    iii. Extend the conveyor belts to the new lines.
    iv. Install a new transport line to the mine face.
    v. Debottleneck the vamping (area where washed ore is held) holding area.
   d. Each of these projects generates a higher return on capital than existing operational improvement opportunities.
4. The improvement opportunities will take nine months to implement and require substantial changes to the operating and management model.
   a. The improvement opportunities will take nine months to implement at a cost of $280 million.
   b. The improvement opportunities will fail with the existing mine management model, which does not measure the correct key performance indicators (KPIs).
   c. More training must be undertaken for workers to understand KPIs.
   d. Remuneration must move to a performance-based system to ensure labour costs rise in concert with production value.
   e. For the new KPIs to work, measurement must be centralised from the head office.
5. Mino 1 must sell and outsource most of its services operations.
   a. Noncore services generate low returns on capital and starve operating initiatives of capital.
   b. Freeing this capital for investment in the core business could lead to a payback within three years.

    c. This would also mean that Mino 1 could fund its improvement programme from its own operations.

    d. Outsourced service functions will also lead to an improvement in quality and accountability.

Max knows this is very far from passing as the final storyboard for several reasons: the story is not very clear, parts of the analyses are missing in the headlines, the numbers are simply placeholders, there is duplication, and the conclusion is missing.

The current storyboard is sufficient enough, however, to allow the engagement team to see their thinking and point out gaps or misunderstandings. It does not have to be perfect. After the model is built, the baseline analyses completed, and opportunities charts received from the engagement team, a much better version of the storyboard will be circulated. Yet, the storyboard should be continuously improved as Max's thinking changes.

While Alana converts the storyboard to slides, Max continues setting up meetings for the next two days to help understand the business, collect the necessary data, and model the operations to produce the baseline analyses.

WEEK 3

day 2

BUILDING THE MODEL

*A*S MAX TYPES UP notes from data collection meetings, he thinks about the pressure on the business case team to produce a solid business case. In fact, it is pretty much all he can think about. This is a key client for the firm. The CEO of Goldy needs support for his bold reforms, and it is unlikely that Mino 1 or any of the regions will accept the need for change without a strong business case. Besides these expectations, the business case team needs to manage expectations within their own team as well as with Sergio and his financial analysts:

1. Sergio thinks the financial model is a key deliverable and is trying to extend the model beyond its purpose. He wants to use the model for capital budgeting and forecasting. This is beyond the scope of the engagement and purpose of the model.

2. The engagement team is deep into analyses and also trying to ensure that all the opportunities they are developing can be measured in the model. Adding the flexibility and capability to simulate and measure every type of opportunity and scenario simply leads to too much modelling complexity. The business case team will focus on trying to create the most accurate analyses for the largest opportunities linked to the core mining business. They will follow the 80/20 principle. They

will only analyse the 20 percent of opportunities that generate 80 percent of the value created and do so in a manner that generates an acceptable answer versus the most accurate answer.

Max must diplomatically and politely remind everyone about the purpose of the model. While it must be robust, it cannot do everything. It must be designed to answer the key questions for the business case team:

1. What is the existing financial performance of Mino 1, and how does this compare with that of its peers?

2. What is the effect of the various opportunities identified, and are they viable?

3. What options exist for Mino 1, and what effect will these have over a five-year time horizon?

Alana asked for responsibility in developing the model and has built an early version. At the moment, it is populated with "holding" data, which is the business case team's best estimate of the actual data. Holding data is used to test the model and ensure that all the links work and the relationships modelled are done correctly.

Now the team is in the process of populating the model with the actual Mino 1 financials and operating data to create a baseline of Mino 1's performance. The baseline is important. Sometimes it is called a financial analysis or financial decomposition. Any improvements from the opportunities generated by the engagement team will be measured against this baseline. The baseline analyses also indicate areas in the business worth examining further. Used effectively, it is like a compass for the team. This baseline must be accurate and approved by Flavio.

BUILDING THE MODEL

In building the financial model, a number of key design principles are used:

1. Only the volume of ore produced will be modelled.

2. The model will be composed of top-down (benchmarks) and bottom-up calculations (opportunity charts and subsequent business cases).

3. Labour full-time equivalents (FTEs) will be measured across the value chain and their numbers linked to the volume of ore produced. In other words, labour will mostly be a variable cost and will change as production changes.

4. Only service functions directly affecting the core mining business will be included in the model. They will also include variable costs. For others, their effect will be calculated separately using ratios. For example, if timber usually is 2 percent of OPEX, once the total OPEX is calculated, it will be increased by 2 percent to include timber.

5. Over time, the four options modelled have become more specific and expanded to become five options:

    a. Continuing as is with no changes to the business.

    b. Implementing all operations improvement recommendations excluding the services recommendations.

    c. Implementing all operations improvement recommendations and some of the services recommendations.

    d. Implementing all recommendations.

e. Divesting mining operations that do not earn the required rate of return.[12]

6. The refinery business will be excluded from the modelling, while the costs to run the refinery will be included as a charge to generate the ROCE for the business.

Realizing they will need to explain the process to the client, they prepare six slides to explain their modelling process.

EXHIBIT 36: Business Case Objectives

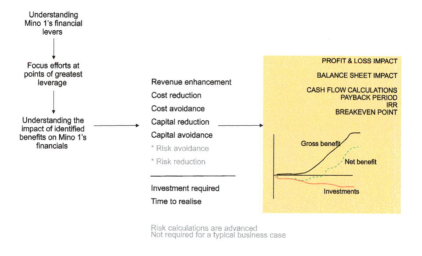

---

[12] The fifth option is not a separate option. It is not mutually exclusive: it could be done as a subset of the other options. It is, however, included as a separate option given the significant impact it would have on the business.

Slide 1, Exhibit 36: The business case team is not trying to re-create the client's budgeting model, forecasting model, or other financial analysis tools. The business case team is trying to determine the drivers of ROCE and the effect of opportunities to improve ROCE. There are five categories of opportunities. Any opportunity generated by the team will fall into one of these five categories.

EXHIBIT 37: Types of Analyses

FIRMSCONSULTING.COM & STRATEGYTRAINING.COM

Four different types of analyses will be conducted over the eight-week engagement

Type	Objective	Analysis
Financial Analysis	What is going on in this company? Understand the business Create urgency Quantify the competition gap Focus on the stream diagnosis	Financial reporting Ratio analysis Breakdown of ROCE Stakeholder value calculation Simple sensitivity analysis
Financial/Economic Modelling	What could potentially happen to this company? Understand future scenarios in the business Set the aspiration Quantify the risks Focus on the strategic analysis	Linked sensitivity analysis Valuation modelling Scenario modelling Optimization analysis
Top-Down Business Case	What are the challenges and associated costs? Establish the link between the financial analysis and bottom-up business case Fine-tune the drivers of the business Understand the economics of the client Quantify the preliminary amount of accessible benefit	Benchmarking exercise Gap analyses P&L and balance sheet impact estimation Cash flow NPV modelling Return on investment calculation
Bottom-Up Benefits Case	What level of benefits do we commit to achieve? Develop fields of opportunities Identify the origins of low performance Quantify and validate the identified opportunities	Opportunity charts Opportunity selection and prioritisation

Slide 2, Exhibit 37: The team decides to explain commonly used and confused terms, such as financial analyses, business modelling, top-down business cases, and bottom-up business cases. It is important the client understands what will be done in each part and how it all links together.

Financial analyses and top-down business cases are linked. They are done in the first two to three weeks of the engagement. They are done to determine the current and historical performance of the business. They generate the baseline against which all improvement opportunities will be measured. The business case team determines the current financial state of Mino 1 by breaking down the existing financial statements during the financial analyses. Benchmarks (top-down analyses) against peers are done using the financial analyses results to determine the magnitude of possible improvement opportunities. It is a gap analysis. For example, if Mino 1 is found to have variable costs 25 percent higher than the highest cost producer, then Mino 1 needs to close that gap. Benchmark-driven gap analyses indicate *potential* opportunity areas. The team will then need to drill down to understand each actual opportunity. Case studies are typically also used in the top-down phase to provide examples of other companies who have done the same things.

Business modelling and bottom-up business cases are linked. They are done after the analyses above allow the business case team to understand the financial situation of the client and magnitude of potential improvements. In other words, they are used to drill down into the gaps and results of the financial analyses. An economic model is developed to simulate the business and assess the effect of different initiatives, scenarios, or opportunities on the business.

A well-designed engagement should always begin with focus interviews, financial analyses, case studies, and some basic benchmarking to identify problems. This should be followed by the business modelling to estimate the impact of changes to fix the problems. An engagement bypassing the four top-down steps should raise some alarms because it is not validating hypotheses early enough.

EXHIBIT 38: Bottom-Up Versus Top-Down Analyses

FIRMSCONSULTING.COM & STRATEGYTRAINING.COM

The four analyses will be brought together to produce the final benefits case

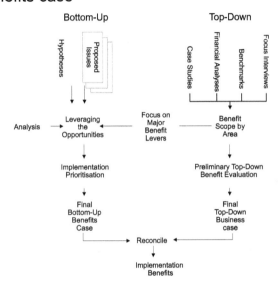

Slide 3, Exhibit 38: Describes how the different pieces of analyses come together to produce the final business case. Attention is paid to ensuring the client team can see where the benchmarking and opportunity assessment is done and how it is assembled to produce the final recommendation. The team believes this will be an important slide in explaining the process to the client.

The top-down work is done first and sets the general direction and outlines the scope of the problem, and if it is worth solving. The bottom-up work then determines if this is true.

Data for the bottom-up part of the analyses will be collected by the rest of the engagement team and fed to Alana through the opportunity charts. She will include each significant opportunity in the model to measure the effect against the baseline and test the change in the benchmarked gaps.

Bringing the bottom-up and top-down analyses together is difficult. Top-down analyses are based on benchmarked data, financial analyses and case studies developed at a higher level with little detailed analyses. These indicate "what is possible" but do not explain how it can be achieved. The bottom-up analysis focuses almost entirely on "how it can be achieved." Yet, it is not exhaustive in nature. Many of the bottom-up analyses will need to be verified during the implementation. At the end of the engagement, both have to reconcile. For example, the top-down analyses may indicate a 4 percent productivity gap, and the bottom-up opportunities must explain how they will close this gap. This is generally difficult to do, and it is the responsibility of the business case team to reconcile the differences and ensure that opportunities are valid. The hard part is rejecting an opportunity from a colleague. That makes the role of the business case team different from any other stream since judgement, in a manner of speaking, is passed on a peers' work. That is not easy to do and a business case consultant lacking in confidence may struggle in this role.

EXHIBIT 39: Business Case Storyboard

FIRMSCONSULTING.COM & STRATEGYTRAINING.COM

Certain parts will be more difficult than others, and we have designed our approach to manage this

This is your financial situation . . .	We think a value gap exists of this size . . .	Numerous financial opportunities exist . . .	When you combine these, the validated benefit is . . .	After subtracting costs, the benefit remains healthy
Weeks 1–0	Weeks 1–2	Weeks 3–5	Weeks 5–7	Weeks 7–8
Difficult	Important	Appears Easy	Potential Problems	Home Stretch
Strategic scoping Financial analysis	Financial analysis (client info) Top-down business case (Business modelling)	Bottom-up benefits case (Business modelling)	Bottom-up benefits case (Individual opportunities)	Finalise by drawing together all elements

Slide 4, Exhibit 39: Using the storyboard, engagement timetable, and their own experience, the team can generate a general understanding of the challenges they will face in analysing the numbers. There can be no surprises. The client must know well in advance that some parts of the engagement will be more difficult than others, that this is normal, and it must be expected. This is known as pre-presenting: telling the audience the message well in advance so the consultants have time to gauge the client's reaction, ensure the client understands the message, and do any further work to ensure the recommendations are accepted. Surprising a client is *never ever* an option. It is a rule of the firm.

EXHIBIT 40: Model Structure

FIRMSCONSULTING.COM & STRATEGYTRAINING.COM

To ensure ease of use and to save time, we will use a consistent Excel methodology

Data is only inserted in the model once.
Only one analyses sheet is necessary.
Excel is big enough (255+ sheets).
No need to link workbooks.

Slide 5, Exhibit 40: It is difficult to understand financial modelling. To make the process easier and ensure there is no misunderstanding, the team uses a standard and simple approach to build economic models. This approach ensures that it is much easier for the results to be understood and used. A consistent approach means there is no misunderstanding of the model or time wasted to understand a new financial modelling approach.

EXHIBIT 41: Worksheet Structure

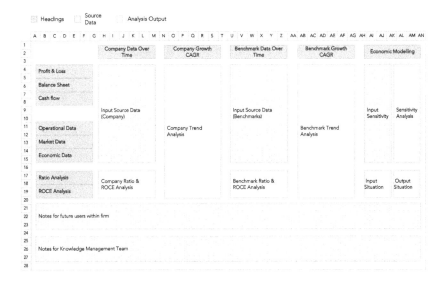

Slide 6, Exhibit 41: The same discipline and design ease goes into constructing every worksheet. They are all designed to be easily understood, printed, used, and validated. Complex economic models will almost certainly result in the key information being misunderstood, and precious time can be wasted in deciphering complex models. This is avoided by using a standardised approach.

Comfortable with their logic and robustness of the model, Alana continues populating their model with the baseline analyses. Max hopes to provide the engagement team with the early version of the numbers at the next team meeting on Friday.

WEEK 3

day 5

OUTPUT FROM THE FINANCIAL ANALYSES

THIS WEEK'S TEAM MEETING will follow a different format. The meetings typically last about 30 minutes, with each team providing a brief status update read off an update chart. Update charts are presented at every weekly meeting and are the primary formal means to communicate with the team. Today's meeting will last 60 minutes, as the business case team will present their update chart followed by a 30-minute update on their findings thus far.

The update chart is designed to present a compact view of progress and force decisions. Details are only provided at the level where decisions can be made between team leaders. Done well, like the example below, and presented well, the update chart helps demonstrate to the engagement team and the client that a team is in control of their deliverables and able to handle the workload. It instils confidence. It has both tangible and intangible purposes.

It is critical to never mislead or misrepresent progress, problems, issues, or information on the update chart. This is an opportunity to have an honest discussion about the progress and ask for help if it is needed. As an engagement-tracking tool, update charts can be called up later if the client challenges the engagement outcome. In the worst case, they may be used in a court of law. Material misrepresentation may not be on a consultant's mind at the time, but it must be remembered that anything a consultant writes to a client is effectively communication between the client and consulting firm, and all these items are on the record. Hence, the engagement manager always checks them internally before they are shared with clients.

To give Alana more exposure, Max asks her to prepare and present the update chart:

EXHIBIT 42: Update Chart

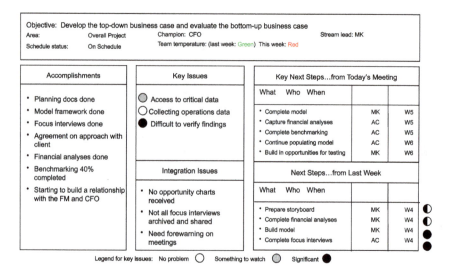

WEEK 3 - DAY 5: OUTPUT FROM THE FINANCIAL ANALYSES

Alana does an excellent job of presenting the update chart in an actionable format. She only presents items that need explanation, are crucial to the progress of the overall engagement team, or where the business case team needs help. This ensures that any discussion leads to progress rather than having detailed discussions that do not contribute to the engagement:

1. She indicates that the team stress levels (temperature) have risen from green to red. Green means the team is calm, orange indicates some stress, and red means very stressed. The team has been working about 18 hours a day to complete the financial analyses. Collecting data and verifying the figures has been difficult. She expects the time requirements to drop as the financial analyses and modelling are completed.

2. The team has completed almost all their "next steps" from last week's team meeting.

3. They feel confident that all the next steps from today's feedback session will be completed on time.

4. Alana uses the meeting to outline some delays and problems the business case team has been experiencing integrating with the rest of the engagement team:

    a. They have not yet received a single completed opportunity chart.

    b. Given the number of focus interviews to be conducted, no one person can attend all the meetings. It is critical that all focus interviews are documented and stored in the engagement archives. Several important focus interviews with the mine management, financial analysts, and ore reserve managers have not been documented, and the data from these interviews is not contributing to the engagement. She implores all team members to try to finish their write-ups as soon as possible.

    c. She recommends that the meeting planning sheet be updated as soon as possible. She explains that the business case team sometimes finds out about meetings after they have happened. There are two problems with this arrangement. First, Max tries booking meetings with clients who are already meeting other members of the engagement team. This can appear uncoordinated and unprofessional to the client. Second, knowing who will attend which meetings can help with preparing team members for the meeting.

Alana summarizes her presentation by stating that the business case team is running on schedule and will present the results of their financial analyses in a few minutes. She outlines that the next critical step is for her colleagues to forward their completed or draft opportunity charts.

A few questions are raised about the modelling approach and data collection. Overall, Alana handles all the questions well and hands over to Max, who will present the findings from the financial analyses and early findings from the benchmarking.

FINANCIAL ANALYSES

The findings from the financial analyses, any case studies done, and partial benchmarking are critical. They will set the direction for the engagement team, disprove some initial hypotheses, and could have a dramatic effect on the final message to the client. Max knows that he must take his time and explain the findings and their implications carefully. He will likely receive questions to test the robustness of the analyses. He must be prepared for such questions. This is the management consulting way. It is better to test findings in a safe setting than in front of the client.

WEEK 3 - DAY 5: OUTPUT FROM THE FINANCIAL ANALYSES

Max takes over the presentation. He explains that although he was given 30 minutes to present his findings, he actually has more information that will affect the engagement. He asks the team if he can extend his session by 15 minutes to 45 minutes. He also thanks the rest of the engagement team for their help in sourcing the data and often helping them conduct the analyses. Max points out that while the business case team presents the financial analyses, it is a result of the engagement team's collective efforts.

Max begins by reminding the engagement team that the business case is split into four phases:

1. Completing the financial analyses to determine the baseline performance of Mino 1
2. Completing the benchmarks
3. Building the financial model to run simulations, test scenarios, and options
4. Validating the bottom-up benefits cases and testing the options

The financial model has been developed but is not fully populated. As per Luther's and Max's earlier compromise, the focus has been on only populating the model to complete the financial analyses of the existing Mino 1 business. Following the correct management consulting approach, Max follows standard protocol in presenting slides:

1. Each slide consists of:
   a. A headline
   b. One piece of data analysis to support the headline
   c. References, sources, and calculation approach fully described at the bottom of the slide

d. As little inappropriate text as possible since data is more important

   e. Simple, clean slides with a headline, data graphic, and sources

2. A well-constructed storyboard so that the engagement team may follow the findings

3. A summary of the findings is presented first. This way, the team knows what to expect and can see how each slide fits into the overall message. Simply diving into the slides without setting the context will not help the audience understand how the information will be used.

Max presents the slides:

Overall Finding

1. Mino 1 is destroying value, as the ROCE is 4.57 percent versus a cost of capital of 7.7 percent.

2. Mino 1 has seen a 1.8 percent CAGR reduction in ROCE over the last six years.

3. When benchmarked against mining peers, Mino 1's ROCE is in the lower quartile.

Revenue

1. Operating revenue has increased by 3.3 percent CAGR driven by a rise in gold price, while production volume has dropped by 2.1 percent CAGR over the last six years.

2. Both production and productivity declines have been masked by rising gold prices.

3. Productivity improvement opportunities, which could raise operating revenue by 8 percent and generate returns of 10.2 percent, have not qualified for funding.
4. Eleven key debottlenecking initiatives are starved for capital and de-prioritised.
5. The capital allocation decisions appear to be made incorrectly and fund low-return initiatives.
6. Even if the initiatives were approved, the current mine KPI system makes it impossible to transfer targets to the workers at the mine face.
7. 82 percent of employees did not like the existing mine management model.

Costs

1. Costs are poorly tracked, and the SAP database is unable to reconcile costs.
2. A manual reconciliation of invoices, expenses, and costs disproves that deeper mining is leading to higher costs.
3. Costs have increased 34 percent as salaries and support costs have increased.
4. Although labour has resulted in a 34 percent increase in costs, salaries are below the benchmarked group.
5. Mino 1 has a higher cost structure on every benchmarked category except labour.
6. The services function is a significant drain on Mino 1's cash flow.
7. Services accounts for 18 percent of operating costs and 12 percent of capital expenditure, while peer gold mines maintain lower expenditures.

8. Despite these large costs, it is unclear how important the service function is to Mino 1.

9. Benchmarked to peers, Mino 1 is spending approximately 20 percent less of its Opex and 17 percent less of its Capex on core mining activity.

10. This has led to a direct loss in revenue.

11. It is very difficult to allocate and account for at least 12 percent of the rise in costs and 18 percent of yearly Opex.

12. A contract for $20 million/annum has never been audited, and there are no performance benchmarks in place.

13. This situation appears to be the norm for six contracts valued at $183.5 million per annum.

The presentation expectedly raises numerous questions. Luther kicks off the question and answer (Q&A) session by requesting more detail on how some of the conclusions were developed, especially those where data would be more difficult to find. He asks about three conclusions in particular:

Q - "Key debottlenecking initiatives are starved for capital and de-prioritised."

A - Max:

"During our focus interviews, we asked for a complete list of all initiatives/programmes/pilots/projects that went through the approval stages for capital budgeting.

A list of 734 such projects was compiled, with all projects undertaken over the past six years. We then further filtered the list into those directly related to the core mining operations versus support services or refinery improvements. This generated a list of 442 projects.

From this list, we then worked with the financial manager and analyst to further filter them into three groups:

A—Large impact on production

B—Large impact on cost reduction

C—Large impact on safety

We only examined groups A and B, which consisted of 212 projects. Using the assumptions presented in the original requisition for capital and making adjustments for what we know today about the mine, we recalculated the return-on-capital from these initiatives.

We then compared the ratings of the 212 projects against those approved. There is no correlation between those approved and superior returns or increases in production. Many key initiatives that should have been approved never were. Many that were approved should not have been. We think it is a systems problem in the way projects are approved. The incorrect measures are used.

Even if the initiatives were approved, the current mine key performance indicator (KPI) system makes it impossible to transfer targets to the workers at the mine face."

Q - "82% of employees did not like the existing mine management model."

A - Max:

"During the focus interviews, we included a set of questions to determine the effectiveness of the new management model, how many were using it in the mines, and whether or not it encouraged adherence to KPIs that improved ROCE.

Across all levels of the organisation but especially at the lower levels, employees did not approve of the new mine management model. When we enquired about the reasons for their dislike, they mentioned the following reasons in order of importance:

1. Previously, the employees were rewarded for increases in production. With the new model, they are rewarded based on the performance of the entire company. It is not clear to them how to improve their salaries, so they see little reason to work harder.

2. The previous CEO constantly spoke about increasing value and decreasing costs. How could they do that? To employees, they believe they are already paid little and could not even begin to think about what effect they could have on value.

The interviews showed a clear dislike for the management model. More time may be needed to understand the reasons, but the outcome is clear—employees overwhelmingly do not like the current management model."

Q - "Costs are poorly tracked, and the SAP database is unable to reconcile costs."

A - Max:

"How we found this is very interesting. We went down to the stores (equipment storerooms) to see how costs are captured. We had the hypothesis that because the requisition system was not fully automated, there must be huge delays in getting material from the stores above ground to the workers on the mine face. These delays would probably affect costs a little but mostly impact lost revenue.

We paired up with the operations improvement team that actually conducted the analyses. So thanks, guys, for letting us tag along. We spent a day-in-the-life (DILO)[13] of a store's clerk. We agreed on everything with their supervisor and confirmed the employees were not

---

[13] A DILO study entails following an employee for a complete day and tracking the time spent on each activity. Thereafter, poor use of time, inefficient processes, or broken processes can be deduced from analysing the data.

being reviewed in a way that would affect their employment, salaries, or performance bonuses. The results of the analyses would not be revealed to their supervisors. We followed two different clerks in different parts of the mine to ensure the findings were not skewed by an individual's behaviour.

Our initial hypothesis was totally disproved. There are storage rooms above and below ground. When a clerk above ground receives an order for explosives or equipment, he is not supplying the miner underground; he is simply replenishing the underground storage room that has already supplied the miner. The miner is not experiencing any delays. When we initially saw the orders come through during our site visit in Week 2, we did not realise the delays were about replenishing the stores. We thought they were about getting supplies to the mining face.

Although that hypothesis, which was a central improvement area in our initial thinking, was disproved, we noticed something else. Clerks did not like the graphical user interface to capture orders and invoices. They were drawing up invoices on an Excel template, and they were being approved. Consumption of stock was also not captured on SAP. They were captured on Excel templates.

We collected the Excel templates for just the two sites over the last three weeks and compared the data in the templates with the SAP database. We found that 8 percent of the costs and inventory for these two stores was not accounted for in the SAP system. That means Mino 1 could be overstating their profits. These costs are collected somewhere and will one day reflect on the accounts, thereby forcing Mino 1 to take a significant unplanned charge to its statements. We went back a few more weeks and found this to be a recurring problem. Some costs are just never captured on SAP.

At this point, we are not sure where these costs are aggregating. We only finished the analyses last night and did not have time to follow this through. That said, this is likely an opportunity worth pursuing."

Listening to the Q&A session between Max, Alana, and the rest of the engagement team, Luther is impressed with the breadth of the analyses, rigor of the fact checking, and the ability of the team to discuss their findings in great detail. Most importantly, they have followed a critical consulting rule:

Always engage the frontline staff to test ideas and hypotheses.

No amount of data crunching and spreadsheet analysis can replace the quality and usefulness of information found when testing findings with employees at the frontline who face the problems on a daily basis. Even with the correct data, a hypothesis remains a hypothesis until it is validated with the frontline employees because data can sometimes be misleading or incorrectly interpreted.

Provided the analyses are correct, Max and Alana have given the engagement team valuable direction and help in setting priorities.

Alana's preparation has also been thorough. Once Max finished his initial presentation, Alana emailed copies of the model and slides to the engagement team so that the consultants could poke through the numbers and test the logic and thinking. They probably would not have time to do this, but it is shared should they want to look at it. This demonstrated a transparent team attitude, which was important for the engagement. Alana is rapidly learning, and anyone observing the Q&A session would not have noticed that she was a junior member of the team with only four months of management consulting experience.

Despite the overall positive impression, Luther did have some concerns:

1. Working 18 hours a day is not healthy. He needs to find a way to support the team or transfer some of their work to other team members. Thus far, the business case team has been

driving the engagement. That should not be the case for the entire engagement, and their workload should decrease soon.

2. All the numbers and analyses will have to be carefully checked internally and with Goldy employees before they are presented. Flavio will likely want to see the numbers as part of his weekly updates, but the CEO should see them first. After all, the engagement team reports to the CEO.

3. While the individual insights are excellent, Luther is not sure that the overall "so what" of the findings has been made clear. He will have to work with Max to finalise the storyboard.

4. The benchmarking is critical to isolate the size of the gap. This part of the financial analysis is not yet completed.

5. Being three weeks into the engagement with not a single opportunity chart completed is a major concern. From experience, he knows that validating an opportunity chart will take time, and the engagement team will need about two weeks to do this completely and accurately.

As the morning meeting wraps up, Luther and Max discuss validating the financial analysis and completing the final storyboard for the first steering committee meeting. They will need to book time with Selgado next week for the first significant update of the engagement followed by a similar meeting with Heinze and Flavio. This will be followed by a full meeting of the engagement steering committee, which is headed by the CEO.

Max agrees to complete the financial analysis verification next week as well as the benchmarks and presentation. It will be a long week.

WEEK 4

day 1

PRESENTING FEEDBACK FROM FOCUS INTERVIEWS

CONTRARY TO POPULAR BELIEF, findings and feedback from focus interviews are a significant part of the business case. They can rarely be used as the sole proof of a problem, but they should be used to convey urgency and indicate areas that require further examination. Anecdotal evidence presented with hard data can build a compelling argument. Quotes are priceless.

Steering committee storyboards are usually assembled by Luther and Marcus, the engagement manager and engagement partner. The first steering committee meeting is typically driven by the findings from the focus interviews, though you can include the financial analysis findings as we have done in this study, but not the bottom-up financial modeling output. Financial analysis, benchmarking and case studies are usually presented in the second update. At this early stage of the engagement, the financial analyses will comprise the bulk of the feedback and storyboard. It is crucial that all other feedback supports the central messaging of the financial analyses. Although the business case team continues to drive the central message in later updates, the rest of the work teams would be producing sufficient material for future client updates.

For the first update, Max will work with Luther and Marcus to ensure the entire storyboard flows well and caters to the client's needs. The steering committee update will typically comprise information from the following areas, although the order depends on the message delivered:

1. Key Findings
2. Financial Baseline Analyses of Mino 1 (usually presented in the second update, but can be included earlier)
3. Quick Wins (usually presented in the third update, but can be included earlier)
4. Brief Operational Improvement & Services Update
5. Next Steps

Feedback from the focus interviews is usually blended into parts 1 to 3 above. Presenting feedback from focus interviews by themselves is dangerous since they can be dismissed as opinion. A seasoned consultant will be able to manage this pushback, but if you struggle to do so, it helps to include data from the financial analysis. Though the preference is to keep update one to the focus interviews. Linking the statements of employees to problems or opportunities that can be supported with data is much more powerful. The engagement team knows this and works with this in mind.

Feedback from the focus interviews is also a powerful way to reflect and challenge the leadership of a company. It is very difficult for Goldy leadership to debate the significance of strong feedback. It is credible and because it is not analysis and/or opinion from the consultants, it is very hard to challenge. Even if the feedback is dismissed as merely "opinion," enough negative opinion implies an unhappy workforce. In a mining environment, where civil unrest is a major problem, negative opinions don't end with debates in an air-conditioned office. They can lead to hostage situations, rioting workers, and burning buildings. Goldy is all too aware of this possibility. In 1982, its Northern Venezuela operations were shut down for 21 days as workers barricaded themselves in a mining control centre. In 1991, workers in South Africa went on a rioting spree that lasted five days and caused millions of dollars in damage. The situation was only brought under control when the army was called in to protect property and senior management.

A well-presented focus interview feedback pack helps set the stage for presentation of the financial analyses, which can be blended into employees' feedback with performance data. If the feedback is positive and the financial performance is negative, that indicates management and employees either do not understand their business or are oblivious to the problems. If the feedback is negative and performance is negative, that could be due to problems between management and employees or poor working conditions. Irrespective of the permutations, the findings are important.

PRESENTATION

Max and Luther write out their proposed storyboard for the focus interviews:

1. We interviewed 74 employees to understand the reasons for Mino 1's performance.
2. Most managers understand the drivers of value in the business.
3. There is widespread agreement that Mino 1 is no longer an efficient and effective mining hub.
4. The organisation believes Mino 1 is no longer competitive against international peers and other Goldy mines.
5. The organisation is heavily focused on cost reduction versus production increases.
6. Morale is very low across the organisation and cited as a major concern by shift managers.

7. Senior management have not been highly rated by employees.
8. Despite the negative sentiments, employees believe Mino 1 can improve performance.
9. Employees believe performance can be improved by refocusing on the core mining business.

After spending about 60 minutes debating the storyline and structure, Max and Luther believe they have a compelling story to deliver from the focus interviews:

Mino 1 has lost its way, thereby resulting in a drop in performance, morale, and relationships. Despite this predicament, the employees understand what needs to happen, believe in the business, and must be supported with the right business model to turn around the operations.

It is important to note that the focus interviews consisted of approximately 35 questions in all. There were also different questions for different levels of employees. The focus interviews' feedback should never be a data dump of all the feedback. The engagement team must analyse the results and only use the necessary and appropriate information to convey the true state of the organisation. Sometimes this means lengthy storyboards, but it never means slides and slides of data with no conclusive message. It is important to never present data without the key insight. Leaving it up to the reader to deduce the insight may lead him or her to draw incorrect conclusions, which is why headlines and storyboards are needed. This is especially important for focus interviews where insights are much more difficult to decipher.

When the focus interviews' storyboard is ready, Luther, Max, and Alana prepare the focus interviews' slides. They follow two simple guidelines:

1. The storyboard (message) and not the amount of data will determine the number of slides.
2. The slides must be simple:
   a. Simple headline
   b. Clear and simple data to support the headline
   c. Clutter-free slides

Pleased with the final draft of the focus interview storyboard, Luther prints out copies and places them on the engagement team's workspace walls for feedback. He leaves out the first slide until he can confirm the numbers and titles of those interviewed.

EXHIBIT 43: Mino 1 Value

Most managers understand the drivers of value in the business

Revenue Bucket	Driver	Cost Bucket	Driver
Production	Face Length	Labour	Distance to mine face, lack of standardization, lack of mechanization
	Face Advance	Fuel	Poor ventilation, older equipment, multiple lines running simultaneously, dormant backups
	Stoping Width		
	Blasting Cycles	Water	Poor ventilation, inconsistent cleaning
	Vamping Cycles	Equipment	Poor inventory management, lack of standardization
	Hoisting Cycles	Explosives	Inconsistent blasting
	Drilling Width & Depth		
Productivity	Cost of Material	Pillars (Wood)	Inconsistent boarding techniques
	Overtime	Overtime	No procedure and measurement

> Most managers agreed that the biggest costs lay within the mine management model, equipment, and fuel.

EXHIBIT 44: Overall Feedback from Focus Interviews

FIRMSCONSULTING.COM & STRATEGYTRAINING.COM

There is a widespread agreement Mino 1 is no longer an efficient and effective mining hub

Key Themes from Focus Interviews

Lack of strategic vision for the hub
Lack of focus on mining basics
    Need growth in revenue
Cost containment is a key
    Yet costs are still exploding
Capitalisation and funding of Mino 1 – becoming financially independent
Management capability – both top management and operational
Changing the attitude of people within Mino 1
Downsizing support and administrative functions
Restoring profitability
    Cutting costs even further
    Developing costing models
Sorting out SAP and systems constraints
    Systems integration
Creating a positive culture

EXHIBIT 45: Mino 1 Competitiveness

FIRMSCONSULTING.COM & STRATEGYTRAINING.COM

The majority of managers believe Mino 1 is no longer competitive against peers and other Goldy mines

How competitive are we?

How well are we meeting targets?

Very poor	Poorly	Average	Well	Very well
	47%	27%	20%	7%

"Currently not very competitive, yet Mino 1 has all the capabilities and taught the rest of the business"

"Most expensive – I know we are not benchmarked or sourcing effectively. I shudder to think of the aggregated impact"

"We are discounting our business away"

"Competitive only because we use benchmarks from 2019"

"If someone could tell me our run-of-mine, I would answer that question"

"Nope – we are not competitive, and if anyone says otherwise, ask them for a proof!"

"We will be competitive if we are consistent – our competitors are…"

"Define competitive – do you mean from a time to ore perspective?"

"We have no targets on the mine face"

"My remuneration is not linked to performance"

"We work in a tough environment. We do the best we can"

"Rarely"

"I have never seen consistent targets that make sense, and I am part of the management team"

"I ask for this at every session, but my colleagues believe this mine cannot be changed"

EXHIBIT 46: Mino 1 Priorities

FIRMSCONSULTING.COM & STRATEGYTRAINING.COM

The organisation is heavily focused on cost reduction versus production improvement initiatives

	Mining	Technical	Operational	Finance	HR
Revenue enhancement		Development of a MIS to support business decisions	Costing model development		
Cost avoidance		Ensuring the SAP system implementation is signed-off		Cash flow management	Disciplined work force Attraction & development of analytical capability
Cost reduction	PL project Cost efficiency	SAP functionality	Improved cost efficiency	Finance function restructuring	
Working capital reduction			Migrating PX Intact system to SAP	Debtors days reduction Cash flow	
Capital expenditure avoidance					

> Very few of these initiatives have validated business cases, project plans, or reporting mechanisms in place, and none are focused on mining.

EXHIBIT 47: Morale at the Site

FIRMSCONSULTING.COM & STRATEGYTRAINING.COM

Morale is very low across the organisation and cited as a major concern by shift managers

"How would you describe the culture within Mino 1?"

"Nothing happens here, and we do not understand our priorities"

"Stifling and controlling"

"Living in a bubble – that's management"

"The most popular Internet site visited during work hours is for job search"

"Us and them management and employees"

"When they changed our compensation structure, we had no reason to work"

"Bureaucratic"

"Management is waiting for their pension"

EXHIBIT 48: Rating Senior Management

FIRMSCONSULTING.COM & STRATEGYTRAINING.COM

Senior management has not been highly rated by employees

Strengths	Opportunities
The Mino 1 Leadership Team . . .	The Mino 1 Leadership Team . . .
"They stick together no matter what happens"	"Shows a lack of direction and focus"… "is rudderless"
"Is positive and enthusiastic about making the business work"	"Has reverted to a crisis mode"
"Has a fair understanding and experience of the business"	"Does not have depth of industry experience"
"Has cut down on theft dramatically"	"Is not sharing the vision of Mino 1 with the employees"… "is uninspiring"
	"Is involved in too many things"
	"Is not focused on the core business"
	"Does not engage with employees"

> Further analysis will provide greater insights into Mino 1's leadership issues.

EXHIBIT 49: Employee Feedback

FIRMSCONSULTING.COM & STRATEGYTRAINING.COM

Despite the negative sentiments, employees believe Mino 1 has the capability to improve performance

What do you believe are Mino 1's key strengths and weaknesses?

Strengths	Opportunities
"Oldest mine"	"We are expected to fail"
"Developed techniques used on other mines"	"We employees know better – unleash us"
"Good people"	"Staff morale"
"Access to the best equipment"	"Lack of leadership"
"A lot of skilled and competent people….."	"The finance function"
"Survived this loss of direction before"	"Lack of coherent MIS, lack of process documentation, internal controls"… "We are spending more on the system but getting less"
"Leadership been working together a long time"	
"We know mining"	"Overheads are way out of proportion if compared to competition"
"Key members in the management team"	"Horrendous drop in mining techniques"
	"Inflexibility of operating model"
	"We are very bad at implementing, e.g., SAP and mechanization"

EXHIBIT 50: Employee Advice

FIRMSCONSULTING.COM & STRATEGYTRAINING.COM

Employees believe performance can be improved by refocusing on the core mining business

"Change the mining model – allow us to mine"

"Fix Oracle"

"You need to find skills at the right level"

"Back to basics"

"Start doing the right things instead of trying to do the wrong things better"

"Connect our performance to our remuneration. Please!"

"Management must walk around, inspire us, and tell us war stories"

"Don't give up; it's not that bad!"

"Tell the lower levels how the company is doing"

"Don't trust all the people you are trusting at the moment"

"Commit to break even by year-end; don't set weak targets"

PANEL BASHING

This is what Luther expects and what all management consultants must be prepared to do and accept. "Panel bashing" is the term used when the slides (panels) are criticised and torn apart under the unyielding and rigorous assessment of the engagement team. It is the duty of the team to undertake the harshest possible assessment of the slides. This is the least the client expects. Panel bashing ensures that any presentation receives its greatest scrutiny in the safe environment within the engagement team.

There is no room for egos, and the consultants who prepared the slides are not allowed to defend their work. They can provide explanations and clarifications, but largely they must listen or carefully respond to feedback if it is left through post-it notes. Consultants undertaking the critique are trained to deliver their assessment in a constructive manner. This is not an opportunity to attack individuals, and such behaviour is not tolerated. This is a forum for open and honest feedback.

WEEK 4

—

day 1

—

PRE-PRESENTING

THE CEO, FLAVIO, HEINZE, AND GAVRILO have all agreed to individual hour-long pre-presentation meetings on Thursday. This will be followed by a three-hour engagement steering committee meeting on Friday morning. This is the first major update of the engagement, and the client will have high expectations. To prepare for the pre-presentations and steering committee meetings, the team will have to continue their analyses but also find time for the following during the week of the steering committee meeting:

1. Panel bash the steering committee presentation
2. A workshop to discuss the opportunities and quick wins
3. Develop a strategy for pre-presenting

PRE-PRESENTING

Pre-presenting is the process of taking the audience through the complete presentation *before* the day of the actual presentation. This could be a week before the presentation or a day before, provided there is sufficient time to explain the details of the presentation, answer questions, and most important, make necessary changes to the agenda, analyses, or recommendations.

There are two reasons for pre-presenting. First, think about the times you have been invited to any meeting with little or no agenda or any guidance as to the topic for discussion. How did the meeting go? Was it useful? Did you feel prepared and want to contribute? Were any decisions made?

In such cases, the meetings are rarely productive. The same thing happens on management consulting engagements except the stakes are higher. A management consultant does not have the luxury of time to build a relationship with the client. Every chance must be taken.

Second, have you ever been in a large meeting where you were outnumbered by the attendees, they did not like your message, and you had never met them before? Is it easy to control the situation? When someone attacks your presentation, what do the others usually do? Do you understand how to respond to the attacks?

Even the most rational people can act irrationally when part of an enthused and unrestrained group. Moreover, if you have never met and built a relationship with someone, it is unlikely they will come to your defence, and it is almost certain they will not help you deliver your message.

Now we can take these two reasons back to a management consulting engagement to explain the importance of pre-presenting:

Steering committee meetings are held to make decisions. If the audience's first viewing of the results is on the day of the steering committee meeting presentation, they would not have had time to think about the significance of the findings. They may not fully understand the implications of the analyses. They are likely to ask questions and seek clarification during the steering committee meeting, which forces the steering committee meeting to become an educational session as opposed to a decision-making session. Pre-

presenting before the session allows the session itself to focus on the correct agenda item: making decisions.

Clients do not like to be surprised. Clients, especially senior clients, want to avoid the impression they are learning something about their business for the first time, especially when they are around their peers or superiors. This applies to a greater degree when management consultants are providing the new information. An executive will be really unhappy to hear critical information at the same time as his colleagues and even more so if it is bad news about an area of the business under his or her control. Surprising clients could damage relationships and possibly derail an engagement. The consulting team must try to create allies throughout the organisation.

Explain the analyses and answer questions. It is important to never take for granted the rigor and complexity of performing a thorough business analysis. If it takes weeks to conduct the analysis, it will surely take some time to explain the detail behind the numbers. Moreover, any worthy executive will challenge the numbers. It is unlikely they will take the analysis at face value. For these two reasons, pre-presentations provide an opportunity to explain the analysis and convince the executive of the validity of the findings.

Build relationships and make allies. Pre-presentations allow the engagement team to build trust and a relationship with the steering committee members. The audience is unlikely to attack a presentation if they understand the validity of the findings and the care taken to find evidence to support the recommendations. This prevents clients from forming groups that attack the presentation or derail the agenda.

Consultants can rarely tell the client what to do. They certainly cannot do so in a meeting with a large client group. They can merely recommend and advise. A senior member of the audience needs to help reinforce the consultants' message for it to have any traction. Pre-presentations allow the engagement team to find steering committee members who support the engagement team's message and can serve as champions to deliver this message.

The engagement team needs to identify sources of resistance. The engagement team must identify who will likely resist their findings and recommendations. The aim is not to sideline the executive. The goal is to create sufficient time to understand his or her reasons and then to build a stronger case.

Should this not be possible, the team may consider adjusting the agenda or even agreeing with the executive to discuss concerns outside the steering committee meeting.

The engagement team needs feedback and guidance. It is one thing to have the correct data and insights, but it is quite another to understand how to position the findings and deliver the recommendations. The engagement team must find allies in the steering committee and organisation who will guide them in understanding the internal politics, turf wars, preferences, and dislikes of the audience. Poor planning of this key point usually results in consultants being labelled "too analytical" or "lacking emotional intelligence."

No amount of financial analysis can ever enable the engagement team to understand the emotional dynamics at work. They need to have built strong enough relationships with allies in the businesses who are willing to volunteer this information as the consultants plan their presentation. The aim here is not to change the message to make the audience happy. Rather, it is about understanding how to deliver the message to create action.

An agenda is crafted around facts and personalities. The agenda is *never* crafted exclusively around the message the engagement team wants to deliver. It is crafted around the action and decisions they

WEEK 4 - DAY 1: PRE-PRESENTING

seek. For example, in some cases, the engagement team may believe that certain findings are too controversial to share with the steering committee. The engagement team may take them to the CEO and recommend that it would be better for the CEO to speak to the executive in question and thereafter present a watered-down version of the findings in the meeting. The key findings will still be delivered. They will just be done at a higher level, and less time will be expended on them.

If the objective is to get the executive in question to accept that his or her division needs help, it may be best for the CEO and the executive in question to meet one-on-one. A group discussion could make the executive defensive and will certainly hurt his or her ego.

Pre-presentations allow the consultants to better understand if actions are required before steering committee meetings and to plan for it should they be needed.

The engagement team all agree that this is the case for the Goldy engagement. Gavrilo actually believes his division is performing well. They must update the CEO first, and he must decide how to present these findings to Gavrilo before the steering committee meeting. The team can safely make this decision because they were hired by the CEO and report directly to the CEO.

Given the rather painful news they will deliver, Marcus asks for a session with Luther and Max for the next morning. He wants to discuss some of the quick wins they can present. This will be critical in demonstrating to Goldy that, despite the negative news, there are short-term initiatives that would build morale. Quick wins are a primary tool to manage the morale of the employees at Mino 1. It is one thing for employees to learn they are underperforming, but it will be quite another if they cannot generate any result worth celebrating in the short term.

Max and Luther agree to meet with Marcus at 7 a.m. the next day for a quick-wins discussion.

WEEK 4

—

day 2

———

IDENTIFYING
QUICK WINS

SITTING IN HIS HOTEL ROOM the night before the quick-wins meeting with Marcus and Luther, Max cannot help but worry about the progress of the teams. The services and operational improvement work teams have submitted 47 opportunity charts, but these charts have problems. Halfway into the engagement, many of the opportunities are ill defined, and some explanations are missing. With four weeks of the engagement to go, the teams still have sufficient time, yet they should have at least sketched out their opportunities in more detail. He will have to spend more time with both teams to better understand the opportunities.

One bright point is that the operations improvement team has developed an excellent storyboard but need to find the data to prove their hypotheses. Max thinks they can do it since they have carefully constructed the analyses to run and have most of the data required. Both Max and Alana are keen to visit some of the areas of the mine themselves to gain a first-hand view of the opportunities.

The services team seems to be having greater difficulty. While they have conducted some excellent analyses and found large savings areas, Max believes they are overlooking a crucial step. They have not yet clearly explained why the service functions are not a central part of the infrastructure to deliver the core business of mining. That is where much resistance is occurring. The client accepts that the hospitals, schools, housing, and more are costly, but they do not accept it is not a core business. Max thinks it is critical for the client to accept the argument that service functions not be managed in-house. He will speak to Nadia tomorrow about her thoughts on this matter.

Turning his mind back to the opportunity charts, he thinks that only five opportunities can be classified as a quick win. A quick win is defined as an opportunity that can be implemented and the savings banked quickly with limited disruption to the business. Quick wins are critical to raising morale.

He lists these five opportunities:

1. **Ensuring that all orders, expenses, receipts, and inventory are processed directly into SAP.** This is an unusual quick win. It will immediately lead to an increase in the costs, as more costs are captured as they are incurred, and it will lead to a drop in the reported operating margin. The win here is actually a better view of the business' cost structure and, therefore, an ability to identify which costs can be lowered.

2. **Transporting workers to the mine face.** The operations team developed an excellent opportunity to use dormant rail carriages underground, taken from above the mine, to serve as a transportation service to take workers directly from the elevator shaft to the mining face. Early estimates indicate this would be cheap to do since the carriages are compatible with the transport lines underground. This would effectively add about 16 percent of extra productive time to the average workday, reduce fatigue among workers, increase morale, increase output, and raise operating margins. It is a good idea that needs to be carefully checked before the presentation day.

3. **Consolidating support staff.** Each mine in the hub maintains separate information technology, finance, human resources, administrative, and training crews. Each mine support staff team and mine crew only operate at about 80 percent capacity. The reasoning is that due to the distance from any other centre and complexity of the operations, should any worker become sick and unable to come to the office, there is spare capacity to manage the shortfall of staff. Overall, this makes little sense because the capability to automate most of the features exists, there is excessive duplication, little sharing of ideas, and no pooling of resources. Simply put, not all the mines will experience the same problem on the same day. Accordingly, duplicate spare capacity is not needed. It can be drastically reduced and shared between all the mines.

4. **Enforcing contracts and service-level agreements.** Both the services and operations teams' analyses of contracts indicated that approximately 45 percent of contracts are not delivered by vendors as per the terms of the agreement. Approximately 80 percent of these contracts have had none of the penalties or revenue clawbacks imposed when the terms were breached. Given the size of the Mino 1 hub and the thousands of contractors used, this is a major opportunity area. Pursuing all the contracts will not be a quick win by any measure. Max has proposed initially targeting three large contracting vendors where the breach in terms and conditions are clearer and easier to enforce.

5. **Mino 1 is paying its creditors within 15 days.** It could realistically do so within 30 or even 45 days. The interest saving alone is a significant opportunity. In some cases, Mino 1 is actually paying in advance, *i.e., they are paying the complete fee before delivery.* They are currently doing this for

the excavation and development equipment bought from a variety of suppliers. The capital cost of excavation and drilling equipment, maintenance, and spare parts was $121 million in 2009. There is no material reason for this to happen.

NEXT MORNING

Luther agrees with Max's concern about the client's views on support services. Nadia, the services work team leader, and Luther have had several discussions about how to explain their thinking to the client. They have decided that a workshop to bring the executive team along in their thinking is probably best. A session is scheduled later in the week for Nadia to discuss her ideas for the workshop.

Luther quizzes Alana about populating the model with the needed data. At this point in time, the client has been sent Excel templates into which the data must be inserted. Understanding the usual misinterpretation that occurs, limited time of employees, and sometimes limited interest, Alana has set up an hour with each source to help them find the data and populate the template. It will probably take her the entire week to complete the data gathering. It is not the most glamorous work, but this attention to detail and collection of the appropriate information is vital for building an effective business case.

Alana points out that the greatest difficulty will be in understanding the correct cost structure. In some cases, she is working with the accounts team and auditors to review invoices and build an estimate of the true costs. It is not the kind of work expected in a top-down business case, yet with Goldy's poor management of its finances, it is a necessary step. If Alana can accomplish this in time, it will add significant credibility to the engagement.

WEEK 4 - DAY 2: IDENTIFYING QUICK WINS

Marcus arrives in the middle of this discussion and is intrigued with the analyses being done. It is a very bottom-up approach to build a model. While he is happy with Alana's initiative and solution, he reminds her that time is not on their side. This level of analysis is good but impossible to do for the entire engagement. She needs to follow the 80/20 rule and must either get Goldy's financial analysts to do more or get the auditors to provide data they already have. Max acknowledges that he can ask Sergio to have the Goldy financial analysts spend more time on this and also place some pressure on the auditors. Max makes a note to speak to Sergio before the end of the day.

Once everyone else arrives, the group discusses the story for the first steering committee meeting. Distilling the findings from the financial analyses, focus interviews, and quick wins creates the following key messages:

1. Mino 1 is destroying value and underperforming on every key metric.
2. There is little control of costs, and poor mining techniques are stifling production.
3. Key organisational checks, balances, and systems are not in place.
4. Left to run as is, Mino 1 will continue destroying value.
5. Employees believe management has neglected its core business.
6. Employees do not think management is sufficiently engaged.
7. Despite these problems, most employees believe the business can be turned around.
8. There are opportunities to demonstrate results quickly.
9. A full turnaround will take three to four years.

Marcus is generally comfortable with the messages for the steering committee. He spends most of the time ensuring that the data and analyses to support the message are correct and the right conclusions have been drawn. Despite Max's enthusiasm for the quick wins, Marcus does not believe they have been sufficiently validated. Marcus believes that more validation must be done before they can be presented. For example, he thinks the idea of dismissing excess staff will be difficult to do under Brazil's tough labour laws. It's definitely an opportunity but most likely will not be a quick win. He also believes that given the dire assessment of Mino 1, the CEO must make the call about how much will be presented in the steering committee session.

With a full working day still to go, the team heads off to complete their tasks.

WEEK 4

—

day 5

———

STEERING
COMMITTEE
MEETING

*t*HE ENGAGEMENT is now officially at its midpoint. It is the last day of the fourth week of an eight-week study. The engagement team was in the office until 2 a.m. the night before updating the final steering committee storyboard by incorporating the feedback from the pre-presentations. They were back in the office by 7 this morning to do the final reviews and fact checking for the three-hour steering committee meeting starting at 11 a.m.

The pre-presentations the day before did not go exactly as planned. The team flew into Rio de Janeiro at 9 a.m. and started their presentations at 10 a.m. Selgado was clearly surprised at the state of Mino 1's performance. Throughout the meeting, he kept referring to the financial analyses prepared by his own analysts. The numbers differed substantially, and 12 minutes into the meeting he called in Flavio, who, in turn, called in his own analyst responsible for preparing the reports. The bottom-up analyses Alana prepared paid off. The engagement team was able to clearly refer to invoices and receipts for constructing the data. It became very apparent that a difference existed between the actual financials and the financials reported to the head office. Mino 1 did not have a firm grasp on its operations and shared this erroneous data with the head office.

After the initial confusion about the numbers and differences on the basis of the assumptions made, Selgado seemed even more convinced that Goldy needed a radical overhaul. The refined quick wins were also presented and again indicated that many of the problems were due to poor management controls within the business and an insufficient focus on mining fundamentals. Selgado did not seem surprised at Mino 1's excessive employee numbers when compared with those of the benchmarked peers, but this was the first time the differences had been quantified. Both Selgado and Flavio were interested to understand how other companies achieved the superior benchmarks metrics presented. Hendrik could talk in some detail about the benchmarks, as they were his former clients. He was careful to do so without divulging confidential information.

Overall, the pre-presentation to Selgado and Flavio went well with the exception of one item. While the CEO agreed with the engagement team that the service functions were not core to the business, he felt that it was not enough to state this point. The engagement team needed to find a way to make the executive team understand this as well. The idea of the workshop was raised, and the CEO asked that he be invited to this session.

It was finally decided that both Heinze and Gavrilo should see the complete presentation before the steering committee meeting. The CEO was adamant that changing the culture of the company must start at the top. To him, if they did not already know this information, they were not doing their jobs anyway. The executive committee must be able to have frank and open discussions about the performance, culture, and health of the business.

Both Gavrilo and Heinze were taken aback by the findings and implications. Hendrik was very careful in presenting the insights only and not delving into the detail about why this was happening. Given that the problems lay squarely with both Heinze and Gavrilo, they would naturally be defensive. Since the engagement team was not ready to present the diagnosis, any speculations would only damage the team's credibility were this to change in the future. Although surprised by the findings, neither challenged them. They accepted and acknowledged that things could be better, but Gavrilo ended the meeting by stating that although performance could be better, it could only improve at the expense of Mino 1's culture, and he was not prepared to "hurt his employees." It was just not the Goldy way, and he needed to preserve the culture.

After these four sessions, the engagement team decided to do the following preparation for the steering committee meeting:

1. Ensure that every data point presented could be traced back to verified evidence.
2. Assumptions and estimates were clearly marked.
3. Earlier versions of the storyboard contained hypotheses about the root causes of the problems. These were removed, and only validated examples or observations were provided.
4. Hendrik also felt that the storyboard was too "busy" and "cluttered." He insisted that the engagement team only have the following on each slide:
   a. Headline with a clear and direct message
   b. *One* piece of analysis to support the headline, which could be a graph, set of quotes, or another graphical representation
   c. "Kicker" stating the "so what" of the slide
5. Draft versions of the presentation consisted of 35 slides. Hendrik requested this be reduced to 15 slides at most. This would allow four minutes of presentation time per slide, thereby resulting in a 60-minute presentation, followed by a 120-minute discussion. The other slides could be included in the appendices and brought up if needed.

6. Hendrik also believed the objectives of the presentation were not clear. They needed to start the session by telling the audience what decisions needed to be made or what was expected of them.

   a. The decision needed was the level of analysis required for the service functions. It was clear that significant benefits lay here, but the client needed to understand that this would be a change in scope and effort. Like any good partner, Hendrik has already positioned the engagement team to do the work, but he wants the client to believe this is over-delivery from the engagement team.

STEERING COMMITTEE

All the presentation facilities are tested ahead of time, and colour printed and bound copies of the presentation are taken in. Given the fees paid by the client and the tradition of the firm, the consultants understand that image is important. All documents must be error free, and they need to be prepared to discuss their findings and observations in great detail should that be required. Only Hendrik, Marcus, and Luther will participate in the meeting. Given the seniority of the client, it is important that every participant contributes to the session and can add to the discussion.

The composition of the steering committee says much about the intentions of the primary client, the CEO. Typically, steering committees comprise executives who are closely linked to the operation analysed and who can steer the engagement to benefit the operation. The CEO decided that a scaled-down executive committee should serve as the steering committee for the engagement. He has invited the EVP of HR and EVP of Risk Management to attend.

WEEK 4 · DAY 5: STEERING COMMITTEE MEETING

The presentation itself goes very smoothly. A few clarifying questions are asked during the presentation. By far, most comments ask for examples when data is provided. It would appear the pre-presentations have worked well.

At the end of the session, four debates occur among the committee members:

1. Why is there a need to increase the focus on services when the operations clearly need the most help?
   a. The argument is that Goldy is known as a company that cares for its employees. Providing complete support services is essential to maintain this image and morale in the workforce.
   b. The counterargument is that Goldy can still provide some services, but many others could be outsourced. Goldy does not need to own them all to provide them.
2. How is it possible that Goldy's internal view of its operations is so different from reality?
   a. This places the CFO, Flavio, in the hot seat. He explains that the previous CEO decentralized the finance functions and the regional finance managers report to the hub leaders. He has no control over them. Flavio did not approve of this arrangement, but it was endorsed by the previous CEO.
   b. The COO, Heinze, and Gavrilo insist that the current structure is best. They note that if things are not working, any number of reasons could be the cause, e.g., lack of training, poor support, etc. They insist that the structure remain as it is, but it should be improved. Gavrilo insists that gold mining is a unique and challenging business. The finance managers must be linked into the operations.

3. Does the focus interview feedback reflect the broader employee sentiment? What does this mean for the business?
    a. The one view is that it has always been like this. The focus interviews are simply measuring what is already known. Nothing needs to change.
    b. The counterargument is that just because this is the status quo does not make it right. In any business, a deeply unhappy workforce would raise alarm bells. If Goldy is so interested in providing support services to maintain employee morale, why is employee unhappiness dismissed under the excuse that this is normal? This does not support the previous arguments made.
4. If this is true, what should the business do?
    a. The CEO throws open this question to the steering committee. Despite the insistence from the members that things will be better, it seems the group is unwilling or unable to offer any compelling solutions. The CEO does not push the matter further, but he does indicate that he is unhappy with the ideas presented and will decide what to do when the consultants complete the study.

The consultants understand their role. They have briefed the CEO on each of these likely topics the day before and expect him to lead. It is critical that the consultants do not appear to be making decisions for the CEO, which would only undermine his credibility and make it all but impossible to effectively drive change.

Despite all the data and the presence of 80 percent of the executive committee, the group is unable to reach a consensus on any of the points. Given the lack of consensus, the CEO decides the way forward:

WEEK 4 - DAY 5: STEERING COMMITTEE MEETING

1. Focus should be given to the service functions but not at the expense of the operations opportunities. If needed, the engagement team should be expanded.
2. Flavio and his team should, even though they agree with the consulting analyses, reconcile the financial differences to understand if this is a company-wide issue.
3. For now, the steering committee should think through how to manage this situation. The consultants should continue their work and present the detailed services and operations assessment in the next meeting. Then decisions will be made.

The team is overall pleased with the session. The engagement team achieved what they wanted; the CEO delivered the correct message, and the initial analysis has withstood an examination by the most senior executives at Goldy.

WEEK 5

day 1

MID-ENGAGEMENT
REVIEWS

THE FIRM UNDERSTANDS the importance and value of honest and constructive feedback. Without clear and descriptive feedback, consultants cannot grow as professionals, and clients do not benefit. In the long term, the culture of honesty can atrophy, and this strikes at the heart of the management consulting ethos: doing what is in the best interests of clients.

The firm follows a simple process when providing feedback on an engagement. The final rating is provided at the midpoint of the engagement.[14] Although counterintuitive, the process works for the following reasons:

1. The firm discovered years ago that given the pressures of delivery and strained timelines, engagement managers and partners sometimes do not spend sufficient time thinking through constructive feedback. They tend to provide consultants ineffective feedback during the course of the engagement.

---

[14] Midpoint reviews are atypical in most firms and have been piloted in only a few offices.

2. By their nature, most people try to avoid a conflict midway through an engagement and avoid outlining clear problems that need to be addressed. There was a tendency to "sugarcoat" problems. There was also a tendency to withhold negative feedback in the hope that a consultant's performance would improve over time. A consultant does not receive sufficient guidance until the end of the engagement when it is too late to effect change.

3. The outcome of the above was that consultants were getting watered-down feedback or very little feedback at all. Hence, the consultants felt they were doing well and did not try to improve. They were very surprised when, at the end of the engagement, they received harsher ratings. They invariably asked, "Why was I not told earlier?"

Most of the firm's competitors, and even most of the firms' offices, only provide feedback at the end of an engagement. To avoid the problems above, feedback is presented in the following manner as a pilot:

1. Consultants receive their final rating at the midpoint of the engagement, i.e., they are rated on the assumption their performance over the entire engagement will be similar to the first half of the engagement.

2. This rating can change at the end of the engagement if the consultant's performance changes.

3. This forces the manager and partner to think through the rating and present their recommendations with supporting evidence.

4. Consultants understand they are receiving a rating based on a thorough review. Should they not be satisfied with the review, they can seek clarity, feedback, and guidance.

WEEK 5 - DAY 1: MID-ENGAGEMENT REVIEWS

5. If the consultant is unhappy, they have half the engagement left to improve. If the consultant is pleased with their performance, they can simply maintain their level of performance.
6. This process forces clear and honest communication.

Max spent time from Thursday through the weekend thinking about Alana's performance. He has spoken to other team members and the client. He spent time reviewing the model and the progress she has made. As a business analyst, Alana will be reviewed along the following dimensions:

1. Demonstration of firm values
   a. Placing the client's interests first
   b. Teamwork
   c. Intellectual rigor and honesty
2. Financial analyses and general analytical skills
3. Ability to structure analyses under guidance
4. Ability to design hypotheses under guidance
5. Ability to test hypotheses under guidance
6. Ability to prepare storyboards under guidance
7. Client interaction
8. Understanding of engagement issues
9. Assessment of deliverables against the dimensions above

In their three-page assessment, Max and Luther must think about whether or not she can rise all the way to partnership. If at any time it is believed she has reached her peak and cannot rise through the firm, it is in her and the firm's best interest for her to leave. Of course, the firm will help place her into another external role so that she transitions well.

The analyst has scored very highly on the quantitative elements from points 2 to 6 above. The client seemed very happy with her performance, and the financial model was developed to best practice standards. She grasped all the concepts very well and was able to work independently, but she received negative feedback[15] from her colleagues regarding the firm's values:

> *"Likes hoarding information and does not volunteer critical information."*

> *"Does not genuinely appear to see teamwork and regular interaction as the golden thread through the engagement. Her interaction seems forced and focused on benefiting her rather than the team."*

> *"Tends to like working in isolation and can therefore drift in the evolution of her ideas."*

> *"To her, consulting is about numbers and facts. She is less concerned about the people issues, which are just as important."*

> *"Seems unable to work comfortably in groups."*

> *"Very good business analyst but a bit of a loner."*

None of these quotes will appear in her feedback. Written feedback is very diplomatic, and one has to avoid the tendency to assume that minor development areas are not important. It's the little things that matter and the feedback is written in a diplomatic way to depersonalize the tone and focus on the issues, versus the person. The minor things matter even if they take up just 5 percent of the feedback summary.

---

[15] Even in the most critical cases, feedback is always presented in a diplomatic manner.

Max understands that this is Alana's first engagement. She has also not worked with the rest of the team as much as she has worked with him. While he has not seen any indication of the issues listed above, he acknowledges the concerns are consistent: six similar improvement areas from six different people.

In providing Alana with feedback, he is careful to use wording that indicates thus far there is only a perception of a problem. This makes it clear that he is not sure if these issues are indeed real issues, but the perception does exist, and she needs to be aware of it.

Here are some examples of the language used to describe development areas for her:

> "*I wish I knew* if you were comfortable working more closely in a team-based environment."

> "*How to* include the organizational and people issues when considering recommendations."

By using the phrase "I wish I knew," Max makes it clear that he has not yet reached a judgement on Alana's performance. He is allowing her the opportunity to explain the perception and gives her a chance to change her behaviour, should it be needed. The same happens when he uses the phrase "How to." Max is again placing the responsibility on Alana to respond to these concerns. Should his perceptions be incorrect, he has raised them in the correct way without reaching a conclusion prematurely.

Max and Alana spend an hour discussing her performance. Overall, she will receive a "met expectations" rating unless she demonstrates her ability to live the firm's values. The firm does not negotiate on its value system. Even the brightest consultants are marked down or counselled to leave if they cannot uphold the values held dear. It is critical for Alana to show demonstrated competency and the capacity to do these things. Only actual examples will be used as opposed to speculations about her abilities. This ensures she receives a fair performance review.

Alana agrees that she is much stronger on the analytical side and needs exposure to opportunities where she can demonstrate her ability to handle clients and work as a team with her colleagues. It just so happens that the services work team leader needs assistance preparing and hosting his services workshop. Although Alana is busy completing the financial model, this may be a good chance for her to be exposed to a less analytical process. She can also develop a better relationship with the rest of the team through the preparation process. Max recommends that Alana focus on the financial model for now. The model must be her primary responsibility, but she should join the brainstorming sessions to contribute to the planning. Any other preparation for the workshop should not be her responsibility. Max will make the arrangements with Luther and Nadia.

WEEK 5

day 4

SERVICES WORKSHOP

*A*LTHOUGH BOTH the financial analyses and engagement steering committee concluded that services can contribute significant opportunities to the business case, there was widespread disagreement on how the service functions should be managed. Executives understood the costs generated by the service functions, yet no one agreed on what should be done to fix this problem.

Given the size of the opportunity, the number of Goldy executives in disagreement, and the opportunity's potential contribution to the final business case, a workshop appeared to be the best way forward. It was important to get everyone thinking in the same way. All through Week 5 of the engagement, the services team has been designing the workshop. Initial discussions earlier in the week focused on the key objectives of the workshop. Initially, the team wanted to go broad and were ambitious in their objectives:

1. Obtain a plan for the service functions
2. Quantify the size of the opportunity
3. Discuss potential exit plans for each service function

Marcus thinks the team is being too ambitious. He reminds them that the engagement is diagnostic in nature. They need to determine the problems in Mino 1 and identify the magnitude of the business case in addressing them. There is no time to start thinking through exits and divestments. Moreover, he indicates that given the nature of the steering committee and the differing views among executives, the team should focus on just one objective.

He reminds them that workshops almost always take longer than planned to achieve their objectives. A good rule of thumb is to plan the ideal agenda and then divide this by 3. This will create the ideal agenda length. He points out that the discussion on the service functions is pivotal and could be a turning point for the engagement and Mino 1. *If the executives do not buy in to the concept that their core business is mining, it is unlikely that any of the other recommendations will work. This workshop needs to cause a shift in their mindset.* The workshop should be designed in such a way that the outcomes and agreements can be used as a reference point and precedent for future decisions. It is critical to use this work as an opportunity to refocus the executives on their core competency: mining and extraction of gold.

He believes they should not start the workshop discussing the service functions. They should start by discussing Goldy's core business. This would disarm the executives and get them to open up to a topic they should know well. Once Goldy's core business is agreed upon, they can then begin the services discussion and its position in Goldy relative to the core business. If the workshop could accomplish this goal, it would be a successful session. The workshop could end once the executives have accepted the position of the service functions. They could then be presented with the detailed analyses and options for managing the functions. The team agrees on the objective of the workshop:

Making the executives understand Mino 1's/Goldy's core business, and that the service functions are not a core competence.

With the objective agreed, the team thinks through the best way to accomplish this goal. They know from prior experience that such concepts as core competency and the core role of a business can quickly and dangerously spiral into a philosophical and theoretical debate. In extreme cases, the attendees can understand what the consultants are trying to achieve and can try to hijack the agenda or manipulate the process to achieve their own goals. As a starting point, the team lists all the service functions at Mino 1:

1. Human Resources
2. Housing
3. Security
4. Marketing
5. Procurement, Equipment, and Supply Chain
6. Legal
7. Treasury
8. Internal Audit
9. Finance
10. Printing
11. IT
12. Public Affairs
13. Workshops
14. Engineering (consists of 12 sub-services)
15. Asset Management (consists of eight sub-services)
16. Engineering Specs (consists of five sub-services)
17. Project Management

18. Mine Development (consists of four sub-services)
19. Laboratories
20. Properties (consists of four sub-services)
21. Hospitals
22. Recreation (consists of seven sub-services)
23. Shopping Centres
24. Environmental
25. Health Care
26. New Business (consists of four sub-services)
27. Transportation
28. Training
29. Family Support
30. Schools
31. Training College
32. Management Information Systems
33. Investor Relations

Some of these service functions, especially the engineering service functions, consist of large subdivisions. In total, there are 73 services and sub-service functions employing approximately 13,000 workers. This is approximately 20 percent of the overall workforce at Mino 1. Marcus suggests that the process used should try to avoid getting into the detail of each function. The workshop is only scheduled for three hours, and there would never be sufficient time to analyse each of them.

WEEK 5 - DAY 4: SERVICES WORKSHOP

Nadia recounts a workshop held on her last engagement. Several executives understood that the workshop would result in their having to give up control of their IT resources. Since they understood the planned outcome, they did everything to stonewall the process. It was a frustrating session that did not achieve the desired outcome. The lesson from this workshop is that the attendees need to logically arrive at the desired outcomes rather than being told the preferred outcome. If they know where they are being led, they may think the outcome has been predetermined and will try to disrupt the process. The executives should arrive at the desired conclusion by themselves as they progress through the workshop.

Given the advice above, the team deploys an innovative approach for the workshop:

Step 1: They present a series of short case studies on other mining companies and how they have defined and bolstered their core competency. They have asked the CEO of a mining company, a client, to take part in a six-minute videotaped interview where he discusses the journey he and his executive team undertook to define their core business.

Step 2: The team sends each attending executive two questions to answer before the workshop. Each executive needs to answer each question in no more than one minute.

1. Why does Goldy exist?
2. What must Goldy do really well to accomplish the answer above?

As the attendees read their responses, they are captured in real time on large white flip charts and placed up along the boardroom so that everyone can follow the discussion and refer back to comments made. The attendees need to discuss and debate the answers and agree as a group on the best answer. If they cannot agree on the best answer, they need to work together to develop the appropriate answer to both questions. This step forces them to agree on their core business.

Step 3, Exhibit 51: The facilitator now asks the workshop attendees to discuss each service function and plot it on the following matrix. They must plot the service functions as they are *currently* managed. They need to use their *older definition* of their core business and not the definition of core competency agreed in this meeting. The consultants have created a huge matrix on a brown paper so that all the executives can see the evolution of the matrix and contribute to the discussions. Each function is characterised by a post-it note so that the position of a function can be easily changed as the debate changes.

EXHIBIT 51: Services Matrix

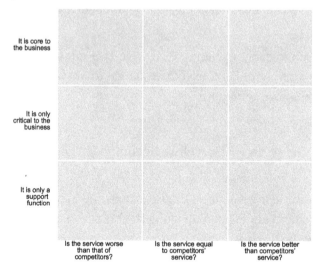

It is critical to be prepared. For each of the service functions, the engagement team has prepared a single-slide analysis listing key business information, such as the function's primary role and responsibility, location in the business, number of employees, cost trends and usage trends, its internal customers, and more. The aim is to present an objective analysis so that the workshop attendees can make informed decisions. They have not assumed the attendees have all the information at hand.

Step 4, Exhibit 52: The executives must now change the order of the functions (post-it notes) based on their new and agreed-upon definition of their core competency. Would a function's positioning change if the new definition of the core business were used? If so, they must agree on the new positions. The objective of doing this is to demonstrate that many, if not most, service functions are not core to the business.

EXHIBIT 52: Completed Services Matrix

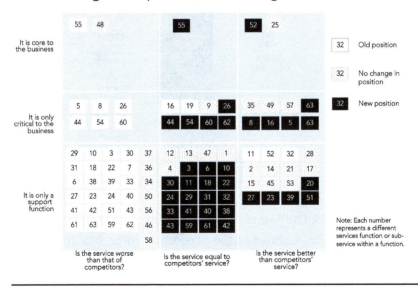

Step 5, Exhibit 53: At this point, the executives are still not aware of the implication of the quadrants. This is done intentionally. Allowing them to understand the implication of the quadrants at the start of the workshop may have led to some executives changing their answers to manipulate the outcome. When the process is done, the meaning of the quadrants is explained, which is accomplished by collapsing the 3X3 matrix into a simpler 2X2 matrix.

EXHIBIT 53: Explaining the Services Matrix

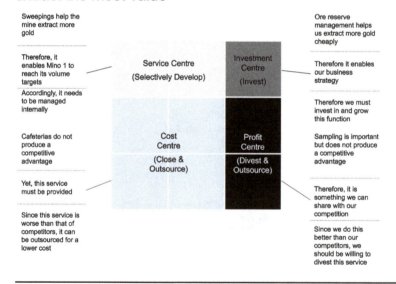

Step 6, Exhibit 54: Only when this is completed do the participants understand the implications of the process. By now, it is too late to change what has been said. They have already debated the positioning extensively and cannot renege on their agreement.

EXHIBIT 54: Managing the Services Functions

Is Goldy managing the service functions correctly?

FIRMSCONSULTING.COM & STRATEGYTRAINING.COM

	Cost Centre	Service Centre	Investment Centre	Profit Centre
Definition	Lowest possible cost levels	Enhance business competencies	Directly enables the strategic intent of the business	Deliver product/service in external market
Management Practice	Efficiency Cost avoidance Cost reduction Outsource	Customer requirements must always stay in mind Balance between optimal service level and internal service guarantee	Competitor awareness Customer requirements Portfolio management Maintain in-house	Financial and nonfinancial benefits Market driven Prepare for sale or sell immediately
Illustrative Products/Serv.	Maintaining workstations Data centres	Business process redesign Internal corporate services, e.g., accounting	Ore reserve management	Hotels Hospitals Schools
Measurement Criteria	Absolute and relative cost levels (relative to benchmark)	Service quality indices profiled over time and benchmarked Client satisfaction	Return on investments Effectiveness relative to competitors	Market-based benchmarking Realised profit levels Market experience

The facilitator asks the attendees several questions:

1. *"After we plotted the functions based on the core competency agreed upon this afternoon, our classification of the service functions changed significantly. What does this imply?"*

2. *"If our core competency is mining and extraction, how should we manage the service functions?"*

3. *"How do we deal with each quadrant?"*

Using this process, the engagement team stages a very successful workshop on Thursday afternoon. There was overall agreement that not only was the bulk of the service functions not a core business, but also that Goldy should not be managing many of these businesses at all. There are a number of reasons for a successful workshop:

1. There was a clear and simple objective for the workshop.
2. When a workshop process is not known to the attendees, it is important to make it as simple as possible. Having to explain a complex process to numerous attendees creates much confusion and delays.
3. The process was visible to all participants, and feedback was constantly captured and updated with flip charts and post-it notes.
4. The engagement team was prepared. They had analysed each service function and could present these on a separate screen as needed. They removed as many information gaps as possible.
5. There was an "aha" moment at the end when the 3X3 matrix was collapsed into the 2X2 matrix. Attendees now had to decide how to manage the services business. They must feel a workshop building to a natural conclusion.
6. The engagement team facilitated the process, but the attendees arrived at their own conclusions. This is a much more effective process than merely telling the audience the answer. This leads to attendees feeling a sense of ownership for the conclusions. Yet, the process must lead the attendees down a well-defined path.

WEEK 6

—

day 1

———

WHAT IS BIG-PICTURE THINKING?

THE ENGAGEMENT is now moving into its last three weeks, which presents both opportunities and challenges. On the one hand, the consultants should by now have a firm grasp of the client's business and likely conclusions from the study. They would have also received their performance rating and could use this as guidance and motivation to improve their performance. On the other hand, this is really the most important time of the engagement, and it introduces some risks. The team will have about two weeks to complete the key parts of their analyses and validate their findings and recommendations. The remaining week will be used to educate the client about the findings and build support for the recommendations. The team does not have the full three weeks to complete the engagement. They have about two weeks. Given the busy schedules of their clients, it is also likely that the pre-presentations for the next steering committee session will be spread out over a two-week period. This could result in their having even less time to prepare.

While the team has been consistently sharing information, placing updates on the engagement room walls, and holding their weekly update meeting, consultants tend to lose sight of the bigger picture over time. This occurs naturally as the team becomes focused on their analyses. Unless they are reminded to see the big picture, they can become too focused on their work and forget how it fits into the overall picture. All consultants must be constantly aware of how their work fits into the bigger picture and how the engagement fits into the broader client context.

Monday morning of Week 6 begins with such an opportunity. Luther has arranged a breakfast meeting for the team away from the client's offices. They will stay in Rio for the day and return to Mino 1 in the evening. Such meetings away from the client offices are very effective and valuable for team dynamics. Given the highly pressured and deadline-driven structure of management consulting engagements, it is essential for the team to decompress in a relaxed environment. A breakfast overlooking the famous Rio beachfront followed by a working session overlooking breaking waves can go a long way to reduce burnout and build camaraderie.

Luther has structured an agenda that gives all the consultants time to speak and present their views but also ties together the work into the overall recommendations they are likely to make. The following agenda items are listed:

1. A partner of the firm has been invited to join the team and deliver a 45-minute talk about a similar engagement done for a Chinese mining company. There are many similarities. This would help the team step back for the day and see the same problems in a different context.

2. The business case team would present the scenarios, options, and assumptions from the model. This is particularly important since *all* of the opportunities developed in the operations improvement and services team will need to be run through the model. Due to this, high-level design decisions for the model are critical.

WEEK 6 - DAY 1: WHAT IS BIG-PICTURE THINKING

3. A discussion on the findings thus far. This agenda item will have a full three hours dedicated to ensure that the team can understand the insights generated thus far.
4. Next steps from the meeting.

CASE STUDY DISCUSSION

The partner presents the case study of Chinese Gold (CG). The company bears a striking similarity to Goldy. It was created in the 1980s by a businessman who bought one mine shaft in the interior of the country. Through a series of shrewd acquisitions, he managed to build it up to become the third-largest gold miner in China and the 10th largest in the world. The company was also characterised by its tough, non-traditional culture. As a result of a focus on M&A-fuelled growth, the company had lost its ability to effectively operate its assets. Revenues were dropping, production was down, and morale was low. Surprisingly, despite the frugal nature of CG, costs were very high.

The partner mentioned that the CG engagement appears to be very similar to Goldy. Similar analyses were done. Structure and variability of the mines were also approximately the same. The culture was similar as was the historical animosity between management and employees. CG was continuously losing senior executives who went on to be very successful in the mining sector. Talent acquisition, retention, and development were critical. The company had an antiquated financial reporting system, which was failing. To prop up the failing share price, the company tried to branch out into different areas, such as nickel production, and even commercialise its support services as separate but wholly owned divisions. The CG study made five key recommendations:

1. Create a new corporate office that had control over all operations. CG's operations were too decentralized, and the head office was too small and had limited knowledge about the individual operations. For example, the CFO only saw the financial reports a few days before the quarterly announcements. Regional finance managers did not even report to the CFO.

2. Exit the noncore businesses, such as hospitals and nickel production. Exit the service functions.

3. Divestiture of 12 mines that were unable to earn the required rate of return.

4. Launch a back-to-basics programme to improve operating performance. A variety of measures were introduced, such as a new mining structure, continuous operations,[16] salary and bonus scheme, a new shift programme, and more.

5. Morale and culture were significant hurdles. The leadership of the company needed to actively engage their employees who felt disconnected from the business. It would be difficult to address any of the points above unless the company moved to a more accountable and open style of management.

Although CG did eventually turn itself around, this only occurred when the board ousted the CEO whom they felt was unwilling to implement the far-reaching changes. The partner's parting words were, "spend time with the client to ensure they understand the implications of the recommendations. They need to understand that change is tough, and it will disrupt everyone's life. They must be prepared for this."

---

[16] Continuous operations (CONOPS) are a technique to run a mine continuously for an extended period of time. This requires changing the employee shifts, bonuses, and vacation structures.

The key lesson for the team was that they may have been too focused on presenting analyses to substantiate their recommendations and not enough time ensuring that the client understands the implications of the changes. The client does not fully grasp the difficulty of rolling out such substantive changes. Moreover, it took a long time for executives to accept the concept of exiting noncore businesses. More time should have been taken to ensure everyone was on the same page.

SCENARIOS, OPTIONS, AND ASSUMPTIONS

Presenting feedback on a financial model is similar to a movie review. If you asked a colleague for a summary of the award-winning Pixar animated movie *Up*, what would your reaction be if they said the following?

"The movie started with a scene of a boy in a movie theater followed by a scene with a boy wearing goggles, holding a balloon, and playing in what looked like a middle-class suburb in rural America. The balloon was blue and wobbled through the air. It seemed to be summer. The boy in this opening scene was running toward the camera, and the camera then zoomed out, showing a wide shot of a boy looking at an abandoned house."

That is not a proper review of the movie. It is too detailed. It is not reviewing the movie; it is explaining every element of the movie and *leaving* it to the listener to draw conclusions. The listener also does not know where the movie storyline is going and will be lost until the very end. The objective should always be to provide a complete review at a high level, but with sufficient information for the listener to understand. Tell the audience what you intend to tell them. If required, the listener can then ask for more information.

A much better review would have been:

"It is the story of childhood sweethearts who meet while playing out their dream of visiting a waterfall in South America. Throughout their marriage, they collect all their savings to make this visit. Sadly, the wife dies before they can realise their dream. The husband becomes desolate and lives a life of isolation. When his home is scheduled for demolition, he decides to fulfil his wife's wishes and go to South America. In this fantasy story, he attaches balloons to his house and flies to South America. While on this trip, a boy scout stowaway shares many adventures with the old man and helps him move past his sorrow to find meaning in his life."

Too many consultants make this same mistake when providing feedback on a financial model or feedback on any other piece of analysis. They think it is better to take the first approach. They disclose a list of all the assumptions and slowly talk through them all. This is a poor presentation skill. With this approach, the audience does not understand the final outcome of the model. They will struggle to understand how the assumptions fit within the big picture. Explaining every single cell linkage and calculation is also not necessary. The consultants presenting the financial model are responsible for making sure the technical side works. The audience is not interested in this, and if they are, they will ask questions. It is much more effective to help the audience understand how the model will work at the conceptual level. Once they have this big-picture view, they can better understand the impact of small changes.

Understanding this, Max and Alana present their feedback in the same format:

"At the highest level, the model does four things:

1. *It simulates the Mino 1's current financial accounts to estimate future and historical ROCE.*

2. It models the number of tonnes mined and amount of gold recovered.
3. It uses historical cost/tonne ratios to estimate changes in costs.
4. FTE labour is calculated by estimating the labour requirements in each part of the mining process as a function of the tonnes mined.

The results we run must be done within the context of an economic environment. Each context we model is known by the word "scenario." We have calculated that ROCE is most sensitive to three external variables: the price of gold, real/dollar exchange rate, and cost increases (inflation). We will run only four scenarios. Each scenario will be constructed by choosing different values for the variables:

1. **Scenario One:**
   Rapidly Expanding Brazilian Economy and Strong U.S. Economic Growth = Stable gold price of $880/ounce, fixed exchange rate, and costs increasing by 10 percent/annum driven by inflation.

2. **Scenario Two:**
   Rapidly Expanding Brazilian Economy and Uncertainty in U.S. Economic Growth = Gold price rises to $1,400/ounce, real strengthens against the dollar by 17 percent, and costs increasing by 10 percent/annum driven by inflation.

3. **Scenario Three:**
   Average growth of Brazilian Economy and Strong U.S. Economic Growth = Stable gold price of $880/ounce, fixed exchange rate, and costs increasing by 5 percent/annum driven by inflation.

4. **Scenario Four:**
   Average growth of Brazilian Economy and Uncertainty in U.S. Economic Growth = Gold price rises to $1,400/ounce, fixed exchange rate, and costs increasing by 5 percent/annum driven by inflation.

We believe that Scenario Two is most plausible for the next two to three years, and then Scenario One is likely until year 5.

After we pick the economic environment within which Mino 1 operates, we need to select the actions the company will take. Each complete set of actions to fix the overall production problem is an option for Mino 1. We believe that management has five options. We developed these options based on discussions with you, so please feel free to change them:

1. Nothing changes. Mino 1 continues operating "as is."
2. Mino 1 exits mines not earning the required return on capital. This is not really a separate option, but given its impact, we have elevated it to this level. We can also run any of the options 1, 3, 4, or 5 and then add the effect of exiting some mines.
3. All operational improvement opportunities are implemented, but services opportunities are not implemented.
4. All operational improvement opportunities are implemented, and services opportunities are partially implemented. The definition of partial will need to be decided, but we think it means exiting all service functions that are not at least critical to the business.
5. All recommendations are implemented.

Our approach is basic and very straightforward. We have made a few critical assumptions that affect the ROCE and cash flow of the business:

1. We have produced a total Mino 1 income statement and cash flow statement. We have included all the service costs within Mino 1's income statement. The numbers will differ from the numbers reported to Goldy, which exclude the service costs. This is more accurate since the service functions exist solely to support Mino 1. Service functions are not shared with another

mining hub within Goldy and could not fall into the corporate office charges.

2. We have stripped out corporate office charges as a separate line item. This will allow us to see the impact of corporate-wide initiatives, such as rolling out SAP, licensing fees, and more. Luther, the IT charges you wanted to see will appear here. They are very small.

3. We have assumed that the mines will not expand vertically but develop horizontally. This is in agreement with the ore reserve teams' and mine managers' plans and projections. This lowers costs substantially, but it also lowers revenue so the ROCE remains unchanged.

4. We have added the mine closure and rehabilitation costs for the Mino 3 and 7 complexes. These are the two older mines in the Mino 1 complex, and they will be closing within the next three years. Rehabilitation is expensive and as more mines are closed and need to be rehabilitated, the attractiveness of the complex diminishes.

It is fundamentally important that everyone understands and agrees to the scenarios, options, and high-level assumptions. Max and Alana position the feedback at just the right level. There is sufficient detail and explanation for their colleagues to visualise the overall approach and understand how their pieces of work would fit into the financial model. Team members needing more detail ask for more clarification, and this is provided.

Max wraps up the discussions by making a final plea to their colleagues to complete their opportunity charts by the next day. They need them to make the necessary adjustments to the model.

FINDINGS

The findings have not changed since the previous discussions. The teams are focused on adding more details and finding the supporting evidence. Luther shifts the discussion to a fundamental question that is at the heart of management consulting: *"Are the consultants doing what is in the best interests of the client?"*

Although this is a core firm philosophy, it is always worth asking this question. It is also a core philosophy that everyone has the right to dissent and speak out constructively without fear of reprisal. Nadia raises the point that there is tremendous value to be gained from fixing the service functions. Although the scope has been limited in this engagement, it is the team's duty to raise this with the client and expand the scope as needed. The client will benefit from understanding the amount of value that services provide.

As the reader will recall, this has come up several times. Initially, services were thought to be outside the scope of work. Thereafter, given the size of the service functions, it was included but limited to just those opportunities that affect the core mining and extraction business. Then the client agreed to the expansion of the team and to have a dedicated services team.

Luther indicates the level of analysis is sufficient for this stage. More detailed analyses may be necessary but only at the implementation stage. The benchmarking and root cause analyses are sufficient for the engagement. Nadia agrees but feels more time must be dedicated at the next steering committee meeting to discuss their findings.

This type of constructive debate continues about various topics in the engagement. Everyone is allowed to contribute and debate. The aim is to have a spirited discussion with the entire team, with all the information available and everything open for debate. It is important that the team communicates and understands the reasoning of their colleagues. A key finding in one team could have a material impact on another team. Only through communication can these linkages be established.

The team wraps up the planning session by capturing the next steps in preparation for the next steering committee meeting:

1. Complete the modelling analyses.
2. Finalise the opportunity charts.
3. Complete the services and operational improvement storyboard.
4. Complete the second steering committee message and storyboard.

WEEK 6

—

day 3

———

MANAGING
A CRISIS

MANAGEMENT CONSULTING is a stressful career. Consulting firms hire only the very best business school and university graduates. Joining a consulting firm is, however, not a prize, nor *the* prize. It's the entry point to a process of constant evaluation, constant training, and constant culling of those who do not meet the standards to be a partner of the firm. Making partner or leaving on one's own terms is a prize. *The* prize is taking up a leadership position post consulting. Constant travel, time away from family and loved ones, living out of a suitcase, and the pressure to maintain an exceptionally high level of performance all take their toll.

More is written about dealing with client challenges than the inevitable burnout of some consultants as they struggle to manage the workload and expectations. Some consultants suffer burnout and simply resign, while others are managed out if their performance irreversibly drops. Fatigue can lead to lapses in judgement, which can come back to haunt an engagement team. Nadia finds herself in just such a predicament.

After an exhausting day of discussing the emerging recommendations with the Mino 1 management team, Luther returns to his hotel around 10 p.m. He has plenty of work to do in preparation for the second steering committee meeting as well as reviewing the feedback from the services workshop, storyboards, and findings from the completed financial model. Exhausted, he collapses into bed and sets his alarm for 5 a.m. He convinces himself it is better to rest than try to push through this wave of exhaustion. He calls the office and asks the team to lock up on his behalf.

Luther arrives by 6 the next morning. He is not the first to arrive. Alana is already in and building a huge visual map[17] to explain the financial model. She is running a workshop with the Mino 1 financial analysts to obtain their sign-off on the model approach and outputs. By 7 a.m., an exhausted Nadia arrives. Given that she started one week late on the engagement, she has been working 18-hour days to catch up with the rest of the team. After Nadia sets up, she spends about 10 minutes looking for some of her documentation. She goes around asking each person if they have seen a folder labelled "Hospital and Treatment Analyses." After 20 minutes of searching and no progress, Luther decides to help out. Once everyone is assembled in the room, Luther asks Alana if anyone entered the room after she had opened up in the morning. She knows no one entered but also indicates that she was not the first person in that morning. The room was open when she arrived, and no one was there. Alana simply assumed the person who opened the room had stepped out.

Luther is now worried. It is an engagement rule that the workroom is always locked, or if it is open, a consultant must always be in the room. Clients are never allowed in the room unaccompanied since

---

[17] A visual map is sometimes called a brown paper. It consists of a large brown paper with tape over the borders to prevent fraying. The visual map can contain any information required for a visual display. They work well for workshops and the sharing of information. Slides, charts, and even explanations can be pasted onto a visual map.

confidential material or work in progress may be in full view. It takes a few minutes to determine that Nadia forgot to lock the engagement room when she left the previous night. She had also forgotten to lock away her analyses in the storage cabinets. These are two serious mistakes.

Although unhappy with his team's breach of management consulting protocol, Luther needs to understand what is missing and the significance of the information. He needs to do damage control. Nadia had been working out the treatment costs for the HIV/AIDS antiretroviral treatment Mino 1 was providing to its workers. Any data could be damaging in the wrong hands, and it is important to find out what had happened to the folder. Luther determines from building security that the only people who entered the building at night were the five-man cleaning crew. They were in from 2 a.m. to 3 a.m. It is likely they simply placed the folder in the trash, but it is better to know for sure. The security crew promises to let Luther know once they have contacted the cleaners.

Luther immediately launches the following damage control procedures:

1. He requests a copy of the folder's contents to assess the damage. He also requests that building security speak to each member of the cleaning crew.
2. He immediately leaves a message for Marcus summarizing what he knows and asking for his call to be returned.
3. He books time with the engagement team later that afternoon to discuss protocol while on the client's site.

Unfortunately for Luther, the information in the folder is potentially explosive. The analyses clearly show that the hospitals are receiving government-subsidized antiretroviral treatment but storing them as opposed to distributing them to employees because the hospital has had its testing budgets cut and is unable to track all employees who are infected. Should this ever get to the labour unions, Goldy will face a firestorm of criticism. The analysis is thorough, and it will be difficult to refute the evidence. The damage to the consulting client relationship would be too great to imagine.

As Luther waits for feedback from the security firm and a call from the engagement partner, he carefully thinks through the sequence of events and wonders if this could have been avoided:

1. Nadia clearly made an error of judgement. She did not lock the room door or lock away her analyses in the storage cabinets.

2. There may be other deviations from consulting protocol that must be addressed.

3. In her defence, she had been working 18-hour days for effectively four weeks and through all weekends.

4. There were other signs that she was fatigued and under stress. All her update charts in the Friday meetings indicated high stress levels. She was usually the last person to leave the office and the first to get in. She has also been struggling with meeting deadlines.

5. Firm rules clearly state that consultants working at that rate must be given three days of leave after the third week irrespective of the importance of the engagement. That was Luther's oversight.

The firm places the interests of clients at the top. The welfare and health of the consultants are not far behind. Any deviations from consulting protocol are thoroughly discussed and used in performance evaluations. It is important for Luther to provide a balanced perspective of the events.

By this time, the security team has tracked down the cleaning crew. At least there is good news. One of the cleaners found the folder, and because it looked important and the "consultants had always been kind" to her, she sealed it in an envelope and pushed it into one of the drawers. The consultants find it exactly where the cleaner said she put it. Relieved, Luther is pleased the consultants have upheld the firm's values of treating all employees with respect. This certainly paid dividends in this situation.

Before the team meeting, Marcus calls. Luther quickly provides a rundown of events and his recommendation. This is not entirely Nadia's fault. She did make two mistakes but had been working much too hard over the last four weeks and should have been given more support or time away. If anything, this is a lesson in better engagement management. The engagement partner agrees and endorses the idea of a refresher meeting to ensure everyone is following the correct protocols. They both agree it would be wise to bring in a consultant from "the beach"[18] to assist Nadia and reduce her workload.

These kinds of crises are not uncommon on engagements. They occur far more frequently than one would think. Most consulting firms have a protocol for avoiding these problems, and should they occur, detailed damage control steps are undertaken. In this case, the lapse probably occurred because the protocols to avoid these problems were ignored. Another important point to note is the value system employed by Luther and the system of checks used by the firm. First, Luther did not place the blame solely on the services team. He provided an honest appraisal of the situation and divided

---

[18] "The beach" is a term applied to consultants based in the consulting office. They are either not staffed on an engagement or working on internal projects.

responsibility. That demonstrates strong consulting values. Second, the reason he does this is because the firm takes these and other engagement matters seriously. If they did not, and Luther knew these issues might never be discussed, he could be enticed to sweep the situation under the rug, so to speak, and place the blame squarely on Nadia. The midweek scare does jolt the team a little and forces them to be extra alert as they complete the study.

WEEK 6

day 5

OPERATIONS
IMPROVEMENT
& SERVICES
FEEDBACK

***T**HIS FRIDAY MORNING* update session will again be an extended session. Both the operations and services teams will provide their feedback. To ensure a more robust discussion, Luther has asked both teams to circulate their presentations the night before. This will afford everyone an opportunity to familiarise themselves with the information and develop questions. It will also help the new business analyst, Rafael, who had been sent in to support Nadia. The feedback would only consist of a high-level review of the complete storyboard and just key slides of analyses that support the recommendations.

With just two weeks left in the engagement and one more week until the second steering committee, not much room remains for significant changes to the recommendations. Pre-presentations will begin next week for steering committee two, and the final draft of the recommendations will also be presented. The team has also decided to treat the second steering committee as the final session. This will ensure they only have to make minor changes to the presentation for the final steering committee. The few days before the final steering committee meeting will be used as an opportunity to validate recommendations and hold discussions with the executives.

SERVICES

Despite the challenges faced by Nadia, she produced an outstanding storyboard. Given the number of service functions to analyse, there was always a danger she would become bogged down in bottom-up analyses and unable to synthesize the information to produce the headline messages. That does not seem to be the case here.

The services storyboard is short, compelling, simple, and insightful—the hallmarks of great management consulting. Although Nadia has supported this with more detailed slides, the main storyboard delivers a strong message:

1. Over 20 years, Mino 1 has accumulated 67 different service functions.
2. Services employs 10,000 employees, uses 18 percent of operating expenses, and 15 percent of capital expenditure.
3. On 27 occasions in 2009, services capital needs have siphoned $57 million from essential operations projects.
4. Despite the investments, the functions perform much worse than benchmarked peers.
5. Ninety-four percent of all functions create no competitive value.
6. Building services to the levels required to support the core business will cost $288 million over three years and not create value.
7. Most service functions are not core to Mino 1 and should be divested.
8. Divesting ancillary support services could save Mino 1 $45 million over three years and create a once-off gain of $223 million.

WEEK 6 - DAY 5: OPERATIONS IMPROVEMENT & SERVICES FEEDBACK

9. Redesigning the metrics in the retained services could save another $22 million/annum over three years.

10. These savings could be redirected to needed operational improvement programmes.

11. We recommend continued analyses to design the restructuring of the service functions.

There are slides for each of the headlines above, but Luther wants to just review the analysis slides. Nadia only pulls up four analysis slides to support her recommendations:

EXHIBIT 55: Core Services at Mino 1

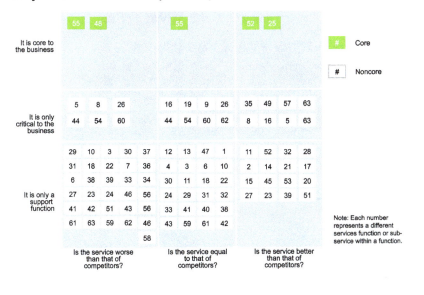

Slide 1, Exhibit 55: This is the summary from the services workshop. It outlines the executives' view on which functions should be controlled by the company and which should be divested. The slide reiterates that over 70 percent of service functions are not essential to maintain in-house, and only five are core to the business.

EXHIBIT 56: Measuring Value in Services

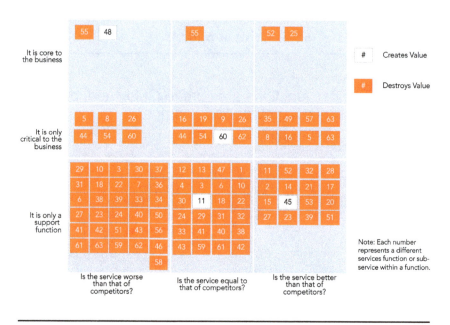

Slide 2, Exhibit 56: This is the same as slide one, but each function is either coloured red/black or white. White services are creating value, while red/black services are destroying value. The slide is mostly red/black. This slide means little by itself. Service functions typically do destroy value since their primary function is to support the profit-producing parts of the business. They are measured more by the value they bring to the operations' units; they are measured by customer service ratings and the cost of delivery.

EXHIBIT 57: Customer Ratings of Services

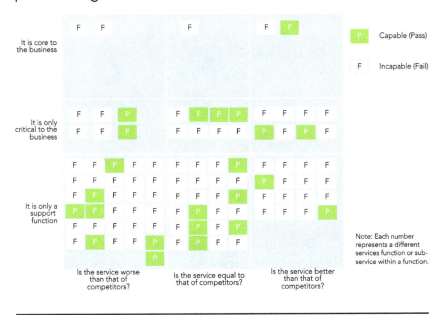

Slide 3, Exhibit 57: Again, it is the same slide with added detail. It is the natural follow-up from the previous slide. This is the overall rating of each service as provided by the users in the core mining and extraction business. A major argument about retaining the service functions in-house is that by doing so, the functions can develop a deeper understanding of the operations and provide a better service than external providers, but the feedback from the mining and extraction teams says otherwise. The service functions are actually worse at their jobs than external providers.

EXHIBIT 58: Investment Required in Services

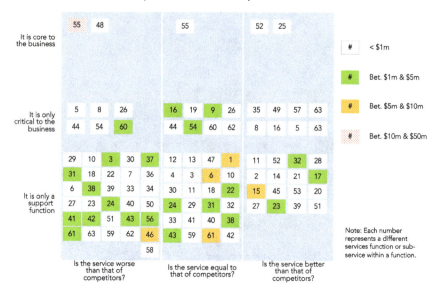

Slide 4, Exhibit 58: Again, the same slide, but each function is shaded in a different colour based on the amount of investment needed.

The shade indicates the amount of investment required to bring the function to benchmarked parity. This indicates the enormous investment needed just to make the function competitive. It raises a question: Why should Goldy make this investment in an area that is not their core business?

Nadia has done a significant amount of work in a very short period of time. The engagement team is intrigued by the methods used to arrive at some conclusions in a very short space of time. The questions reflect this interest.

Q – How did you determine the value created by the service functions?

A – Nadia:

"First off, value is a term developed for this engagement. Value does not have its traditional economic meaning. As you are aware, the service functions are not separate legal entities and do not have their own income statements and balance sheets. Therefore, we worked with the accounting department to create income statements and cash flow statements over a two-year period and also projected future expected costs. We used the internal charge-out sheet to estimate the revenue they earned. It is not real revenue. It is simply allocating costs from the service functions plus a fixed mark-up fee as a cost to the operations centres, which operations must settle. Basically, the service functions charge the business on a cost-plus-mark-up model.

We now know the total amount that service functions charged the operating division for work. We then called external providers to determine how much they would have charged for the same work. We then calculated the difference between the amounts. In all cases, the service functions' fees were lower than the market quotes. Yet, this does not mean that the lower price of the internal service function creates competitive value.

Lower prices by the services team could mean they provide lower-quality service. This lower quality will have a cost attached to it, which will show up somewhere. We went hunting for these costs. So we worked with the operations team to estimate how much extra it cost to fix problems created by service functions or the amount of revenue lost from using the service functions. We did the same analyses for housing, hotels, and so on. We added these back to the total cost of the service and recalculated the difference between prices for the internal service functions and competitors. When we did this, the majority of service functions added no extra value.

The methodology is good enough, but we admit the data is not perfect. Many estimates have been made, and we needed to conduct many telephone interviews to obtain competitor pricing data. In many cases, we had proposals submitted to Mino 1 from external contractors and could see the costs to provide services based on Mino 1's requirements. We also had to speak to other gold mining companies to ensure the competitors' work was up to standard, or we would need to work in the cost of their flawed work. Luckily, we encountered very few such problems. For this engagement, we really tried to provide focus to the implementation teams, and this analysis accomplishes this task."

Q – The analyses are great at presenting the problems. Well done. However, we don't see much analysis around the possible causes.

Response from the services team:

"You are correct. We have focused more on understanding the true extent of the problem. There are several reasons for this:

1 – Conducting this analysis was not easy. The data, systems, and reports frankly did not exist for any kind of comparative analyses to be done. Therefore, we spent much of our time creating the framework for the analyses. We thought that would be a valuable tool going forward.

2 – As you can see, we have presented a top-down analysis by making benchmark comparisons. We think, for this stage of the engagement, that should be sufficient. This directly leads us to the third point.

3 – We do not need, at this time, to analyse every single service function to determine the root cause of the issues. We only need to do so for those functions Goldy decides to retain in-house. Since Goldy has not decided which services will be retained, we wanted to wait. For those not retained, it will be unnecessary since they may be sold or shut down. As a result, an outcome of our analysis is a decision on how to manage the four different quadrants. Once we know which functions will be retained, an extension to the engagement or an internal team within Goldy needs to determine the root cause issues."

Q – Have you given much thought to how the service functions should be managed in the future?

A – Nadia:

"Yes. We have many ideas on streamlining the hospitals before divestiture. We have similar ideas on the hotels, shopping malls, and more, but at this stage, they are merely hypotheses. We stress that a more detailed analysis will be required.

At the end of this engagement, we need a decision on what stays and what does not. Our quadrants analyses must be taken forward and a decision made on what stays and what will go.

Q – What are the main opportunities in the services area?

A – Nadia:

"We can group them in waves:

Wave 1: Agreement on what will be sold or bundled out and the proceeds from the sale as well as investment avoidance in these functions.

Simultaneously find external suppliers and negotiate new supply agreements and terms of service.

Wave 2: Redesigning the metrics, structures, and performance contracts for the service functions retained. There are substantial opportunities here. You can see the opportunity charts in the appendices.

Wave 3: Taking these lessons across the Goldy business.

We believe waves 1 and 2 can commence at roughly the same time, but wave 2 will certainly be completed before wave 1. Conducting the due diligence, developing divestiture options, and actually selling or closing down the functions will take time. We would also need to determine the severance packages to be paid and understand how this can be done under Brazilian law.

The earlier matrix mapping is a great approximation but needs to be validated."

Nadia does a commendable job of defending her approach and explaining the rationale. Given her late start and frantic push in the last few days, she has not had much time to properly brief her colleagues. Besides the services workshop, her colleagues have not seen the thought process behind her work. Despite this, she has been able to present a logical and highly rational storyboard. She was also able to explain her ideas and thinking in a short space of time without losing the audience. These are all good signs.

Nadia faced problems common in many management consulting engagements:

1. A significant number of businesses required analyses. At least 73 service functions needed to be analysed, and recommendations had to be provided. She needed to do the right kind of analysis and just enough of it. The approach used for the analysis must be both accurate and cater to the time constraints.

2. No reliable data was available to use. A lot of data was available but not much in a form that could be used by the team. This is another common problem. Sometimes the data just does not exist to complete the analysis planned. Another analysis needs to be developed. Flexibility is important.

Nadia managed this by thinking through what the likely outcomes would be. She logically concluded that the divestiture of some functions was likely. She further realised that this decision could not be made soon irrespective of the data available, and the recommendation also needed buy-in from the steering committee.

Understanding that delays were likely irrespective of the data available, she developed a new process that allowed the steering committee to understand the rationale for divestiture and also provided a framework for grouping the functions and sorting them. This would not be the end of the process, but it was sufficient to move to the next level. It is a clever move since the client will now want to move to the next step and is likely to retain the firm for further analyses. Nadia was not trying to sell more work to the client. The firm does not *sell* engagements. Rather, she focused on the best interests of the client, and that will likely lead to more work. By doing excellent work, she knew that more engagements and profits would eventually come to the firm.

Many consultants become obsessed with over-delivering and sticking blindly to the original contract. Engagements change, and it is impossible to always follow the original agreement. A consultant must over-deliver in terms of insight and quality, not the volume of slides, and be flexible to change their approach as understanding of the client's situation evolves.

OPERATIONS

The operations update is less eventful than the services update. For one, operations issues have been central to the problems in Mino 1 and have driven most of the discussion and debate within the team. The storyboard presented by the operations team merely confirms their earlier discussions. Even so, there are a few surprise findings:

OVERALL FINDINGS:

1. Mino 1 has seen a 2.7 percent CAGR drop in ore production since 1995.
2. Bottlenecks effectively constrict production by 27 percent.
3. Gaps in key processes constrict production by another 10 percent.
4. Revenue fell 3.5 percent CAGR over the last five years as the mine moved into less profitable reserves.
5. Mino 1 overspends its peers on every benchmarked cost category.
6. Mino 1 is underutilising its asset base by approximately 18 percent.
7. By moving back to within 10 percent of best practice benchmarks, Mino 1 can increase its ROCE by up to 50 percent.

VOLUME:

1. Rising gold prices have masked production and ore grade declines.
2. At the same time, the cost of Mino 1's support structures, assets, and employees have increased.
3. Volume decreases can be directly traced to ore reserve guidance, bottlenecks, gaps, management structure, and capital allocation.
4. Poor ore reserve guidance is forcing Mino 1 to increase its asset base over an increasingly uneconomical ore body.
5. Diminished returns from the ore body have led to capital constraints and key projects starved for capital.
6. One critical debottlenecking project that did not receive capital could have increased production by up to 15 percent.
7. The capital allocation approach is unclear, as many approved projects have not met their hurdle rates in the planning stage.
8. This has been compounded by limited funding to critical projects to remove gaps in the production process.
9. The new management structure has removed critical incentives that indirectly drive ROCE.
10. New performance measures have not been audited since implementation two years ago.
11. The management structure is extremely unpopular and encourages the wrong values and behaviour in employees.

PRODUCTIVITY:

1. Mino 1 is 35 percent less productive than the leading gold mine.
2. Reducing this gap to within 10 percent of best practice levels could increase productivity by 18 percent.
3. Asset purchases are not consolidated, and $30 million worth of duplication has occurred in the last two years.
4. Consolidating the procurement functions could generate annual savings of $20 million.
5. Fixing SAP alone would account for savings in working capital of $15 million/annum.
6. Of the departments analysed, there seems to be excess staffing capacity of between 10 percent and 20 percent.
7. Support functions could be centralised and cut by up to 66 percent.

RECOMMENDATIONS:

1. Mino 1 must address nine different areas to successfully turn around its operations.
2. Continuing as is will lead to closure of Mino 1.
3. Poor control over purchasing and cost structures needs immediate attention, as the company could be exposed to liabilities.

The operations team supported their primary storyboard with a detailed list of 40 slides providing the root cause explanations for the problems they have encountered. Given the detail and earlier discussions, not many questions are raised. Max, however, is keen to follow up on a comment made in the interviews by Heinze:

Q – During the focus interviews, the COO mentioned that numerous operations improvement programmes have been tried at Goldy. Did you guys find out what they were and why they failed? Were they done at Mino 1?

A – Klaus:

"Yes, Max, we did spend quite a bit of time searching for these operations improvement efforts. Despite the claims of the COO, the on-the-ground reality was very different. All the programmes he mentioned as well as the others we found were not real operations improvement programmes. In each case, a financial analyst and engineer had been assigned to conduct desktop research to identify best practices and work out the impact of implementing them. The engineer was usually very junior and saw the effort as a training programme. Given the limited seniority of the engineers, these efforts went nowhere and were of really poor quality. We looked at the documents, and they were really summaries of competitor websites and a few telephone interviews. It was not at all at the level of analysis and insight needed.

To summarise our reasons for why they failed:

1. It was done in the wrong way. Desktop research was inappropriate.
2. The team was junior and had no authority in the business.
3. This approach did not have the buy-in of the Mino 1 operations team.
4. There was almost no interaction with the operations team.
5. There was no senior support for this. It was almost never discussed at Mino 1 management meetings or operations meetings.

To answer your final question, yes, these were mostly done at Mino 1."

With two weeks to go, the teams look to be in good shape. It is now up to Luther to work with the teams to build a compelling steering committee 2 storyboard and for the business case team to finalise the business case.

WEEK 7

day 2

AGGREGATING THE BUSINESS CASE

*t*O ENSURE THERE IS SUFFICIENT TIME to make changes, the consulting team will treat Week 7 as the final week of the engagement, which means all the outstanding analyses must be completed at the start of the week, the final storyboards must be completed, and pre-presentations must begin. One steering committee has been completed successfully where the team has stated the depth of the problem. The second meeting will have to be focused on the potential solutions, and a discussion on the options available to Mino 1 will be the focus of the third meeting. This plan fits perfectly into the deficit model selected by the business case team.

Alana has successfully built the financial model. It has been populated and tested. With Max, she has also set the model to operate in a scenario of high costs and low U.S. economic growth for the first three years followed by high costs and high U.S. economic growth for the fourth to the fifth year. For this scenario, they also tested each of the options available to Goldy management. They have further tested all the options against the other three scenarios developed. Goldy management can then examine all the options for the future of Mino 1 in four different scenarios.

In total, they were presented with 43 opportunity charts. Eleven were not mutually exclusive and had to be removed. The team had to build each of these opportunities into the options since the options are effectively different combinations of opportunities.

Each opportunity must be measured against the following eight criteria:

1. The dollar size of the opportunity
2. The returns
3. The cost to achieve the returns
4. The payback period and cash flow
5. Will the funding come from operating expenditure or capital expenditure?
6. Can it be implemented given company constraints and legislation?
7. Will it be easy to implement?
8. Who can do the implementation (consultants or employees)?

It will be worthwhile explaining this further. If you recall, five options were built into the model:

1. Nothing changes. Mino 1 continues operating "as is."
2. Mino 1 exits mines not earning the requisite return on capital.
3. **All operational improvement opportunities are implemented, but services opportunities are not implemented.**
4. All operational improvement opportunities are implemented, and services opportunities are partially implemented, which meant exiting all service functions that are not at least critical to the business.
5. All recommendations are implemented.

Look at the third option above to see how it is built into the model. This option means that the business case team must do the following:

WEEK 7 - DAY 2: AGGREGATING THE BUSINESS CASE

1. The model variables must be set to Mino 1's actual operating conditions. When this is done, the model output must mirror Mino 1's actual performance. This is a test of the model. Does the simulated output correctly represent actual performance?

2. Now the model is set to operate in the economic environment (scenario) they have chosen to run. To "set" the model, they will manually need to change the values of the macroeconomic variables (inflation, the exchange rate, and gold price) to reflect this economic environment.

3. Then they would need to ensure the model is capturing the benefits from all the operational improvement opportunities. That is option 3 above. To explain this, let us look at how just one of the operations improvement opportunities is built in. This opportunity was discussed earlier: *"The operations team developed an excellent opportunity to have unused carriages from above the mine transported underground to serve as a transportation service to take workers directly from the elevator shaft to the mining face. Early estimates indicate this would be cheap to do since the carriages are compatible with the transport lines underground. This would effectively add about 16 percent of extra productive time to the average workday, reduce fatigue among workers, increase morale, increase output, and raise the margins. It is a good idea that needs to be carefully checked before the presentation day."* Remember that the core of the model is calculating the volume of ore produced. Everything else changes as the volume of ore changes. Costs, labour requirements, and purchases all change as volume changes. They are the outputs. Non-variable costs are calculated separately using a combination of benchmarks and actual expenditures at Mino 1.

    a. In this case, the business case team would need to determine how the volume of ore produced increases if the production crews have 16 percent more time in the day to mine. Obviously, it would lead to more ore produced.

    b. If they are more rested, the team can also assume that they will work harder, be more focused, and accurate. They can assume the effect of this may be 1 percent more ore mined.

    c. To mine more ore requires more explosives, electricity, water, supplies, fuel, and wood. The model will calculate this.

    d. More ore means that shaft cleaning and conveyors work longer and harder. This increases water consumption and will lead to higher maintenance cost. These costs must be calculated by the model.

    e. The useful life of some assets will decrease. This will affect the depreciation timeline of some assets. This must be changed in the model.

    f. The costs of installing and running the carriages as well as maintaining them must be included.

4. This must be done for each opportunity. Besides a model of the existing hub, the effect of each opportunity must be layered or added.

5. When all the opportunities that comprise an option have been added, the effect of the option can be tested.

6. Although the technical aspects of financial modelling fall outside the scope of this book, one word of caution is necessary. Good financial modellers will ensure that all this data is inserted in the model only once. Afterward, all the options and scenarios can be tested by simply turning them "on" or "off."

As each option (combination of opportunities) is analysed, the business case team must compare the eight criteria for each option as well as the trade-offs for each option.

WEEK 7

day 3

BUSINESS CASE
SIGN-OFF

*A*SUCCESSFUL MANAGEMENT consulting engagement ultimately comes down to the ability of the team to develop a set of recommendations that add value to the client. Business cases are not only about financial analyses. A successful business case consultant must also be able to understand the business, break it down into the components that generate value, and map this into an Excel spreadsheet to test a set of carefully constructed hypotheses. When all analyses are completed and recommendations finalised, a short written report is often required as a final deliverable in addition to a clear PowerPoint presentation. Given the importance of business cases, getting the client's approval on them is a significant step in an engagement. Effectively, the client must designate someone who has the necessary knowledge and authority to review the opportunities and benefits case and sign off on them.

In this case, the business case will have two people doing the sign-off. Sergio and his team of analysts will examine each opportunity and physically sign each summary sheet. Flavio will sign off on the overall business case, as he is best qualified to understand the impact on Mino 1 and Goldy overall. This is because any changes to Mino 1's finances will affect Goldy's finances.

The sign-off process does not begin at the end of the engagement.

If the business case team is planning their sign-off process after they have completed their work, it is too late. The process must start right at the beginning. Sergio, the analysts, and Flavio must be kept updated on all developments, changes in thinking, and assumptions. They should be involved in developing the thinking, testing the ideas, and providing guidance as the engagement progresses.

Although the business case team is responsible for generating the final case, they cannot work in isolation and must rely on their colleagues and the client to provide information and guidance. There must be joint ownership for the ideas so that the client feels vested in the benefits case. If the client feels excluded from the process or feels his views have been ignored, it is highly unlikely he will be willing to step in at the end and validate an approach that he has never seen develop or has never taken his guidance into account. Frequent communication is essential.

The sign-off is critical. By having the sign-off, the team has the explicit support of the executive who has approved the work. This is a critical requirement going into the final update sessions. Irrespective of how impressive a report is, unless several influential executives support the recommendations, the recommendations could be dismissed. For business cases, both Flavio's and Selgado's approval count the most.

Max and Alana followed best practice in ensuring their sign-off is a smooth process:

1. The team only finalised their planning documents and charter once they had incorporated the inputs and guidance of Flavio, Sergio, Heinze, and Gavrilo.

2. Whenever concerns were raised about their approach, these were not summarily dismissed. The team held a separate meeting with the person raising the issue to understand their concerns and ensure they addressed them or explained why they could not make any changes.

3. Alana had been holding short Monday morning and Friday morning coffee meetings with the financial analysts. Repetitive meetings can become dull and a drain on scarce time. To overcome this problem, Alana kept the meetings interesting by bringing different pastries to each meeting so that the analysts could sample them. She also kept the meetings to 20 minutes and focused on the changes and ensuring that the financial analysts understood what was happening. Over time, she developed a relationship with the financial analysts and found it much easier to work with them and solicit their support.

4. Workshops had been held with Sergio and his team to ensure they understood the financial model and that it adequately reflected Mino 1's financials. They had been given sanitized copies of the model earlier in the engagement to perform checks.

5. Both Max and Alana visited the area managers responsible for the unit where each opportunity would be implemented. Where possible, they wanted their opinion in writing on whether or not the opportunity was viable or would create any unexpected problems that would negate the planned benefit.

Using this process, the business case team had managed to achieve complete buy-in of the approach, model, opportunity charts, and overall business case well ahead of time. Afterward, obtaining the approval of the final opportunity charts and the overall business case was a formality.

WEEK 7

day 4

FINAL STORYBOARD

tHE ENGAGEMENT ROOM is a blizzard of activity. From a distance, the walls look as though they have been covered with bright handmade tiles. Each team's draft storyboard is up along with hundreds of post-it notes capturing comments. Everyone is working long hours to fact-check their findings, test their assumptions, ensure references are inserted, and complete outstanding analyses. Luther is also working on the final storyboard and asking teams to change their slides or create new ones.

The second steering committee meeting will be held on the Monday of Week 8. The team is preparing their submissions for the final presentation to be used. Earlier chapters have discussed storyboards for the *different* work teams. The *overall* engagement storyboard follows similar principles, but given the importance of storyboarding and presentations to management consultants, it is important to understand how this final presentation is developed. Before that is explained, it is worth discussing how incorrect presentations are generated and why they fail on poorly managed engagements. The leading firms avoid these problems:

Teams work in isolation: Each team in the broader engagement works in complete isolation. They conduct analyses, prepare drafts, and hold meetings away from the overall team. They believe that they do not need input from their colleagues, and it is not necessary for them to provide input. In many cases, update meetings are superficial in nature, and the individual teams are more concerned with "looking good" rather than having an honest debate about the engagement's objectives. There is a combative relationship between work teams. At the end of the engagement, each team presents their findings, which are condensed into one overall engagement document. This is similar to how Max's previous employer operated.

Solutions ignore the broader picture: An engagement team must present a recommendation that solves the problem they are studying and does not create an entirely new problem in another part of the organization. Consultants must think broader than their engagement and think about the overall best interests of the client. The correct solution will allow the entire organization to improve.

Forgetting the value tree: As shown earlier in this book, the primary question answered by the engagement team sits at the top of the value tree. To examine the drivers of the value tree, each branch is broken down into smaller and smaller questions that are mutually exclusive and collectively exhaustive. Given the amount of analysis required, parts of the tree are given to different teams. Yet, they are all working to understand the primary question. Many consultants forget this point. They are all working to answer the same question, *and* no one person has all the information. Consultants must share their insights to complete the gaps in their knowledge. Only then can they see the overall picture.

Writing for the consultant versus client: A client is not concerned about the type of analysis done, the amount of data collected, or the pages and pages of analysis required to arrive at a conclusion. They are paying high fees for the answer and, sometimes, an explanation of how the answer was derived. Too many consultants are obsessed with showing clients the amount of work completed to arrive at the answer. That is an example of writing for the consultant and not the client. If required, detailed slides can be included in the appendices, but it is more important to develop an effective storyboard for the client.

Too much data, too few insights: Poorly constructed headlines and presentations lack a "so what" statement, which should be the question a consultant asks of every slide and presentation they prepare. If a consultant asks this of the slide and cannot easily find an answer, the slide represents incorrect information. It is actually the "so what" findings that should make up a slide and presentation.

Clutter does not equal quality: Busy slides with lots of bullets, text in small fonts, and many graphics are usually a sign that the consultants do not understand the point they are trying to make. Accordingly, they fill a slide with as much information as possible, hoping the client will be able to pick out the information needed. This confuses the client and forces them to interpret the meaning of the slide. If the client extracts the incorrect message, the entire engagement could be worthless.

Poor formatting: Poor formatting will damage the brand and ultimately the pricing power of a firm. Great consulting firms understand this and use a consistent formatting standard for every document that goes into the public or client domain. It is easy to recognise documents belonging to major firms just by looking at them without seeing the logo. It is a subtle but crucial point.

Knowing these common pitfalls, let us now look at how to build a proper presentation for the overall engagement. The key point here is that while the teams have been working separately on operations, services, and the business case, they need to bring it all together. Each work team brings one piece of the puzzle and only together does it all make sense. Bringing it together is not about simply having three sections and the insights separated. The team must blend it all together to produce a consistent storyboard.

There are no boundaries: *Just because the business case team was separated as a work stream does not imply it should be a separate section in the final presentation.* That is not how the business works or the client thinks. The overall engagement storyboard must tell the story of why production value has declined and how it can be improved. To do this, the storyboard needs to pull together data and information from all the teams and in the sequence required to build a compelling story. For example, on production issues, the client will want to know the level of production volume, why it has declined, how this compares to peers, and what it will take to correct the situation. This requires pulling together slides from the operations and business case team. The client is not going to see a compelling story if the work is separated into sections. Let the storyboard, not the breakdown of the work plan, dictate the order of the slides and layout.

Everyone's work need not appear in the final pack: The services team conducted excellent analyses of how the hospitals could possibly reduce their overall costs and increase their capacity, thereby qualifying for a higher government subsidy. This was directly linked to the provision of HIV/AIDS treatment drugs. It was a creative piece of analysis, but should it be in the final storyboard? Does it form part of the final message for the client? Not every piece of analysis must be included in the storyboard. No matter how much time was spent on analysis or the level of sophistication employed, if the analysis does not add to the final message, do not force it in. It is distracting and confuses the audience.

In numerous presentations, consultants like to say, "I put this in because it was interesting, but it is not as important, so let's not spend too much time on it." If it is not important and just interesting, it is not worthy of the client's time.

Remember the delivery model selected: Earlier in the engagement, the team debated whether or not to use the aspiration or deficit model to deliver the message. Both models are based on observations of human psychology and ensure the final presentation is a success. Forgetting or changing the model midway through an engagement is dangerous. It could derail the entire effort to mobilise the client. For example, the deficit model requires that the first message to the client conveys just how bad the situation really is, and it must create a crisis. Every major update thereafter must help navigate the client through the crisis and show them the path to success. Changing the model should only be done if the team is aware of the outcome this will achieve.

Offer recommendations: The first week or two of the engagement must be focused on verifying the depth of the problem facing the client. This is essential since the engagement team must be comfortable they are addressing the right issues, but once the issues are confirmed, the engagement team must move on. The team must reach a point of providing recommendations to problems. A drawn-out engagement that consistently refines the key question to be solved has been poorly designed and probably misdiagnosed the problem at the start. Clients pay for recommendations.

Validation: All facts, figures, assertions, and recommendations must be fully validated before they are presented. There is no excuse for not validating information. If necessary, carry copies of emails in a folder to support the validation. Taking in material that has not been validated may result in an executive changing his mind and withdrawing his support. This can be damaging for the teams' credibility. It is not enough to hear that a fact is correct and approved. Make sure evidence is presented, but only when it is called upon.

Employees' support: Getting a set of financial projections approved by the finance executive is one form of validation. Another equally powerful form of validation is to have line management, which will be affected by the changes, review the recommendations and provide their support. This serves two important roles. It first demonstrates that the solution can be implemented and, second, support of line employees indicates that the change management process is possible.

WEEK 8

—

day 4

———

CONSULTING
VALUES

f

RIDAY IS A PUBLIC HOLIDAY, so the team prepares for a much-needed rest over an extended weekend. The engagement has officially ended. The extended weekend will be more special since the consultants will be with their families. The firm has a policy of flying consultants' spouses and partners down to an engagement location if the consultants have been away for an extended period. This team's fly-in happily coincided with a long weekend. To usher in the long weekend, the engagement team will have its final dinner at the Antiquarius Grill on Avenida das Americas. It is a spacious and elegant setting and serves some of Rio's finest Portuguese-style cuisine.

As the consultants and their partners have cocktails on the balcony, Marcus watches the strollers along Pepe beach and recalls the last few days. Steering committee two turned out to be a tough session that lasted six hours. Triple the allocated two-hour slot. When Selgado saw the reasons for the poor performance at Mino 1, he went ballistic. Matters compounded when not only did Heinze and Gavrilo not have credible explanations for the poor performance, but they also tried to defend the performance. Excuses ranged from an entrenched culture in the mines to the fact that the mine was too old and could not do more. Selgado requested that the options for management be presented in the same meeting. At least the consultants had run the analyses, pre-presented them, and were ready to discuss these.

Despite the overwhelming evidence that Mino 1 was underperforming and that services needed to be separated, Heinze and Gavrilo still believed that the operation was doing the best it could. It seemed the two executives were digging themselves deeper and deeper into a hole. The session ended with Selgado endorsing the option to implement all the operational improvement measures and separate the noncore service functions. He requested that both Gavrilo and Heinze develop a plan of action on how they would implement the recommendations at Mino 1. Selgado shortly thereafter presented the findings to the board, which also endorsed the findings. He made two other additional recommendations to the board. Both Heinze and Gavrilo would need to go.

That's why the firm has brought down the consultants' partners. The engagement is moving into the next phase, and consultants will be in Brazil for a few more months before rolling out the programme across Goldy. The successful engagement caps a four-year effort by Marcus to reposition the Brazilian office for the firm. After a slow start, results are gradually starting to come through. Goldy is one of several major relationships developed in the four-year period. Marcus recalls the advice he received 12 years ago when he joined the London office as a business analyst. He had been invited to lunch with the office director, who made it a point to meet all hires and explain the philosophy of the firm.

"Marcus, I am pleased you have chosen to build your career among a firm of professionals. Very soon you will be sitting across from a client and providing advice on his or her business. When this time comes, you must never ever forget that it is a great honour being able to sit across from a client and assist with their issues. It is not our right to have this access. It is privileged access that we nurture and respect. It is access that can be lost with a stray word. It is access that partners before me developed and handed down to me. I have developed those same

WEEK 8 – DAY 4: CONSULTING VALUES

relationships and will pass them down to you and other professionals of the firm. You never own a relationship; you simply nurture it for the next generation of partners.

As you develop your career, always remember the following:

1. As a professional of this firm, you will be expected to hold yourself to the highest possible standards. The partners always hold themselves to higher standards, and you should receive guidance from them. But the greatest guidance should come from within you.

2. Honour and respect your clients. We never sell work. We never chase profits. By placing the needs of our clients first, they come to us, and profits are an outcome of having these strong principles.

3. Don't confuse doing what's in the client's best interests with making a client happy. They are totally different. Sometimes you have no choice but to make clients unhappy when you place their best interests first. If you believe a client's course of action is incorrect, you should say so. If the client chooses to walk away and proceed without us, that is fine. We must always preserve out intellectual integrity.

4. You have the right to dissent at all times. You do not need to agree to everything, but you must state your position. Vibrant debate only makes the firm stronger.

5. Generously invest in others. Give your time and expertise to colleagues. This makes the firm stronger and makes you stronger.

6. There is no hierarchy at the firm. Every single professional is important, and we treat everyone as equals. You have access to anyone and everyone, including myself. You just need to ask, and you will receive access.

7. All the fancy analyses taught today in business schools are wonderful and important to the firm. Invest in it. Yet, never forget the importance of engaging and understanding the viewpoint of frontline employees. They can provide more insight and guidance than any desktop analysis.

8. Don't stop learning. As you progress through the firm, you will need to learn and master different skills. Be humble and keep an open mind. There is always something to learn.

I would recommend the salmon for lunch. Do you have any questions?"

A lot has changed since that time. Yet, the values of the firm have remained the same. They are timeless. The potential future partners of the firm, such as Luther, Max, Alana, and Nadia, all exhibit these values.

WEEK 8

day 5

DID THE ENGAGEMENT TEAM SUCCEED?

OVER THE COURSE OF THIS BOOK, we introduced you to an engagement team at an elite management consulting firm and followed them as they advised a new client. To conclude this book, it is worth discussing the broader skills needed as a management consultant. Throughout a consultant's career, these skills will need to be deployed. In particularly challenging engagements, all these skills will be needed, and they will be severely tested.

The Goldy engagement was by no means easy. It was a difficult environment, within a tough operating culture resistant to consultants, and the team was trying to fix deep and persistent problems. By using the right tools and techniques, they successfully completed the study.

Unfortunately, there is an illusion that analytical excellence alone is sufficient to become a partner. Yet, you need to be excellent at analysing problems and understanding their impact on the business. Without this core skill, you will struggle as a consultant since you will not be able to understand the impact of your recommendations. Moreover, since you are not able to analyse a problem using fundamental analyses, you will rely too much on your experience to generate solutions. Experience is a competitive advantage when it helps you understand the context. It is an Achilles heel when it clouds the ability to look at hard data and draw conclusions based on the facts.

We also saw that none of the analysis is linear. It is not a matter of simply collecting the problem statement and locking yourself away until you produce a report and hand this over to your manager and the client. The most difficult part is in understanding the question you are answering. That takes both time and experience. Once this is done, the question needs to be broken down into manageable sub-questions. For each sub-question, data needs to be collected and analysis completed to answer the question.

Problems arise when the perfectly planned analysis cannot work in reality. The data is not available, time is not sufficient, or circumstances change. Should this occur, the analysis needs to change and so must the data requirements. The consultant needs to make these changes while ensuring that the overall and original question is answered. As we saw in this engagement and this explanation, data hunting does not drive the engagement. It is an outcome of understanding the key questions and the analyses to answer the question. This drives the data hunting.

Changing or even creating new analyses can only be done by someone who understands how to analyse problems at the most fundamental level. No two engagements are the same and most engagements are unlikely to use all the techniques in this book, though many will use most of them. Simply using frameworks and templates without the ability to test their relevance can lead to problems on the engagement.

While this book takes you step-by-step through an engagement, there are many more detailed ways we could have examined an engagement. The full study training programmes on StrategyTraining.com teach these in exhaustive detail.

WEEK 8 - DAY 5: DID THE ENGAGEMENT TEAM SUCCEED?

Analytical brilliance is the most basic building block of a management consultant, but it is not enough. The stress levels during a consulting engagement are very high. Time is limited, and the situation is fluid. Clients are not static. They respond or don't respond. Either way, the consultant must find a way to work through these challenges to complete the study.

If analytical brilliance is one building block, emotional intelligence is another. The ability to engage and work with clients who may not appreciate your presence or like working with consultants is critical. A consultant who is able to provide coaching and guidance to colleagues without demeaning them is a successful consultant. Such a consultant builds a strong network of peers who want to work with them and want them to succeed.

True consulting means using your advanced training to find proof that may not exist in the most comfortable locations. It could mean following mine workers underground to determine where they are delayed the most during a typical workday or following a cleaning crew to count the number of trucks they send out and the time it takes to reach the client. It means engaging the frontline employees. None of this is glamorous, and in some cases, you will not be speaking to formally educated people. You will need to empathise, build relationships, and influence them to want to work with you. That takes skill. Finding the information may be messy, but management consulting is about the insights you develop from these tasks and how you translate it into recommendations for the client.

Another building block is political awareness. When management consultants are called in, there is a high probability that the client will implement the changes and thereby cause some level of turmoil in the organization. Pending organisational changes by themselves always cause employees to jockey and jostle for power. This happens all the way from the most senior executive to the most junior employee.

A management consultant must be aware of the impact their presence is having. They must know that every employee is trying to paint a positive image of themselves or their business. The consultant needs to be aware of this and be extra careful to verify and check everything in duplicate, if not triplicate. In some cases, executives try to discredit consultants. A consultant needs to read an employee's personality to understand who is an ally of the company and who is an enemy. Experience usually generates this skill.

To become a partner at one of the top firms, you need all three skills cocooned in your constant display of a firm's values. Yes, a firms' values are fundamental. While the leading firms all have similar values, they also have important differences. To be a successful management consultant, not only must you know these values, but you also need to *be* the values and *live* them every day. They need to be a part of who you are. Consulting values are not an intangible concept. They are the invisible hand behind actions taken by management consultants every single day. Every time you do something, it is either a chance to honour or dishonour the values.

If you master every technical skill but fail to internalize the value system, you most likely will never be a successful management consultant.

Deploying these skills, the engagement partner who secured this study knows that one of the unspoken objectives of the study was to provide the momentum for the CEO to institute the change needed to turn around Goldy and improve his business standing. In other words, the results of implementing the recommendations must make the CEO and Goldy successful.

There are stated and unstated reasons for launching this study. Of the stated reasons, the consultants have done well on a number of challenging objectives:

WEEK 8 - DAY 5: DID THE ENGAGEMENT TEAM SUCCEED?

1. Determine the causes for the drop in production value.
2. Develop recommendations to address the issues.
3. Develop a working relationship with Mino 1 executives.

Therefore, the client did obtain the desired results as they relate to stated reasons for launching this study. One unstated objective was to ensure that Goldy executives understand the true state of Mino 1 and accept the analyses of the business. This was also successfully accomplished. The most significant unstated objective was to assess the will, capability, and capacity of the Mino 1 executives. The engagement partner will not provide his judgement of the Mino 1 executive team. That is not why they were hired, and it would be unprofessional to do so. The engagement team, however, has provided an assessment of Mino 1's current performance for the CEO to determine if the Mino 1 team is up to the task of leading the change required. He ultimately decided they were not up to the task.

Goldy eventually implemented all the recommendations provided. It was not an easy experience. Initially, there was internal resistance from the Mino 1 executives. The change process only began when Mino 1 stumbled through another two months to post a devastating loss that plunged Goldy into a crisis with investors and creditors. The CEO was able to stabilise the company and replaced the entire Mino 1 management team. The consulting firm was tasked with rolling out the same analyses across all mining hubs worldwide. Change still took time. A new corporate office was created to centralise operational control of the business. A shared services platform was rolled out to control excessive support costs. Improved procurement practices were the largest source of savings in the shared services platform.

Goldy sold most of its service functions. It retained even fewer functions than originally approved in the second steering committee meeting. The large divestiture programme allowed it to implement a series of layoffs that were initially resisted by the labour unions. Yet, they were implemented over time. Three years later, Goldy is obtaining better service through outsourced contracts and at a much lower cost. The company exited many operations that were not earning the required rate of return and exited all noncore ventures.

Tackling the cultural and performance issues proved to be more difficult. A new management model was created and implemented. New performance metrics and remuneration criteria were introduced. Initial surveys indicated that employees were optimistic the change would be positive. Time will tell if this will all work. Goldy's ROCE is up and closing the gap with peers. So is its share price. The government has retained its large shareholding in Goldy but has remained a passive shareholder. It has publicly affirmed its support for Goldy to become an international mining champion.

EPILOGUE

A**LTHOUGH THIS ENGAGEMENT IS FICTIONAL**, this book is based on real management consulting engagements, and the real experiences of the writers when they were management consultants, to present to you the most authentic learning experience. Yet, all the names, places, and other confidential details have been changed.

For us, it was important that you, the reader, could learn how to use the consulting techniques of leading firms in a realistic setting, but we needed to do more. We needed you to understand the challenging and sometimes messy environment within which engagements are taking place. No engagement goes according to plan, but the top firms have the processes, protocols, and values in place to navigate these issues.

This book introduces the reader to many powerful tools and techniques used in management consulting. While we have carefully explained how each one is used on an engagement, more information is available.

In-depth training on skills and techniques used in this book, as well as on other consulting skills, is available on Firmsconsulting.com and StrategyTraining.com.

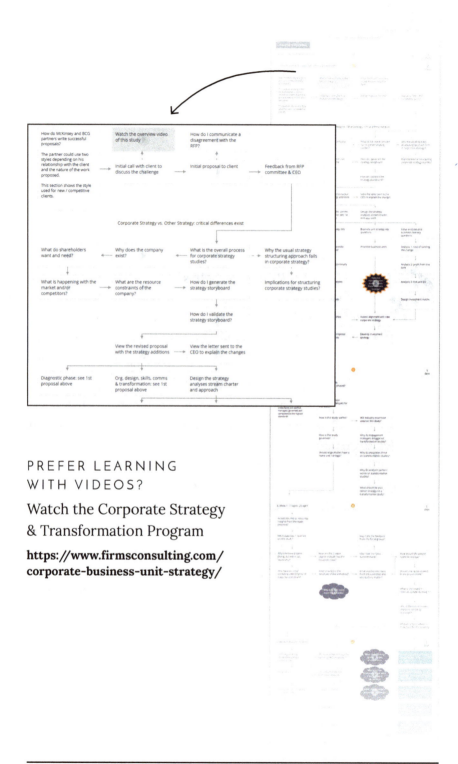

PREFER LEARNING WITH VIDEOS?

Watch the Corporate Strategy & Transformation Program

https://www.firmsconsulting.com/corporate-business-unit-strategy/

PREFER LEARNING WITH VIDEOS?

Watch the Market Entry Strategy Study

https://www.firmsconsulting.com/market-entry-strategy/#!step-2

FREE EPISODE FROM BOOK'S COMPANION COURSE AT FIRMSCONSULTING.COM/SAAMC 455

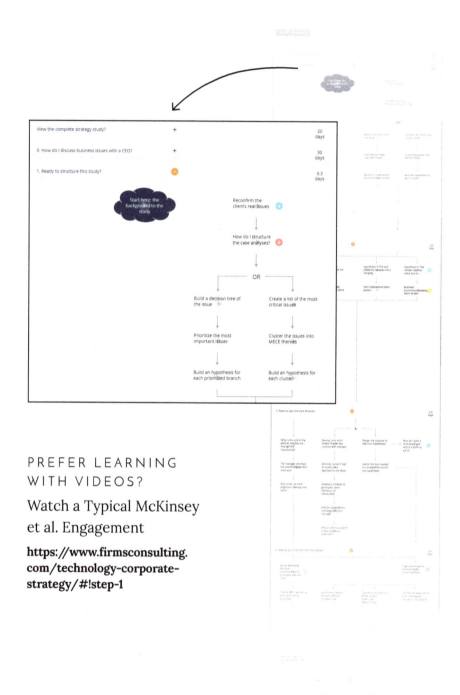

PREFER LEARNING WITH VIDEOS?

Watch a Typical McKinsey et al. Engagement

https://www.firmsconsulting.com/technology-corporate-strategy/#!step-1

ABOUT THE PUBLISHER

THE STRATEGY MEDIA GROUP

At the Strategy Media Group we believe in the power of critical thinking, creativity, and storytelling to teach our clients to solve mankind's toughest problems. Our mission is producing original long-form content to empower a loyal, hardworking, inspiring, well-meaning and ambitious worldwide audience to solve the most important problems and, as a result, make a positive and meaningful impact on the world.

Our clients make a difference because they aspire for more than that which society had intended for them. They do not confuse aspiration for ambition. They choose the latter. They act.

We provide a full range of content development, financing, marketing and distribution services for wholly owned educational programs, documentaries, feature films, and podcasts teaching business strategy, problem-solving, critical thinking, communication, leadership and entrepreneurship streamed in >150 countries 24/7 through feature-rich Apps and websites.

At any given time >1,000 unpublished episodes are in post-production. Our digital properties include **StrategyTraining.com**, **StrategyTV.com** and **FirmsConsulting.com**. Our apps include Strategy Training, Strategy TV, Strategy Skills and Bill Matassoni A Memoir.

In addition, we own some of the world's most popular business strategy and case interview podcast channels with >4.5 million downloads and counting, and the world's largest business strategy OTT platforms with >6,000 episodes of original programming distributed on iOS, Android, Roku and Apple TV.

We have financed, packaged or distributed more than 45 premium programs through our wholly owned OTT platforms, including "The Electric Car Start-Up," "The Digital Luxury Atelier," "The Gold Miner," "Competitive Strategy with Kevin P. Coyne," "The Bill Matassoni Show," and we try to focus on social causes like championing the rights of disenfranchised workers.

We take an equity ownership positions in businesses we are documenting to produce programming for our platforms. Such as a gold miner, electric car start-up, luxury brands start-up, and new age cosmetics start-up.

Our programming is analytically and conceptually deep, in that we dig into the numbers and details to help you understand the economics at work, and help you replicate our thinking. "The US Marketing Entry Study" and "The Corporate Strategy & Transformation Study," with >270 videos each, are programs used worldwide to understand the nuances of restructuring a retail bank and turning around a troubled power utility.

In the scripted space, we create original content combining education with entertainment to deliver business teachings.

Our publishing arm releases original books on strategy, business and critical thinking, such as "Marketing Saves the World" by Bill Matassoni, McKinsey's former senior partner and world-wide head of marketing and "Succeeding as a Management Consultant."

We teach business and critical thinking skills to children and young adults, with original and entertaining novels and programming merging entertainment and business training. We believe children

ABOUT THE PUBLISHER

and young adults will have a formidable advantage in life if they start learning to think like a strategy partner early in life. STEM skills should be complemented with critical reasoning skills. It should be strategy, science, technology, engineering and mathematics.

We invest in and have exposure to the world's fastest growing market segments and market geographies, including the BRICS. Our subscribers include senior government officials, and leaders of industry and consulting firms, all the way to the executive committee members of the world's leading consulting firms.

We work with eminent leaders such as ex-McKinsey, BCG et al. partners who plan, produce and/or host all our programming. The type of content we produce does not exist anywhere else in the world and is hosted exclusively on our platforms.

Kris Safarova is the Presiding Partner of Firmsconsulting.com, which owns the world's largest strategy streaming OTT channel. She works with a network of ex-McKinsey, BCG et al. partners to produce original strategy/leadership training programming and books. She manages several of the top podcast channels worldwide for strategy and management consulting, with >4.5 million downloads.

Kris Safarova was born in Samara City, the Russian Federation. She received a Dipl. in Music with a concentration in Classical Piano from DG Shatalov Music College, a B.Comm from UNISA, cum laude with highest distinction and an MBA from Ivey Business School, University of Western Ontario in Canada, on the deans list with highest distinction, where she was President of the Public Sector Club and Editor of the Public Sector Journal. Prior to obtaining her business degrees, she worked in management consulting and post-MBA she was a banker and consulting engagement manager in Toronto, Canada. Prior to consulting Kris was a master classical concert pianist and official representative of the Russian Federation who toured Europe. She joined Firmsconsulting.com as a Partner, Corporate Finance in 2015 and was appointed Presiding Partner in 2016.

RECEIVE ACCESS TO EPISODES FROM OUR VARIOUS TRAINING PROGRAMS:

firmsconsulting.com/promo

GENERAL INQUIRIES:

support@firmsconsulting.com

COLLABORATION/PARTNERSHIP INQUIRIES:

kris@firmsconsulting.com

BULK ORDER REQUESTS/ GROUP MEMBERSHIPS:

support@firmsconsulting.com

SUGGEST A GUEST FOR OUR PODCAST CHANNELS:

support@firmsconsulting.com

CPSIA information can be obtained
at www.ICGtesting.com
Printed in the USA
LVHW051418250621
691051LV00010B/875